WHAT THE LEGO COMMUNITY IS SAYING ABOUT
THE UNOFFICIAL LEGO BUILDER'S GUIDE

"I owe a great deal to Allan and this book. His writing was excellent in illustrating techniques and made the art of LEGO interesting enough for me to devote an entire career to it."

– JASON POLAND, WINNER OF THE 2006 LEGOLAND MODEL BUILDER SEARCH

"Brilliant! Bedford guides you step-by-step through the wonderful, limitless LEGO system using his uniquely engaging writing style and passion for the brick. A must-read for every LEGO builder."

–TIM COURTNEY, LDRAW.ORG, CO-AUTHOR OF *VIRTUAL LEGO*

"*The Unofficial LEGO Builder's Guide* is an excellent resource for both the beginner and the expert LEGO builder. For the beginner, it's a great introduction to the hobby and reference to many of the building tricks that the advanced builders use. For the expert, it's a great reference for methods and approaches to building in new themes and scales. I recommend it highly for anyone who is interested in LEGO building."

–JOE MENO, EDITOR IN CHIEF, BRICKJOURNAL

"This is the book I wished I had as a kid and as an adult returning to the hobby. It's a great resource, and is going to have a cherished place on my work table for the foreseeable future."

–JACOB H. MCKEE, LEGO COMMUNITY DEVELOPMENT MANAGER FOR NORTH AMERICA, AUTHOR OF *GETTING STARTED WITH LEGO TRAINS*

"*The Unofficial LEGO Builder's Guide* should be considered the benchmark on all aspects of the LEGO building hobby. A 'must-have' for those who are just starting to experiment with LEGO and experts looking for areas to expand."

–KIETH JOHNSON, AEROSPACE ENGINEER, UNITED SPACE ALLIANCE

"*The Unofficial LEGO Builder's Guide* will make for a great beginning for any future architects or LEGO hobbyists. The detailed model instructions not only show how to build the example models, they also inspire you to go further and build anything you can think of, the only limit being your imagination."

–GARY ISTOK, LEGO BUILDER, COLLECTOR, AND HISTORIAN

"*The Unofficial LEGO Builder's Guide* is a great tool for both young and old. It explains in clear and concise language the things you will need to know to get started and develop your skills as a LEGO builder. From the different types of building techniques and styles, to a comprehensive guide of important parts, this is a great springboard to unleashing the inner Master Model Builder that is in us all!"

–BILL VOLLBRECHT, FORMER MASTER MODEL BUILDER FOR LEGOLAND CALIFORNIA AND OWNER OF WWW.BRICKCREATIONS.COM

How many things are waiting to be created?

UNOFFICIAL
THE ^LEGO®
BUILDER'S GUIDE

by Allan Bedford

no starch press

San Francisco

10 – 10

ISBN-10: 1-59327-054-2
ISBN-13: 978-1-59327-054-4

Publisher: William Pollock
Production Manager: Susan Berge
Cover Design: Leslie Harrington
Interior Design: Octopod Studios
Developmental Editors: William Pollock, Peter Spear
Copyeditor: Rebecca C. Rider
Compositor: Riley Hoffman
Proofreader: Stephanie Provines

For information on book distributors or translations, please contact No Starch Press, Inc. directly:

No Starch Press, Inc.
555 De Haro Street, Suite 250, San Francisco, CA 94107
phone: 415.863.9900; fax: 415.863.9950; info@nostarch.com; http://www.nostarch.com

Library of Congress Cataloging-in-Publication Data

```
Bedford, Allan.
   The unofficial LEGO builder's guide / Allan Bedford.
     p. cm.
   Includes index.
   ISBN 1-59327-054-2
1.  LEGO toys.  I. Title.
   TS2301.T7B44 2005
   688.7'25--dc22
                                    2005013747
```

To my wife Kathie and our little family.
For believing that I could do this.

Creativity is just having enough dots to connect.
—Steve Jobs

BRIEF CONTENTS

Acknowledgments xv

Introduction xvii

Chapter 1: The LEGO System: Endless Possibilities 1

Chapter 2: Back to Basics: Tips and Techniques..19

Chapter 3: Minifig Scale: Oh, What a Wonderful Minifig World It Is!................37

Chapter 4: Miniland Scale: The Whole World in Miniature................................63

Chapter 5: Jumbo Elements: Building Bigger Bricks 81

Chapter 6: Microscale Building: More Than Meets the Eye................................99

Chapter 7: Sculptures: The Shape of Things to Build 115

Chapter 8: Mosaics: Patterns and Pictures in Bricks 133

Chapter 9: Technic: Not as Technical as It May Seem 153

Chapter 10: Putting It All Together: Where Ideas Meet Bricks 173

Chapter 11: Beyond Just Bricks: Other Things to Do Besides Building 195

Chapter 12: Sorting, Storage, and Sitting Down to Build Something................209

Chapter 13: Making and Using Tools for LEGO Projects 227

Appendix A: Brickopedia..239

Appendix B: Design Grids: Building Better by Planning Ahead 299

List of Key Figures 311

Index 313

CONTENTS IN DETAIL

ACKNOWLEDGMENTS   xv

INTRODUCTION   xvii

1
THE LEGO SYSTEM: ENDLESS POSSIBILITIES   1

A Brick Vocabulary 2
    Sizing Up the Elements 2
    The Stud 3
    The Tube 4
    The Brick 5
    The Plate 6
    The Slope 7
    Specialized Elements 8
    Technic 9
    Arch Pieces 9
    Tiles and Panels 10
    Cylinders and Cones 11
    Baseplates 12
    Decorative Elements 12
Precision, Geometry, and Color 13
    Why Precision Manufacturing Matters 13
    Fun with LEGO Geometry 13
    The Colors 15
Review: The LEGO System 17

2
BACK TO BASICS: TIPS AND TECHNIQUES   19

Decisions, Decisions: The Best Ways to Connect Bricks 20
    Stacking 21
    Overlapping 22
    Staggering 24
Building Walls 25
    Connecting Walls 25
    Straight Bricks Can Make Round Walls 27
Bracing: Unseen but Not Forgotten 29
    Bracing = Beams + Columns 29
    Beams 30
    Columns 32
Review: Basic Building Principles 35
    1. Build big but think small. 35
    2. Pick the right bonding pattern. 35

3

MINIFIG SCALE: OH, WHAT A WONDERFUL MINIFIG WORLD IT IS!   37

Scale: It's All Relative 38
    Calculating Scale 38
From the Ground Up: Creating a Minifig-Scale Building 40
    Building Two Versions of the Train Station 40
    Bill of Materials: The Parts You'll Need to Make This Model 41
    Step by Step: Train Station Construction Details 41
    Submodel: The Train Station Roof 51
Substitution: When Other Parts Will Do 54
    Substitute Walls 55
    Substitute Arches 55
    Substitute Windows 56
    Substitute Roofs 57
Review: Building Techniques and Alternatives 61

4

MINILAND SCALE: THE WHOLE WORLD IN MINIATURE   63

Miniland Scale: Bigger but Still Small 64
Creating a Basic Miniland Figure 65
The Best Bits: Useful Pieces for Miniland People 66
Basic Miniland Figure 68
    Mix-and-Match Parts 69
    On The Run: Making Miniland Figures Come to Life 73
Miniland Buildings 75
    Creating a Scene: Combining Figures and Buildings 75
    Street Life: A Simple Downtown Scene in Miniland Scale 76
    Behind the Scenes 79
Review: Miniland Scale, Big Possibilities 80

5

JUMBO ELEMENTS: BUILDING BIGGER BRICKS   81

Scaling Up: How It's Done 84
    The Walls Are Closing In! 87
    Other Parts, Same Technique 89
    Building with Jumbo Bricks 92
Other Scales: What Scales Work, and Why 94
    Picking the Right Scale 95
    Approximation 96
Review: Jumbo Bricks Are Just the Start 98

6

MICROSCALE BUILDING: MORE THAN MEETS THE EYE   99

Microscale: Small Scale with Big Possibilities 101
Getting Started: Ignore the Details 102

Translating Ideas into Bricks 105
    Recap the Technique 107
How Do I Know What Scale I'm Using? 107
    Decide on a scale before you begin building. 107
    Figure out the scale after you're done building. 108
Replacing Full-Size Parts with Microscale Stand-Ins 108
    Microscale Wheels 109
    Microscale Windows 109
    Instructions for Microscale House 110
    Recap of Replacement Parts 113
Review and Suggested Subject Matter 113

7
SCULPTURES: THE SHAPE OF THINGS TO BUILD   115

Spheres: Round and Round They Go 116
Divide and Build: Two Sections Means Twice the Fun 118
Beyond Spheres: Sculpting Other Subjects 126
    Choosing a Subject 126
    Getting Started on the Sphinx 127
    Analyzing the Angles: Building the Head 127
    Special Features: Special Techniques 128
    Building the Foundation Last 131
Review: Sculptures—In the Eye of the Builder 132

8
MOSAICS: PATTERNS AND PICTURES IN BRICKS   133

Two Types of Mosaics 133
What Can You Do with Mosaics? 135
    How Big Should a Mosaic Be? 135
What You Need to Make a Mosaic 135
Designing a Studs-Out Mosaic 136
    Geometric Patterns 136
    Copies of Pictures 140
Designing a Studs-Up Mosaic 146
Design Grids for the Studs-Up Technique 147
Mosaics on Edge 148
Review: Mosaics of All Sizes and Shapes 150

9
TECHNIC: NOT AS TECHNICAL AS IT MAY SEEM   153

Technic: A System Within a System 155
Technic Pieces: An Overview 155
    Bricks 156
    Studless Beams 157
    Gears 158
    Pins/Axles 158

Bushings 159
Couplers 159
Getting Started with Technic: Assembly Notes 160
Gear Trains 160
Going Vertical 164
Technic Meets Basic Elements 165
Putting It All Together: Building a Technic Model 168
Review: What Is Technic? 171

10
PUTTING IT ALL TOGETHER:
WHERE IDEAS MEET BRICKS

173

Thinking Like a Model Designer 173
Limit Your Scope 174
Getting Started: Pick Your Subject 175
Work from the Bottom Up 176
Let Reality Guide Your Design Decisions 179
A Different Perspective 180
Pick a Scale, Any Scale 181
Color Concerns 181
Elements of Design 182
Bringing It All Together: The Final Design 185
Step by Step: Shuttle Construction Details 187
Something's Wrong: Redesigning Doesn't Mean You've Failed 193
After You're Done 193
Review: Taking On the Role of Model Designer 194

11
BEYOND JUST BRICKS:
OTHER THINGS TO DO BESIDES BUILDING

195

"I Give It a Nine Out of Ten": Writing Reviews of LEGO Sets 196
A Simple Review 196
Sharing Your Review 198
How It's Made: Creating Instructions for Your LEGO Models 198
Step-by-Step Pictures 199
Computer-Assisted Instructions 200
Having Fun: Making and Playing Games with LEGO Pieces 201
Games You Already Know 201
Original Games 203
An Example of an Original Game: Connect-Across (Basic Rules) 204
Designing Your Own Game 207
Review: Enjoying Every Aspect of LEGO 207

12
SORTING, STORAGE, AND SITTING DOWN TO BUILD SOMETHING

209

Sorting vs. Storing: What's the Difference? 210
Sorting Bricks: Divide and Conquer 211
    Small-Sized Collections 212
    Medium-Sized Collections 212
    Large-Sized Collections 214
Storing Bricks 216
    Start Small, Keep It Simple 217
    Containers with Compartments 218
    Shoeboxes: Not Just for Shoes Anymore 219
    Keeping Track of the Little Pieces: Tackle Boxes to the Rescue 221
    Reuse Containers You May Already Have: Tubs and Buckets 221
    Deep Storage: Taking Care of Larger Quantities 223
Setting Up a Building Area 223
Review: Unique Solutions for Every Builder 226

13
MAKING AND USING TOOLS FOR LEGO PROJECTS

227

Presser Tool 229
The Ruler 230
Pin Stand Tool 231
Brick Separator 233
Non-LEGO Tools 236
Other Useful Items 237
Review: The Right Tools for the Job 238

A
BRICKOPEDIA

239

Brickopedia Breakdown 240
Review: Bricks, Plates, and So Much More 298

B
DESIGN GRIDS: BUILDING BETTER BY PLANNING AHEAD

299

Downloading the Grids 299
About the Grids 300
    Design Grid #1 300
    Design Grid #2 300
    Design Grid #3 301
    Design Grid #4 303

Using the Grids Effectively 303
    Same Model, Different Views 304
    Sketching or Planning 304
    Description and Date for Future Reference 304
    Drawing on Grid #1 305
    Drawing on Grid #2 308
    Drawing on Grid #3 308
    Drawing on Grid #4 310
Review: From Grids to Bricks 310

LIST OF KEY FIGURES   311

INDEX   313

ACKNOWLEDGMENTS

I want to first thank my wife, for the little and not so little things she did to support me during the writing of this book. For more than once putting a blanket over me when I'd fallen asleep on the futon after a night of creating yet more images for the book. And for seeing me through my illness and surgery just months after the book was started. I know all of this was more than she had bargained for, but her example and her determination helped me get back on track and get to the end of this rewarding project.

My parents deserve more than just a little credit for their role in this book's creation. First, for having the foresight to not dispose of my LEGO bricks when I went off to college. But seriously and more importantly, for letting me rediscover those bricks as an adult and at the same time reconnect with the nine-year-old kid still inside me. It's impossible to express how comforting it is that no matter how old (or young) I am they are there every step of the way. Not just when it comes to LEGO, but everything else too. Their support for and belief in this book has been remarkable and unwavering.

I want to give a special nod to Grandma B. for lessons in patience and grace that no book could ever teach me.

The picture from LEGOLAND California that opens Chapter 4 was used with the kind permission of Tim Strutt of Ottawa, Ontario, Canada. The rest of the chapter was easier to write knowing that people could visualize the building style I was talking about.

A special thanks goes to all of the software and parts authors in the "virtual" LEGO community. Many of the images in this book were produced with their tools and without them the book would not be nearly as interesting. Be sure to visit http://ldraw.org to get started building your own virtual LEGO models.

Thank you to John Fiala, Joe Meno, and Frédéric Siva. I appreciate all the time they put into reading and reviewing the book and I'm grateful for all of the honest and insightful feedback they provided.

To the gang at No Starch Press I offer my thanks for not only believing in this book from the beginning but for their limitless patience in helping me get it to the end.

Special thanks go to my friend Derek Robson for helping me source out a computer to handle the huge volume of image rendering and file storage that was required to complete the book. The machine I had when I started writing would never have made it to the end.

My friend Derek Iddison is a LEGO builder whose work I greatly admire. He was the first to know about the book but more importantly the first to encourage me to actually pursue writing it and getting it published.

INTRODUCTION

LEGO bricks have been engaging builders, both young and old, for decades. However, during this time, surprisingly little has been written about this unique building system and its many uses. True, a number of "idea books" have offered building instructions for a variety of projects, and thousands of printed instructions have accompanied the enormous range of products released over the years. In most cases, however, these instructions were only for one or two finished models. In recent years, books and articles have been written that supply information about LEGO robotics, virtual computer-aided designs, and even about the LEGO company and its many facets. Up to this point, a book that addresses the system itself and its greatest function—building LEGO models—has been missing from this list.

This book fills that gap by offering a broad spectrum of topics all connected by the thread of building real models with actual plastic bricks. Most chapters present best practices, tips, and techniques that you can apply to almost any building project. Woven together with these ideas is background information on such subjects as architecture, design, engineering, color theory, and so on.

I hope that this book will serve LEGO builders who are prepared to move beyond the instructions supplied with official sets and who are ready to begin making their own original models. My target audience may include younger builders who are working on their own or parents who are working alongside their children. Adult builders returning to the hobby may also find useful information they can use to refresh techniques long forgotten or perhaps develop those they never had as a young person.

I round out the book with a unique feature that I hope helps builders of all skill levels see the LEGO system at a glance. The *Brickopedia* (Appendix A) is a graphical reference tool that presents the most common and most reusable elements from available LEGO pieces. Although it does not contain an entry for every single piece ever produced, it does thoroughly examine the LEGO bricks, plates, slopes, and other elements that best define the highly flexible nature of this building system. I have categorized the Brickopedia using some traditional techniques but also using some newly defined criteria and classifications. I set this up intending that you use it as a stand-alone tool; therefore, it does not require a computer or Internet access to be useful.

So sit down with a bunch of LEGO bricks and get ready to build!

1

THE LEGO SYSTEM:
ENDLESS POSSIBILITIES

For millions of people around the world LEGO bricks
have always had a common meaning: creativity.
Regardless of age, we all seem to recognize the sound
the bricks make as we rummage through a bucket full
of them or a pile on the floor.

Whenever you look at that pile of LEGO pieces, you are looking at
something remarkable and yet at the same time remarkably simple. You are
looking at the different parts of a *system*. A system is not only a collection of
different bits and pieces but also the ways in which they connect with each
other to become a larger object or series of objects. In this chapter, I discuss
the LEGO system and what makes it so amazing. I then show you a number
of the pieces that make up the system and how they relate to each other.
Finally, you'll take a look at how geometry and color come into play as you're
building with LEGO pieces.

The LEGO system is made up of an enormous number of different
pieces, sometimes known as *elements*. Every piece in that pile is an element.
Every element (with only a few exceptions) can connect to any other element

in an almost infinite number of ways. A handful of pieces can be combined to form a wall; a few more added on create a roof and then a complete house, then maybe a car and a driveway to park it in. Tomorrow those same elements can be taken apart and recombined to create a deep space cruiser, a sculpture of a calico cat, or even a fortress with a group of medieval knights.

A Brick Vocabulary

Take another look at that pile of LEGO pieces on the floor (or imagine a pile) and you'll notice that not all of them are perfectly rectangular. Some have sloping sides, some are cylindrical or cone shaped, and some are much thinner than others. You've got to have a way to identify different features of bricks or you'll have a tough time learning how to build with them. This section describes the various key attributes of LEGO bricks and puts them into useful categories.

As you read about the different types of LEGO pieces, you'll undoubtedly find many that are familiar to you and that already exist within your own collection. At the same time, you are likely to come across others that you haven't seen before and that you may not yet own. Of course, that's part of the overall enjoyment of LEGO as a hobby. As you buy new sets or find used pieces at yard sales or thrift shops, you discover new parts that in turn open up new building options.

Sizing Up the Elements

Throughout this book, I often refer to the size and shape of various LEGO pieces, but before I do, I need to provide you with a foundation for these references. Let's begin with the basic 1×1 brick, as shown in Figure 1-1.

Figure 1-1: 1×1 brick shown much larger than its actual size

When I speak of the LEGO system, I consider the 1×1 (pronounced "one by one") brick to be the standard upon which I base all other measurements. This, in turn, makes it easy to describe the size and shape of other bricks. For example, if you put two 1×1 bricks next to each other, you see that they are the exact same size as the next largest standard-sized brick. They make a 1×2 brick, as shown in Figure 1-2.

In addition, if a piece is the same height as a 1×1, I say it is "one brick high." A brick that is the same height as a 1×1 brick but is twice as long is called a 1×2 brick.

Figure 1-2: Two 1×1 bricks added together equal a
1×2 brick

It's common to put the shorter dimension (the width) ahead of the longer one (the length). Similarly, the element shown in Figure 1-3 is a 2×4 brick (the equivalent of two 1×1's wide and four 1×1's long). I'll use these measurement standards throughout this book to describe the various LEGO pieces.

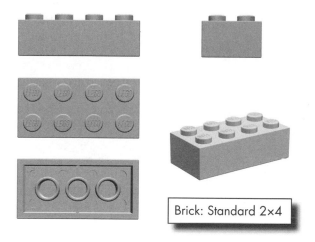

Brick: Standard 2×4

Figure 1-3: Anatomy of a 2×4 brick. When you see it from all sides, you get a sense of its general size and shape.

Another important standard that you will find in this book is the use of the capital letter N as a substitute for a brick's length. For example, I might talk about a bunch of 1×N (pronounced "one by en") bricks that I used to make the outer wall of a building. In this case, the capital N represents a number of possible brick lengths, such as 1×2, 1×4, 1×8, and so on. Rather than list all of the assorted sizes, it is sometimes easier to replace the last number with an N and allow the description to apply to a range of brick sizes.

The Stud

The *stud* is a part of almost every LEGO piece, and you use it to measure the length or width of any given piece. The stud (shown circled in Figure 1-4) helps define the look of a LEGO element and it is integral to how the entire system functions.

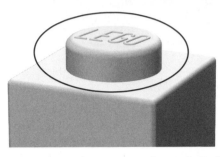

Figure 1-4: The stud gives every element half of what it
needs to connect to almost any other element.

The 1×1 brick shown in Figure 1-4 has exactly one stud. In fact, 1×1 refers to the fact that our base brick is one stud wide and one stud long. Similarly, the element shown in Figure 1-3 is two studs wide and four studs long.

The Tube

The *tube* is the other half of the mechanism that helps bricks stick together. Tubes capture the studs so that you can join LEGO elements and know that they won't fall apart. You can see the tubes by simply looking beneath most LEGO pieces, such as those shown in Figure 1-5.

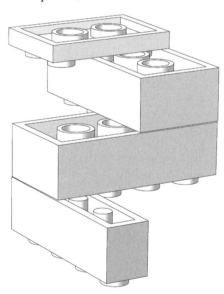

Figure 1-5: The underside of LEGO elements reveals the
other half of the secret that locks bricks together.

Figure 1-5 uses a simple upside-down sculpture to demonstrate the way in which the tubes work with the studs. Different types of elements have variations on the tube design. In Figure 1-5, you can see that the thinnest piece (at the top of the illustration) has shortened tubes, whereas the 2×4 bricks beneath it have longer tubes inside of them. The 1×4 brick (at the bottom of the sculpture) has thin posts rather than hollow tubes. Despite the contrast in their sizes, they all serve the same purpose: the tubes wedge together against the studs of the piece below to hold the bricks together.

The Brick

Although it is tempting to refer to all LEGO pieces as bricks, it is more accurate to use this term only when talking about certain elements. The label *brick* is generally given to a type of LEGO part that is the same height as a standard 1×1 element, like the ones shown in Figure 1-6. A brick should have straight sides and a rectangular shape when you view it from the side.

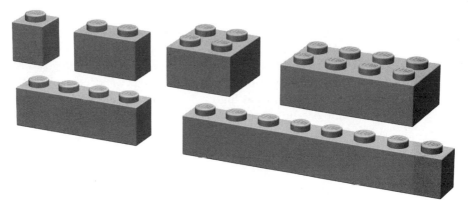

Figure 1-6: An assortment of standard bricks

A LEGO brick is not unlike a real brick that you might find making up the outside walls of a house, an apartment building, or a school. In some respects, the plastic versions are used much as you would use their clay or concrete counterparts. You can use them to create the walls of buildings, but you can also use them to create vehicles, cities, moats, airplanes, and so on.

Using Various Brick Sizes

You will use 1×1 bricks in a variety of ways: they may find their way into mini-land style figures (featured in Chapter 4), mosaics (detailed in Chapter 8), small-scale animals, or just about any model where small detail work is required. In some ways, this is an extremely flexible brick that is sometimes overlooked.

Among other things, 1×2 and 1×3 bricks are handy for creating columns for either true structural support or just for ornamental purposes. I'll explore this technique in-depth in Chapter 2.

In many ways, the longer bricks in the 1×N category represent the backbone of the detail-building portion of the LEGO system. They have an enormous number of uses—far too many to fully represent here. One of the first uses that comes to mind is that they may function as the standard walls for virtually any small building. They provide a reasonable to-scale rendition of the thickness that you would find in real world walls.

Now let's move on to the wider pieces. It's hard to imagine the LEGO system having found as much long-term success without the association it has come to have with the 2×4 brick. For many builders who recall time spent rummaging through a pile of pieces, the 2×4 represents a standard image of a LEGO brick. This piece in particular finds its way into many models; both official sets and original creations by every class of builder.

On their own, these pieces may seem clunky and old-fashioned; they aren't particularly sleek or smooth and don't seem to offer much beyond their rectangular shapes. But for many projects, they represent the core material onto which other elements can be added. They are the true bricks of the LEGO system in every respect.

The Plate

At first glance, the common *plate* (shown in Figure 1-7) may not seem as useful as its big brother, the brick. After all, it takes three plates stacked on top of each other to equal the height of any regular-sized brick. However, that is exactly what makes the plate such an effective building tool. Because it's only one-third as high as a full-sized brick, you can use a plate to add subtle detailing, internal bracing, or realistic scaling to almost any model.

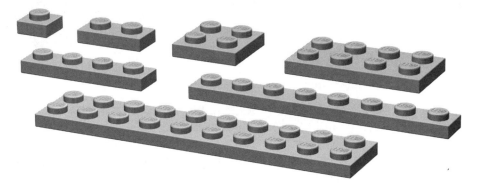

Figure 1-7: An assortment of standard plates

As noted earlier, the underrated plate is often the little piece that could. Plates can be among the most useful of elements and are found in many of the same length and width combinations as bricks—1×1, 1×4, 2×2, 2×4, and so on.

Using Various Plate Sizes

Plates of the 1×1 variety can find their way into almost any model, from the smallest automobile, to artistic mosaics (see Chapter 8 for more on mosaics), right up to helping flesh out the largest of sculptures (like those in Chapter 7). Similarly, you can find 1×2 and 1×3 plates in a range of applications and, thankfully, they are available in an equally large number of colors.

Longer 1×N plates have a huge number of uses; you can use them for projects ranging from building helicopter blades for small-sized rescue machines to creating long colorful stripes on the sides of a locomotive. Another area in which they shine is in helping tie together several columns of bricks or other plates that have been stacked vertically to create a visually interesting pattern. (We'll look more at construction techniques in the next chapter.)

Although the 2×N bricks represent the foundation of the brick class, the 2×2, 2×3, and 2×4 plates are the working class elements that allow you to accomplish a lot with a minimum amount of material. Throughout this book, I will hit on the idea of using a piece that is only as big as it needs to be. Shorter 2×N plates will pop up again and again as we drive toward that goal.

Beneath many a large-scale model are longer 2×N plates that hold even larger 4×N or 6×N plates together. Often 2×N plates allow some areas to remain open or exposed, which in turn allows you to add more detail or structure to the model.

The Slope

When you dig through your LEGO pieces, you'll usually come across what look like ramps for very tiny cars. These are *slopes,* so named because one or more sides slant from top to bottom (see examples in Figure 1-8). Slopes always create an angled surface between the studs at the top of the element and the point at which that element meets the piece beneath it. Slopes come in a variety of angles from 25 to 75 degrees (with 33- and 45-degree angles being the most common).

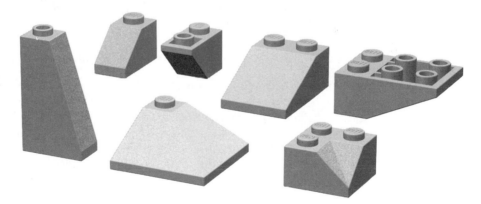

Figure 1-8: Slopes come in a variety of angles and shapes.

Although slopes are sometimes called *roof bricks,* they can do a lot more than simply cap off LEGO houses. They can add character to almost any model by helping to soften the harsh square edges that otherwise result from using only standard bricks. They can give beveled wings to an airplane, create a reasonable facsimile of an evergreen tree, or be used to put the roof on just about any kind of building.

In addition to their standard form, many slopes are manufactured in an inverted variety where the slant is found on the underside of the brick. An inverted slope is what you might see if you put a regular slope on a mirrored surface (see Figure 1-9). Of course, you can put your LEGO elements on a mirror; just don't expect them to realize how gorgeous they are.

Figure 1-9: These two slopes are nearly mirror images of each other. Many slopes come in both a standard and an inverted variety.

Specialized Elements

Within the LEGO system, certain elements defy easy classification. A few examples are shown in Figure 1-10. These pieces are either entirely unique or are just different enough from other elements so that they require a category of their own. Many times these pieces are unique because of their shape or perhaps because of the way in which their studs are oriented.

Although standard bricks and plates are inherently useful, the pieces in this category have some type of extra functionality. They are useful in many ordinary but also many specialized situations.

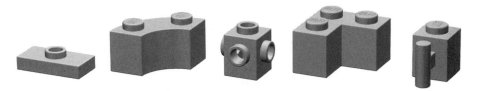

Figure 1-10: Specialized elements can take on a variety of shapes and sizes.

Other classification systems (typically those used on the Internet to catalog, track, or sell elements) tend to sort specialized pieces into existing standardized categories whether the fit is good or not. What happens as a result is that it becomes a challenge to try to find some of these pieces. For example, the well-known offset plate (shown on the left in Figure 1-10) is often described as a plate with a single stud in the center. Other resources label it as a *modified* plate or a *jumper* plate. However, it could just as easily be called a tile with a stud in the center, because its surface is more tile-like than it is plate-like. Without a specialized category, it is not the easiest part to classify.

One subcategory of specialized pieces will be wheels. Although it's certainly possible to use them for other things, they are most often used for one obvious and specialized purpose. See the Brickopedia for a few samples of these elements.

Technic

Originally developed in the 1970s, the Technic portion of the LEGO system was first released in sets known as *Technical Sets.* They promised to add realism and complexity to regular LEGO bricks, and the models certainly reflected that. The key to adding realism was, in fact, that the new pieces (gears, bricks with holes, axles, and so on, as shown in Figure 1-11) were very much compatible with elements already in existence. In other words, if you wanted to buy or build with the new sets, you didn't have to start building your LEGO collection again from scratch. You could buy a little blue go-kart with the working steering and the one cylinder motor, and you could use your own blue bricks to add details to it that didn't come in the factory-made kit.

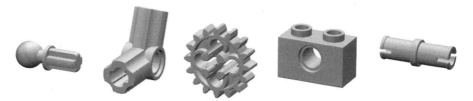

Figure 1-11: Technic parts cover a large range of strange shapes and serve to enable more realistic and functional models made from LEGO elements.

In theory, you could build almost an entire model using nothing but Technic elements, but by adding in some of your regular system parts, you can enhance that model and produce a more finished result.

To classify Technic pieces, you need to add additional subcategories to what is, in essence, already a subcategory. In order to keep things as simple as possible, the number of divisions has been kept to a minimum, and the descriptors have been similarly kept lean. Since Technic gets its own chapter later on (Chapter 9), I'll leave any examination of this category for that part of the book.

Arch Pieces

At first glance, you might think that *arch pieces* (like the ones in Figure 1-12) are too specialized to be of much use for more than architectural detailing. And although they serve their primary purpose without compromise, they can also add character and shape to models of all types, not just buildings.

Arch bricks are useful for creating arches, especially on the exterior of buildings, but they can appear over many things. For instance, you can have an arch over a doorway or above windows. You will also find arches repeated to create visually exciting geometric patterns along the top edges of buildings, or you may find them used on otherwise plain walls to create sections sometimes filled with other colors or patterns.

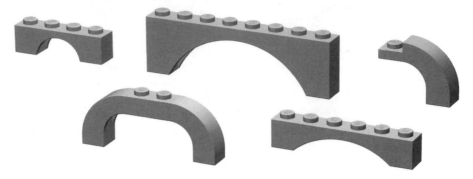

Figure 1-12: Among the most graceful of LEGO elements are the arches. They come in several sizes and styles.

Using an arch as an arch is a no-brainer. Using arches of varying sizes and shapes is a little more difficult. In many cases, it's best to draw your inspiration directly from the building you are attempting to copy, or at least a similar type of structure if you're building a piece of architecture that has never before existed. Picking out how arches are used on buildings is not unlike working one of those brainteaser puzzles where you have to figure out how many triangles are really drawn among the dozens of intersecting lines on the page.

Tiles and Panels

Standard *tiles* are easy to spot (see Figure 1-13); they're like a plate without studs. Cylindrical tiles are similarly easy to figure out because they look like tiny smooth manhole covers.

Figure 1-13: Tiles have a tiny groove at their base that allows you to remove them more easily.

Panels, on the other hand, come in a wider variety of shapes and sizes (see Figure 1-14). In some sense, panels are like tiles with other tiles attached at right angles to form a thin vertical wall or two. Panels may or may not have studs.

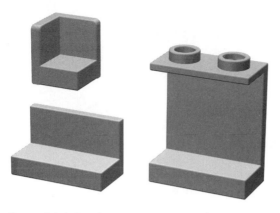

Figure 1-14: Panels come in a variety of shapes and sizes.

Cylinders and Cones

Cylinder elements have a cylindrical shape, like a coffee can or a drum (see Figure 1-15). *Cones,* on the other hand, are sort of like upside-down ice cream cones. Although only a few elements fall into the standard cylinder or cone categories, what they lack in number they make up for in uniqueness.

Figure 1-15: Cylinders come in standard vertical-walled varieties and also sloped versions known as cones.

From tree trunks, to light posts, to the nozzles on the ends of water cannons, you'll find a varied set of uses for cylinders and cones.

Cylinder Plates

Cylinder plates, as their name suggests are just shorter versions of their full brick-height cousins. The tiny 1×1 cylinder plate (sometimes known as a *pip*) and the useful 2×2 plate (both shown in Figure 1-16) are the only two elements that make up this subcategory, making it among the smallest you'll see.

Figure 1-16: A pip sits next to its big brother the 2×2 cylinder plate.

Baseplates

It's not hard to confuse large standard bricks with small baseplates. So where do large bricks end and baseplates begin? For purposes of this text, assume a *baseplate* is an element with a waffled underside to which no other bricks can be attached. These baseplates are, in fact, thinner than even a standard plate, as shown in Figure 1-17. They may be plain (having only regular studs on top) or may have designs (such as roadways) printed on them.

Figure 1-17: A 1×1 plate is used to show the difference in thickness between it and a waffled baseplate.

Baseplates give you a foundation upon which to build a model, whether it's a building, a machine, a sculpture, or just about anything that requires a platform to steady it or allow it to be transported or displayed.

Decorative Elements

Standard bricks, plates, and slopes are obviously useful for creating a basic model. Sometimes though, you need to add a bit of character to your creations. *Decorative elements* can perform that task for you by allowing you to add windows, doors, trees, and so on. As you can see in Figure 1-18, they take many forms.

Figure 1-18: Fences, windows, trees, and flags are just a few examples of decorative elements.

Precision, Geometry, and Color

Now that you have a handle on basic LEGO-related terminology and some sense of how parts can be categorized, let's look at a few other areas of the LEGO system.

Why Precision Manufacturing Matters

It doesn't take very long to realize something very important about LEGO pieces. Every element is manufactured to a very high degree of precision, not unlike the accuracy seen in the manufacture of aircraft parts. Because this precision applies to such a small scale, this tight control of plastic molding may not be evident immediately. If you snap a few bricks together and they are off by a hair's width, it probably won't bother you too much. But what if you begin to stack up more and more bricks? How long will it take before even a small difference in quality control begins to show itself?

Take Figure 1-19 as an example. Imagine you are making a doorway. On the right, you use properly made bricks, each exactly the height it is supposed to be. On the left side, you use a handful of bricks that weren't made with the same precision and care. Perhaps they were made just a tiny bit too short, say, by about the thickness of a pencil mark. It's clear from Figure 1-19 that only a few layers of bricks with such a manufacturing variance would begin to play havoc with your construction. How would you join these two mismatched walls?

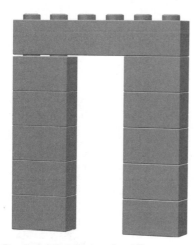

Height, of course, is but one of three essential dimensions that must match in each and every element. Differences in length or width would also quickly become apparent because you would find that a brick wouldn't press down normally onto the pieces beneath it. Studs would be out of alignment and finishing even a modest-sized model would become nearly impossible.

The same attention to detail must also be given to things like the height and width of the studs themselves, the height and thickness of inner tubes, the diameter of the walls of bricks and plates, and so on.

Figure 1-19: Imagine the difference a tiny error makes when multiplied by a number of bricks.

Fun with LEGO Geometry

When you look at the base measurement piece (the 1×1 brick) you'll find that it is a vertically oriented rectangle with a ratio of 5:6 (width:height). Figure 1-20 shows these measurements applied to a 1×1 brick.

This means that five 1×1 bricks stacked on top of each other are exactly the same length as a standard 1×6 brick, as shown in Figure 1-21.

This happens because the five 1×1 bricks are each six units high. So five times six equals thirty. Similarly, each stud of the 1×6 represents five units of width. So six studs times five equals thirty again. Note that we take into account only the dimensions of the brick walls and disregard the height of the last exposed stud. We'll see this interesting geometry come into use in Chapter 8 when we look at mosaics.

Other interesting geometries are available within the system. For example, the tubes under a standard brick or plate are the same distance apart as regular studs, and the inner diameter of the tube is the same diameter as the stud itself. This allows you to place a brick or plate on top of exposed studs where the number of studs is equal to or less than the number of tubes available, as shown in Figure 1-22.

This represents one of the few times, other than when you are using offset plates, that you can offset elements from one another by a value of one-half stud rather than a full stud.

Consider, too, the relationship between the height of a standard plate and a standard brick, as shown in Figure 1-23.

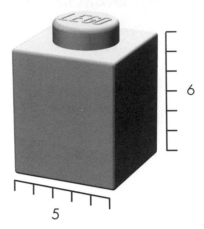

Figure 1-20: The 5:6 ratio of width to height applies to all standard LEGO bricks.

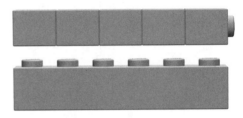

Figure 1-21: The 5:6 ratio of brick height to brick length

Figure 1-22: Studs inserted into tubes, not alongside them

Figure 1-23: Three plates stacked together will always equal the height of one standard brick.

It's quickly apparent that three plates equal a brick, but that is not where things end. This simple and elegant fact represents a wealth of potential building patterns and techniques. One fairly easy application of this fact is that you can use plates to create visual illusions within the context of walls or other structures. For instance, the white stripe seen in the fire truck Figure 1-24 shows how you can stagger plates through several layers of other plates and bricks to create the effect of an angle.

Figure 1-24: Fire truck with stripes made from plates

I'll show you other techniques for using plates throughout the book. As you move on to some of these best practices, you can rest assured that even your wildest designs and ideas can be fulfilled thanks to a system of bits and pieces that have been carefully created to interact with each other as easily as they interact with you.

The Colors

For many years, LEGO bricks were epitomized by the primary colors in which they were available: red, yellow, and blue. In fact, in 1958, when the original patent was issued for the knob and tube design (which defined the modern LEGO brick), only seven different colors were being made: white, black, red, blue, yellow, green, and clear. Of course, today's sets are being released with colors that include mossy green, maroon, pale blue, dark grey, bright orange, and even pink!

Given LEGO's original color limitations, builders had to improvise to create new colors from the limited existing ones. The trick they developed to create new colors was to place one or more colors next to each other to create a sense of blending. For example, a white brick may take on a subtle grey tone when placed next to a black element. Similarly, a yellow piece will shift slightly toward the orange part of the color spectrum when placed next to a red brick.

The colors you chose to use in your models can add realism, character, or even a sense of humor that might not otherwise be telegraphed by the bricks themselves. For instance, a fire engine you model in red or bright yellow will probably look more like the real thing than if you built it from blue or grey bricks. A snowman sculpture will look more like what people expect if he is constructed in a traditional white scheme. (Although you might decide to put red horns growing out of his head to create something playful or mischievous.) A fairground ride might look more exciting and fun if it uses a variety of colors in playful patterns of reds, blues, and yellows. Color plays an important part in almost everything you build.

For the Color Challenged

One problem that often besets new or younger builders is a lack of enough bricks in any one color that they can use to give a model a consistent look. This can be frustrating, but it doesn't have to stop your plans for building sophisticated models. There are two ways you can make the most of the bricks you have, in whatever colors they may be, without spending a fortune topping off your stocks.

1. Match the models you build to the bricks you have. Build small models that let you stay within a single color or perhaps two.

2. Use multiple colors in planned ways to maximize your entire collection of elements. Many vehicles, buildings, animals, and other subjects are either naturally multicolored or allow for adaptation so they can be modeled in other colors.

Even official LEGO sets have used limited color schemes to great effect. Some sets contain only a smattering of colors. Sets like these offer two huge benefits: they provide you with ideas for using limited colors effectively, and they add healthy quantities of two or three colors to your collection.

For example, imagine that you have one or more official sets that contain a lot of red and white elements. Aside from the model(s) suggested in the instructions, you might also find that you have enough parts to build a simple sculpture like a candy cane in time for the holidays (as shown in Figure 1-25).

Or you could use a similar color scheme to put together a small lighthouse like the one shown in Figure 1-26. The point is that your limited palette of colors doesn't need to limit your imagination.

One thing to consider is that you can buy more than one of the same set. Although this may seem silly at first, it makes perfect sense if you are trying to build up your collection of a certain color or colors. This is especially true if you can find the set on sale or perhaps you can ask to receive another copy as a gift.

Figure 1-25: Having limited colors means using what you have to the best of your ability.

NOTE   *For instructions and color images of the lighthouse, visit www.apotome.com/ instructions.html.*

Review: The LEGO System

You may have noticed that you didn't learn much about actually building with LEGO pieces in this chapter. That's okay; there's lots of that to come. You did learn about the basic framework and terminology of the LEGO system. You'll use that knowledge to work through the construction techniques and ideas that follow. Being able to tell a brick from a plate makes all the difference as you move on to those more complicated topics. In turn, those practices allow you to create a minifig-scale train station, a three-dimensional sphere you can hold in your hand, and even a mini space shuttle that you get to design from the ground up. Between here and there, I'll try to explain more of this amazing system, describe its many uses, and hopefully, reveal a few secrets along the way.

Figure 1-26: The stripe on the lighthouse is achieved by carefully placing just two different colors of bricks. Try building this model using red and white elements with brown or dark gray for the base.

2

BACK TO BASICS:
TIPS AND TECHNIQUES

No matter how old you are, when you sit down in front of a pile of LEGO bricks, one thing never changes: you want to snap a few bricks together. Why this happens is not a mystery. LEGO bricks, like grains of sand on a beach, are meant to be together.

But what are the best ways to join bricks? That depends, of course, on what you're building. Official LEGO literature goes to great lengths to point out the many possible ways to connect your bricks. For example, they suggest that if you take six 2×4 bricks, you can arrange them in 102,981,500 different patterns. (Someone at LEGO has a very good understanding of geometry and mathematics or just way too much time on their hands.) Figure 2-1 demonstrates just three of the millions of possible combinations. I'd need an enormous number of pages to show pictures of every pattern.

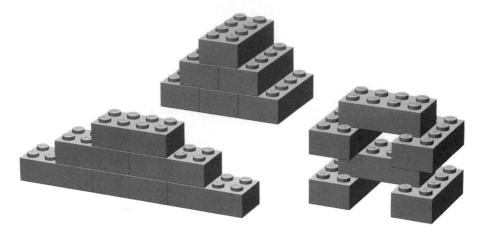

Figure 2-1: You can combine six 2×4 bricks in many ways.

Decisions, Decisions: The Best Ways to Connect Bricks

Perhaps more important than the *number* of ways in which you can fasten bricks together are the principles behind *how* they should be put together.

For example, consider any two 2×4 bricks. You can connect them in three basic ways, as illustrated in Figures 2-2 through 2-4. You can stack them, overlap them, or stagger them.

Is it best to put them together like this?   Like this?

Figure 2-2: Stacked

Figure 2-3: Overlapped

Or like this?

Figure 2-4: Staggered

Each of the diagrams in Figures 2-2 through 2-4 represents a different type of *bonding*, or joining of LEGO bricks. *Bonding patterns* are the ways in which bricks are arranged or connected. Let's look at each of these patterns individually to get a sense of how they can be most useful.

Stacking

Although not the most common way to build, and usually not the sturdiest, at times, *stacking* bricks one on top of the other is necessary. For instance, a small shop in your LEGO town might have vertical stripes of color that you wish to appear painted on the sides of the building. Or perhaps an airplane needs to have a colorful pattern of lines on its tail section.

Typically your decision to use vertically stacked bricks is driven by aesthetic rather than structural needs. The reason for this is simple: as you can see in Figure 2-5, stacks of bricks, unsupported by surrounding pieces or layers, are generally not very strong.

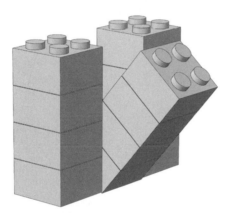

Figure 2-5: Crash! With nothing to support it, the center column of bricks is prone to falling over when you least expect it.

When you do need to stack bricks, make sure that you secure the stacks— both above and below—with longer bricks or plates. For example, as you can see in Figure 2-6, stacked 1×1 bricks create the vertical stripes on the tail section of a plane. The vertical part of the tail sits on several offset plates, but below that, the stripes are held together by a 2×8 plate. Near the top, the stacked bricks are locked together by the 1×4 plate you can see just above the highest slope piece.

Figure 2-6: When it is necessary to stack bricks, make sure you lock them in place to avoid the Humpty Dumpty effect.

Overlapping

No building technique adds as much to your models as *overlapping* does. As with real brick walls, LEGO bricks work best together when they sit on top of each other in overlapping patterns. These overlapping connections strengthen the structure and prevent it from collapsing. (Depending on the size of brick you are using, this overlap may be one-half of the brick below, or as little as a small part of the lower brick.) Figure 2-7 illustrates just a handful of different overlap patterns. The ones you use depend on the bricks you have available and the model you are building.

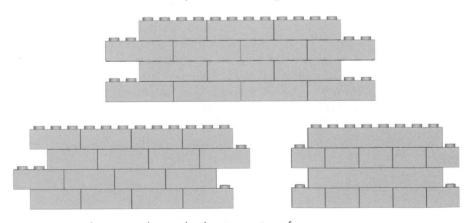

Figure 2-7: Bricks can overlap each other in a variety of patterns.

Overlapping bricks gives your models strength and allows you to fully exploit one of the primary features of the LEGO system: the interlocking feature of elements. Models containing standard bricks and plates almost always utilize one or more overlap patterns. Later in this chapter, I'll show you how to build walls and connect them together. Those tasks both make significant use of the overlap pattern.

Don't forget that other elements need to be overlapped as well. Pieces like doors and windows should be secured using this technique to make sure they are solidly built into a wall. In Figure 2-8, you can see this principle in action.

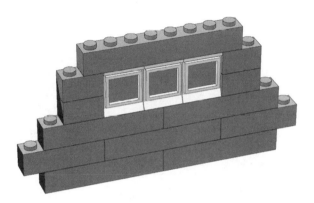

Figure 2-8: A well-placed brick can make the difference between a solid wall and one that will eventually fall apart.

It's clear in Figure 2-8 just how important overlapping is. You can see that the 1×8 brick at the top of the wall overlaps not only the windows, but also the bricks to either side of them. This helps create a solid structure.

The simplest way to achieve good overlapping is to simply remember that you want to avoid too many bricks stacked on top of each other, which creates vertical seams. You can see what I mean in Figure 2-9.

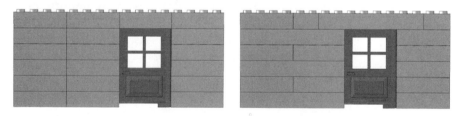

Figure 2-9: A poorly designed wall (on the left) is shown with a properly designed wall (on the right).

The wall on the left in Figure 2-9 was created using the stacking technique you saw earlier in the chapter. You can see how unstable the door would be if you tried to open it because the 1×4 brick on top of it isn't attached to anything else. On the right, you can see the better way to create a wall with a door. Notice that the 1×8 brick over the door is also attached to bricks on either side, just as the windows are in Figure 2-8. This helps anchor the door to the wall and makes sure that they won't come apart when you least expect it.

Staggering

When you *stagger* bricks, you set one layer of bricks back from the front edge of an adjoining layer of bricks to produce a stair-step pattern.

Staggering is a particularly important technique when you're building sculptures (covered in Chapter 7). It allows bricks that are typically square or rectangular to achieve more organic shapes when used in the right combinations. That isn't its only use of course. Figure 2-10 shows a very common way to use the staggering technique.

Figure 2-10: You can apply this simple staggered roof technique to a multitude of models.

In Figure 2-10, you see a small house or perhaps a vacation cottage. By staggering the bricks, you can create a roof out of nothing more than standard bricks. In other words, instead of using sloped bricks for the roof, you create one from ordinary elements; this is a popular technique in the LEGO building world. Figure 2-11 shows a portion of the roof in close-up so that you can see exactly why the staggering technique is so useful in situations like this.

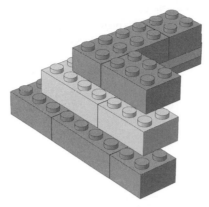

Figure 2-11: Don't forget to overlap bricks as you stagger the layers.

In Figure 2-11, I alternated the colors of the layers in the close-up of the roof so it's easier for you to see how I accomplished the staggering. Obviously 2×N-sized bricks work best for this technique. Notice that even though I stagger the bricks (to accomplish the slope of the roof), I still overlap them from layer to layer. This combination of two techniques results in a sturdier model.

Building Walls

Walls are one of the most common things built from LEGO bricks. They may be walls for a fire station, a hospital, or a police department. They could also be the walls of a medieval castle or maybe even an alien base on some far-off planet. In the "Overlapping" section earlier in this chapter, you saw how to build a strong wall by itself. Now let's move on to learn how to connect two or more walls together.

Connecting Walls

In several of the earlier illustrations (Figures 2-7, 2-8, and 2-9), you saw simple walls built with the overlap technique. However, a lone wall isn't much good if you intend to create a realistic-looking building. The inhabitants of your LEGO world will certainly enjoy their buildings more if you provide them with rooms, doorways, and other basic structures—especially ones that won't fall down.

But don't expect to connect two preexisting walls to each other to make a strong pair. It is much better to build them at the same time and have them draw on each other's strength. Walls should be joined to each other from the very first course of bricks. Figure 2-12 shows the first layer of two walls that will be connected.

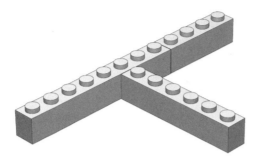

Figure 2-12: The first course of bricks when building a wall connected to another wall

The next course of bricks begins to lock the first layer in place by overlapping, as shown in Figure 2-13. The dark 1×4 brick ties one wall to another, locking the 1×6 to the 1×8.

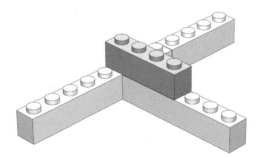

Figure 2-13: The highlighted brick is the cornerstone of the overlap. It connects the two walls beginning with the second course.

This technique is the key to building solid models. As Figure 2-14 shows, as you add the remainder of the second course, the other bricks (in this particular example) aren't quite as important as the one highlighted in Figure 2-13. They are part of the walls, but not part of what is holding the two walls together.

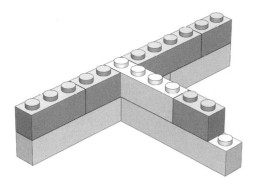

Figure 2-14: The remainder of the second layer is added.

Finally, in Figure 2-15, you can see that the overlapping technique continues to be used to connect the two walls to each other but is also used within each individual wall. This ensures the structure is sound.

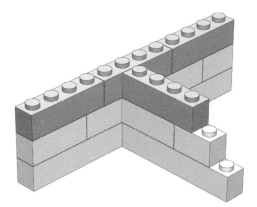

Figure 2-15: Completed example

After just a few layers, you should find that your two walls are firmly supporting each other. Try pushing on either wall, and you will soon see that they can't be easily shifted. The overlap pattern has given you strong walls, and by connecting them together, you have made them even more stable.

Straight Bricks Can Make Round Walls

Of course, you don't always want perfectly straight and perfectly interlocked walls. Sometimes you want to create a model that's a little more organic, or at the very least, less than square.

How can you use straight bricks to form a curved wall? One fun technique is to dig up as many 1×3 bricks as you can find and link them together, as shown in Figure 2-16.

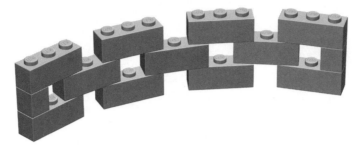

Figure 2-16: 1×3 bricks joined in this fashion make it possible to create curved or even completely circular walls.

This method allows you to curve a wall as much as you want, even to the point of creating a complete circle. You may find yourself using this idea to make a pen for barnyard animals, the body of a rocket, a fence around a house, and so on.

To create a different look, try adding 1×1 cylinder bricks to the openings between the 1×3 bricks. As you can see in Figure 2-17, this makes the wall appear more solid. You won't be able to curve it as much as the example in Figure 2-16, but it's still a great technique that will add new shapes to your models.

Figure 2-17: A few small pieces can make a big difference in how your wall looks.

By playing around with the length of your wall and the curve of the bricks, you may find that you can even link the ends of the wall into existing square structures (see Figure 2-18). For example, you may be able to take two castle walls and create a rounded corner that connects them. Or, you can try to make a guard tower from the 1×3 technique and set it on a castle made from regular walls that meet at 90 degrees. By placing 1×1 round plates at various points under the 1×3's, you should be able to find combinations that allow you to connect your round wall to the other parts of your model.

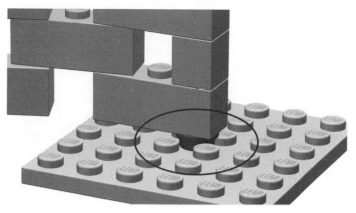

Figure 2-18: Round and square worlds meet. The 1×1 cylinder plate (circled) is used to anchor the curved wall to a flat surface.

Bracing: Unseen but Not Forgotten

Bracing is the art of reinforcing your models, typically on the inside, to make them stronger and more stable. It can be as simple as adding a few long bricks to strengthen otherwise unsteady structures, or as involved as building columns and beams within a larger model to allow it to be handled, transported somewhere, or even just stand up without falling down.

Bracing = Beams + Columns

In Figure 2-19, you see some simple walls. They could be the outsides of an office building, the sides of a grandfather clock, or maybe the beginnings of a tall but slender air traffic control tower. You also see some other bricks (marked A and B) that seem to connect the other walls. This reinforcement, made up of a central column and two horizontal beams, is bracing that is used to make the model stronger.

The amount of bracing required varies from model to model—from none for smaller models to lots for large buildings and towers. Bracing your model properly can give it a very solid structure that is particularly useful for transporting it (to a public display or to a friend's house) or even just playing with it.

Why not just fill in the area inside the building completely and make it solid? Although this might work for some smaller models, it makes larger ones heavier than they need to be, and it most definitely uses more bricks than you probably need. Why hide your bricks needlessly? Use what you need for support and no more. You can use the bricks you save by building efficiently to build other parts or other models.

Bracing is really functional construction and does not necessarily have to look pretty. The great thing about this technique is that you can use just about any bricks at your disposal to beef up a model from behind or underneath. After all, no one is going to see the bricks, so it doesn't matter what color they are or whether they are even the same color.

Figure 2-19: A peek behind the scenes shows how columns and beams come together to form bracing for this representative building.

In Figure 2-19, the column (labeled A) stands away from the walls of the building. The beam on the right (labeled B) extends from the column to the outside wall (labeled D). The dark square (labeled C) in the wall is really the end of beam B. It is built into the wall and creates a strong link between column A and wall D.

To better understand bracing, you need to learn a bit more about columns and beams.

Beams

You saw one form of columns in Figure 2-5. Normally, though, you wouldn't expect to see columns lined up next to each other as in that example. Rather, you would find them as the corners of buildings, the structures on either sides of doorways, or as supports for wide floors or ceilings.

One reason that the columns in Figure 2-5 were able to tumble was that there was nothing holding them together. That's where beams come into play. *Beams* are the horizontal equivalents of columns, and they work hand-in-hand with them to form strong structures.

A beam can be as simple as a single brick (such as the one shown in Figure 2-20) you use to connect two parts of a structure that would not otherwise touch each other. Or, a beam can be a much larger and much more complicated substructure. A *substructure* is a portion of a model that you build separately and then join to the main model. An example could be something used for support, like the composite beam shown in Figure 2-21, or it could be something more visible, like the ladder on a fire truck.

Figure 2-20: A beam can be as simple as a single 2×8 brick.

You can make composite beams (see Figure 2-21) from a mixture of bricks and plates or just several layers of bricks. You can build them very long, yet they still remain strong.

Figure 2-21: A composite beam, made from bricks and plates

Notice (in Figure 2-21) that overlapping plates (with each other or with full-height bricks) is just as critical as it is when you are building with bricks alone.

Given how important they are, building strong beams is obviously a big concern. Let me first show you how not to do it.

How Not to Build a Beam

Set up a few bricks to resemble Figure 2-22.

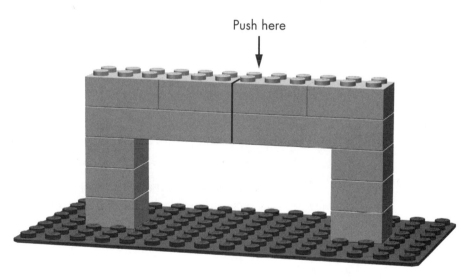

Figure 2-22: When you set up your example, pay close attention to the bond patterns I used.

To conduct this experiment, simply push down with your finger on the brick shown in Figure 2-22. You'll find that with very little effort, the bricks you set up between the two columns quickly break apart and fall down. You have just seen a structure fail, which is typically something that you'd rather avoid in most of your models.

The Right Way to Build a Beam

Now try setting up a similar set of bricks but in a slightly different pattern, as shown in Figure 2-23. Carefully note the positions of the bricks and where they overlap. Now when you push down from above, you should find it nearly impossible to cause the beam to fail. It should become quickly apparent why it is so important to overlap bricks.

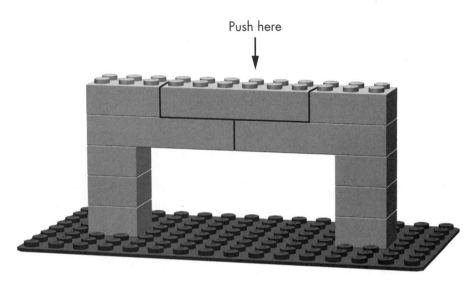

Figure 2-23: This example uses a simple overlap pattern to ensure the beam won't buckle under pressure.

You could use the beam in Figure 2-23 to connect the outer walls of a large building or you might even find it over top of the large opening on the front of a LEGO aircraft hangar.

Columns

Columns are the other half of what you use to brace larger or unstable models. Typically you'll use one or more columns to support beams that connect to the sides of your model. Columns can take many different forms, as seen in Figures 2-24 through 2-27.

The Simple Post

In Figure 2-24 you see nothing more than 2×2 bricks stacked on top of each other. A simple column like this one might suit some of your projects quite well. It's important that you never make anything more complicated than it needs to be. Just be sure the post doesn't get too high, because this type of column lacks the strength of the other examples.

In addition to the 2×2 bricks in Figure 2-24, it is also possible to make a simple post from 2×3's, 2×4's, or just about any other sized brick.

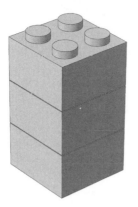

Figure 2-24: The simple post

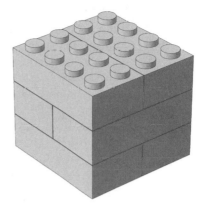

Figure 2-25: The compound post

Figure 2-26: The chimney pattern

Figure 2-27: The keyhole pattern

The Compound Post

Figure 2-25 is a much more sturdy column, though one that obviously consumes more bricks. Unlike the 2×2 version, this 2×4 column can withstand a certain amount of pressure from any side without crumbling. It's also about as simple to build as anything you could ask for. This is an excellent choice when you are creating a number of columns quickly (perhaps even to use as temporary support).

The Chimney Pattern

The column shown in Figure 2-26 is about as strong as the one in Figure 2-25, but it offers some weight (and brick) savings over the previous example. Because the core of this column is hollow, you get much of the horizontal stability of the 2×4 version but at only 75 percent of its weight. This may be important if you are building a model that you want to transport.

One drawback to this column is that you must check it regularly to ensure that its core remains square. Do so by making a 2×2 column of six or more pieces and, as you build, inserting it into the core from time to time.

The Keyhole Pattern

What do you do with all those leftover 1×2's? Make them into a column. The column shown in Figure 2-27 can be varied in both size and shape. The specific arrangement shown here is just one possible pattern based on the principle of creating composite walls out of mostly smaller (1×3 or less) bricks. You can change the pattern slightly and the column can grow in diameter based on your model's needs.

Like the chimney pattern, you must use some arrangement of bricks (built into the shape of the core) to constantly align the keyhole column. Because of its many components, this column has a particularly strong tendency to warp and twist as it rises. However, if you can keep it reasonably straight, it is not only a very functional substructure, but an attractive one as well.

The Hybrid Column

An interesting new pattern comes about when you mix the regular compound post column with the chimney pattern, as shown in Figure 2-28.

By using this hybrid column, you immediately resolve one of the major problems with the hollow-core version: by adding a layer or two of 2×4 bricks (as shown in Figure 2-29) every few layers, you help keep the 1×2 and 1×4 bricks aligned.

Figure 2-28: The hybrid column is both lightweight and self-straightening.

Figure 2-29: An "exploded" view of the hybrid column design showing the orientation of the different layers.

Given the actual inventories of bricks that most builders have, this version may be more realistic to build. It's unlikely that you will build a large-scale model entirely of 2×4 bricks or entirely of 1×2 and 1×4 bricks. In most situations, you are much more likely to mix and match all sizes of bricks as you need them. Therefore, when it comes to having bricks left over for your columns (bricks that you don't need in the main model) you will probably have a good mix of the three sizes.

Remember that your models may not always be so large that they need internal bracing. But don't discard some of the construction patterns you've learned while looking at columns and beams. In Chapter 3, you will see just how useful a simple post–style column can be when you go to create a small building. And you can use beams, apart from linking columns together, to support floors within a building or give you something solid onto which you can add a roof. Keeping the different patterns in mind gives you the essential tools you need to be a successful LEGO builder.

Review: Basic Building Principles

Now you have some idea of the best ways to connect bricks and make your models strong. It's also important to understand how to plan your constructions. You want to build sensibly so that you minimize problems and enjoy your building sessions to the fullest. Here are a couple of basic principles that will help you do that.

1. Build big but think small.

No matter how big you think your model might end up, consider breaking the entire work down into smaller sections that are easier to work on. You'll make the model seem less daunting and make it easy to figure out how to build very high sections or perhaps sections that are constructed at different angles than the rest of the model. For example, if you're building a skyscraper, think about building sections of a few floors each, then attach these sections to each other.

If you're making a model of a real life object, like a building or a vehicle, examine the object and try to find natural separations. This might be where the size or shape changes dramatically or where one color ends and another begins.

Existing separations can help you to determine how to build your model in sections. For example, if you're building a pickup truck, you might want to build the cab separately from the box section.

2. Pick the right bonding pattern.

The decision of which of the three main bonding patterns to use (Figures 2-2 through 2-4) will vary from model to model and even within the same model. You won't always want to use overlapping, despite its obvious strengths. Sometimes you will want to stack bricks and other times you will want to stagger them. Throughout the book, I point out which pattern you're using and why. As a result, as you move on to designing and building your own models, you will have a better sense of the pattern you should use at any given time.

3

MINIFIG SCALE: OH, WHAT A WONDERFUL MINIFIG WORLD IT IS!

The LEGO system is always evolving with the addition of new elements, colors, and updated set designs that reflect the times. Perhaps one of the more significant additions to the system came in 1978 when the miniature figure, better known as the *minifig*, was added. The most basic version of a minifig is shown in Figure 3-1.

Although it is really a collection of three pieces (legs, upper body, and head) the minifig typically arrives as two pieces (legs and upper body with the head already attached). Once you've built a set containing a minifig, you'll probably leave it fully assembled, often with some style of hair or hat and sometimes with a tool or other accessory to hold in its hands.

Figure 3-1: Who is this guy, and why is he smiling?

Over the years, I've seen many different types of minifig, with a wide variety of different styles and costumes—from astronauts and cowboys to helicopter pilots, racecar drivers, and many more.

Scale: It's All Relative

No matter how big your LEGO collection is, you probably have a few minifigs lurking about. It seems only fair then that you look at building a world to their scale.

Simply put, *scale* is how you describe the relationship between the size of one object and the size of another.

But what is minifig scale? For simplicity's sake, assume that from the point of view of the minifig, a minifig is, on average, about 6 feet tall—not the 1 1/2 inches that you measure it to be. In Figure 3-2, you can see that your basic minifig just barely gets to that mark on a ruler.

Figure 3-2: How does a minifig measure up? In our world he's only an inch and a half. In his world he's six feet tall.

Having made this assumption, you know that 1 1/2 inches in the world of minifigs represents 6 feet in our world. Let's take that information and figure out the scale.

Calculating Scale

To convert to minifig scale, do the following:

1. First, convert 6 feet into inches. Because there are 12 inches in a foot, the calculation is pretty simple.

    `12 inches × 6 feet = 72 inches`

2. Then, divide your model/minifig height into your real height.

    `72 inches ÷ 1.5 inches = 48 inches`

In other words, this is the formula:

```
Height of same object in your world ÷ Actual model height = Scale value
```

3. Finally, create your scale. Your minifig is

```
1:48 scale (pronounced "one-forty-eighth" or "one to forty-eight")
```

Scales are shown as two numbers separated by a colon. The number on the left represents one real object. The number on the right represents the number of scale objects it would take to equal the same size. (You may see scale written as a fraction, like 1/48, but the meaning is the same.)

This scale tells you that if you could stack 48 minifigs on top of each other, without having them tumble down, they would equal just about 6 real feet in height.

Figure 3-3 shows another even simpler example. A standard 2×4 brick is shown to the right of a 2×4 Duplo brick. These larger bricks are part of LEGO's line of products aimed at younger children. By comparing these two pieces, you see an easy-to-understand example of a 1:2 scale. In other words, *for every one Duplo brick, you need two regular bricks to equal the same dimension,* because Duplo bricks are twice as high, twice as wide and twice as long.

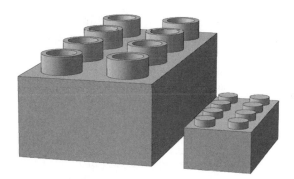

Figure 3-3: A standard 2×4 brick and a 2×4 Duplo brick help demonstrate the 1:2 scale.

Once you have the scale figure, you can use it to work backward, taking a real life object and deciding how big it should be in your minifig world. Let's use an example of a house, because you know every minifig will want one or two. Let's say that the house you want to use as inspiration is 24 feet tall in real life. This time you divide the actual height (24 feet) by your scale value (48).

```
24 feet = 288 inches (converted to inches so that your result is in those
units)

288 ÷ 48 = 6 inches

Real object height ÷ Scale value = Size of scale model
```

It's easy to see that your minifig scale house should be 6 inches tall in order to accurately represent the actual building you're using as your guide.

From the Ground Up: Creating a Minifig-Scale Building

For many years, houses, police stations, hospitals, and other buildings were often used as inspirations for sets put out by LEGO. These days, sets with a town theme aren't as common as they once were, but that shouldn't stop you from making your own.

One thing that always makes official LEGO sets so interesting is the way the designers add architectural details to models of buildings. In the case of buildings, this may take the form of some well-placed arches over windows, a simple chimney rising from the roof, or perhaps some smooth tiles made to appear like sidewalks.

These techniques enhance what might otherwise be boring buildings and turn them into the vibrant places where minifigs like to live and work. When constructing your own models, you can use these same ideas to improve the realism and therefore the appeal of your LEGO town.

For the remainder of this chapter, we'll focus on a single model built to minifig scale. I'll use a small-town railway station as a platform upon which to demonstrate some of the principles you learned in Chapter 2. Starting from the ground up, I'll show you the various parts that go into such a model and I'll teach you how to apply those same building techniques to other buildings in your LEGO town.

As you read along, remember that this building doesn't have to end up as a train station. You can adapt the basic design so it becomes an ice cream parlor, a hamburger stand, or maybe even a ticket booth for a theme park or a zoo. How you use it within your LEGO town is open to your imagination. You are never forced to color inside the lines when building with LEGO bricks.

Building Two Versions of the Train Station

To get the most out of this exercise, we'll need to tackle the building from two perspectives. First, we'll explore how you might build the building as if it were an official LEGO set created from a nearly unlimited range of parts. This way allows you to use specialty pieces to detail the model. Afterward, I'll remake parts of the building using more common pieces, like those you might find in your own collection.

As you can see, I've based the design of the railway station on one you might find in many small towns across North America. A typical station constructed sometime in the late 1800s or early 1900s might look something like Figure 3-4.

Often, these buildings shared a number of common features. Low-angle sloped roofs, arched entryways, and windows dressed in contrasting colors are just some of the traits you can see on many such stations.

Before I can build the roof or any of these other details, I first need to construct the building itself. To do so, I will use a simple overlap technique for the outside walls before incorporating some slopes to complete the roof design.

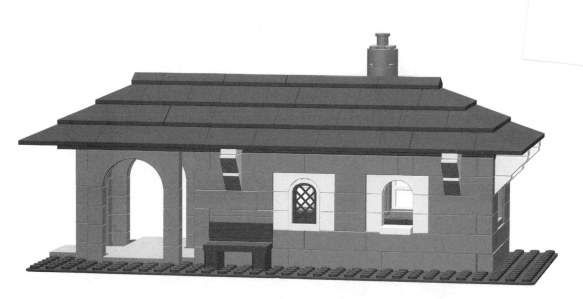

Figure 3-4: Your goal—use the design ideas for this building to create all kinds of structures for your LEGO town.

Bill of Materials: The Parts You'll Need to Make This Model

Figure 3-5 shows you the Bill of Materials you need to build your own copy of this model. The term *Bill of Materials* is used to refer to a picture of all the elements you need to build a model and how many of each you need. Remember that you may not have every single piece indicated in the diagram, but that doesn't mean you can't build the model. For example, if you are short on 1×8 bricks, why not replace each one of them with two 1×4 bricks? Are you missing one 2×2 brick in a certain color? Why not stack up three 2×2 plates to make something that will serve the same purpose? Use your imagination to substitute one or more elements when necessary.

Step by Step: Train Station Construction Details

I've broken the instructions for building the train station down into a series of steps, each accompanied by a picture. Instructions that come with official LEGO sets use similar pictures to represent each building step, but they don't usually have words to describe what's happening. In this book, my main objective is to teach you about building with LEGO—why you should use certain parts and when to use certain construction techniques. By explaining each step along the way, I hope to give you a better sense of what's going on in the picture for each step. That way you're not just following along, but you're also learning how to eventually create your own models.

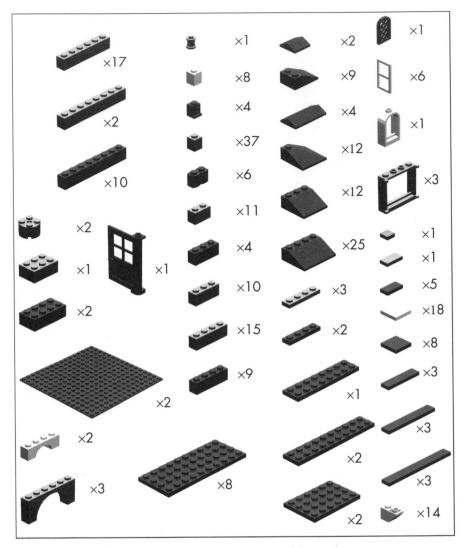

Figure 3-5: The Bill of Materials for the train station model

Step 1

In Figure 3-6, you might notice some 1×1 bricks to the left side of the building. As the building goes up, you'll find that I'm using the stacking technique to create very slender columns based on the simple post technique from Chapter 2 (see Figure 2-24). When I'm done, there will be six of these columns, and they'll support part of the roof. Individually, these columns are very weak versions of the column technique. However, when you use them together, and support them with arches, as you'll soon see, they represent a reasonable balance of form and function.

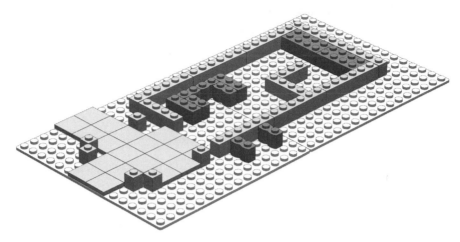

Figure 3-6: Every structure needs a good plan. The layout of your foundation contributes greatly to how the building ultimately looks.

Step 2

In Figure 3-7, you can see what happens after I add the second course of bricks. As promised, this figure shows that I'm using the overlapping technique for the main walls and the stacking technique for the columns.

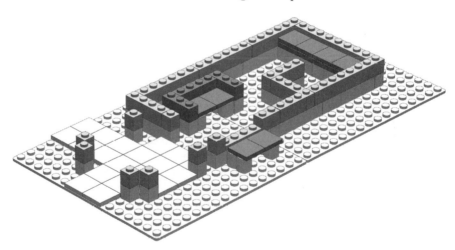

Figure 3-7: Overlapping and stacking techniques used effectively within the same model

Notice how I've applied the overlapping technique to what will become the counter inside the station—the L-shaped wall near the top right of the model, as shown in the instructions. This wall connects to the outside wall with a 1×4 brick and that makes sure it doesn't go anywhere when the train rumbles by on the track.

You can also see three benches. The first is outside the station; it sits on two 1×2 log bricks. The second, inside the station, has armrests. The third, at the very top right of Figure 3-7, is a long bench seat that minifig children can sit on to watch the trains coming along the track.

It's usually best to add things like furniture or inner walls early on in the building process. That way you do not have to take apart the walls or roof to add them later.

Step 3

Next, as the walls and columns continue to rise, I need to install the large windows, as shown in Figure 3-8. It's important to think ahead and decide early on where walls will meet, where windows will be located, and which wall will have the opening for the door. This train station design I've provided you with takes care of all of these.

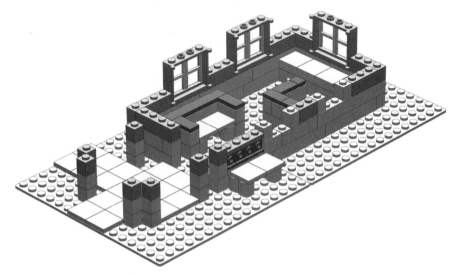

Figure 3-8: The model begins to come to life as the windows are added.

Don't panic if you don't have windows like the ones in Figure 3-8. I'll show you other ways to create the same effect later in the chapter.

Near the center of Figure 3-8, you see four studs facing outward, just behind the bench I'm building there. You're looking at four headlight bricks lined up in a row. These are one of the specialized elements found in the Brickopedia (see Appendix A). Each of these 1×1 bricks has a traditional stud on top but also has a stud on one side. You'll see how I put these to good use in the next step.

Step 4

As you can see in Figure 3-9, things are shaping up. The door is in place and ready to keep waiting minifigs warm while they wait for trains to arrive and depart. I've also added a small, arched, nonfunctional window with a lattice-work screen, just to the right of the outside bench. The opening to its right is where the ticket agent can serve minifig customers. The 2×2 tile sticking out from this opening is meant to represent the counter of the ticket window.

In Figure 3-9, I complete the outside bench, using headlight bricks to do so. I cover the fronts of the bricks (where the studs face outward) with the 1×4 tile; this forms the backrest for the bench. This simple example showcases the additional building techniques you can employ when you're building with pieces from the specialized elements category (discussed in Chapter 1).

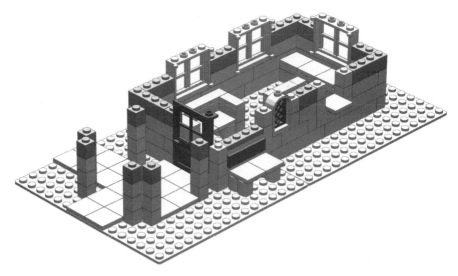

Figure 3-9: Windows and doors add life and realism to your buildings.

Step 5

Figure 3-10 shows how I can add 1×6×2 arches to join pairs of columns together. In architectural terms, such an area is referred to as a *colonnade*—a series of columns sometimes used to support a roof structure. These columns do just that, as you'll soon see.

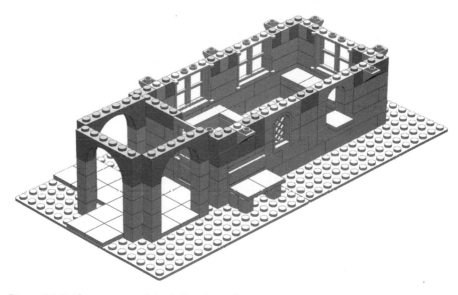

Figure 3-10: The purpose of the 1×1 columns becomes apparent as you add the arches.

Now that the outside walls are almost complete, notice that the two windows at the front now sport 1×4 arch bricks above them, providing a classic look. Also, for this section, I've gone back to the stacking technique for the small section between those two arched windows. I decided on this move because I wanted to create the appearance of frames around the windows. In reality, the frames might have been painted in a color different than the rest of the building. (See the end result in Figure 3-4.)

NOTE   *To get an even better idea of how you can use color in a decorative way, visit www .apotome.com/instructions.html and see the train station in its original red and white color scheme.*

Step 6

Now I'll add the second set of inverse 1×2 slopes that help create the effect of arched supports for the roof, as shown in Figure 3-11.

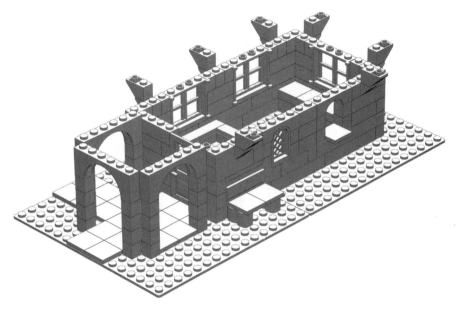

Figure 3-11: The inverse slopes get ready to pretend they are supporting the roof.

Although an inverse half-arch piece does exist in the LEGO system (see the Brickopedia), its dimensions weren't suitable in this case because it would have stuck out past the edge of the roof by one stud. By building your own arches out of slopes, you can produce exactly the look you want.

Step 7

Note how carefully I select the bricks for the top course, as shown in Figure 3-12. Where possible, you must try to tie the lower courses together by making sure that the top layer overlaps as many seams as possible. Consider, for example, the 1×6 brick above and between the two arched windows. That brick is critical to making sure the 1×2's between the windows don't tumble in or out of the building. (Remember, as we discussed in Chapter 2, it's okay to stack bricks as long as you eventually add something to hold them together.)

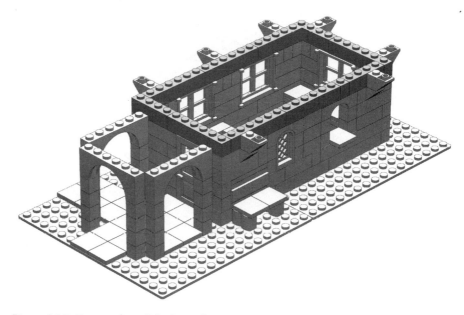

Figure 3-12: Be sure that all the lower layers are stabilized with stretcher bricks along the top course.

Another good example of overlap can be seen in Figure 3-12 when you look at the 1×6 that sits over the door to the building. The door needs something upon which to hinge. In addition, that brick connects the walls on either side of the door.

The opening for the door is something that weakens the walls, not allowing them to interlock. The 1×6 above the door helps restore some of the integrity by holding the walls in place.

Step 8

A roof at last! Well, at least for the colonnade. In Figure 3-13, I begin adding the roof, but not to the entire building. This is a special feature of this design that I explain in the next few steps.

To prepare for the addition of this function, I place a series of tiles around the top of the main walls and on the tops of the faux hall arches.

In Figure 3-13, the plates over the colonnade appear dark gray. In the original design of the building, they were black. For the purpose of actually building the station, they can be just about any color you have on hand. Light gray, brown, tan, or even white would all work fine for these pieces. In the next step, you just cover them up with roof bricks anyway. The plates make up a support structure and are not at all decorative or even visible in the final model.

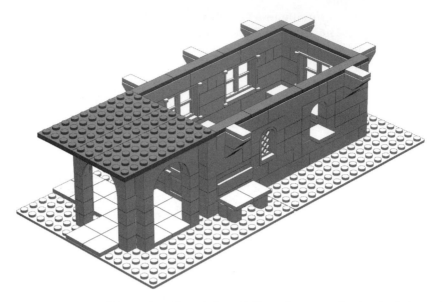

Figure 3-13: Part of the roof and lots of tiles. We'll see the reason for the tiles in just a few more steps.

Step 9

Slopes make such good elements for making roofs that they are sometimes called *roof bricks*. For this model, I use 33-degree slopes extensively to give the roof the gentle angle I want. I begin the first layer of roof pieces by adding them onto the plates I added in the last step. You can see what I mean in Figure 3-14.

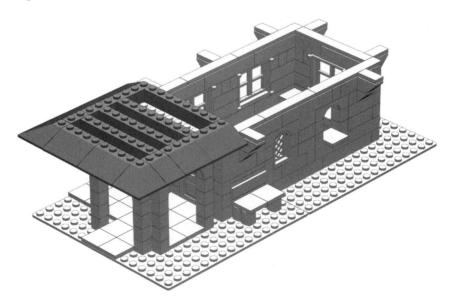

Figure 3-14: The rest of the roof is yet to come. For now, focus on the area directly above the entranceway.

Wait a minute, only half a roof? That might be the question you're asking by now if you're looking at Figures 3-14 and 3-15. Here, I'm creating a nicely sloped and very functional roof, but only for part of the station. This is intentional and helps turn this project into something that you can use as a static display or as a play set. The tiles along the top of the main walls play an important role in creating this dual functionality.

In Figure 3-14, you can see that the lowest layer of slopes extends from the sides of the building out to the same distance as your faux half arches. When I get to the end of the model and reveal the secret of the roof, you'll see that although they aren't really attached, the inverse 1×2 slopes will *appear* to support the roof. Here, I've used LEGO bricks to simulate the look of a real life object without recreating its actual function.

Step 10

As I add the next layer (see Figure 3-15), I'm making sure to overlap the slopes, just as I did with the 1×N bricks I used to create the walls.

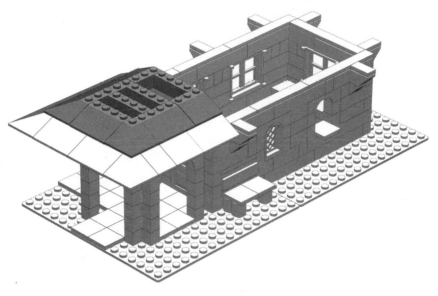

Figure 3-15: The second course of 33-degree slopes

The three 1×4 bricks that I added in Figure 3-15 serve the same purpose as the 1×8 bricks I added in Figure 3-16. They provide support for the layer of slopes above them, which I'll add next.

Step 11

Remember that color isn't everything. Although I intended this building to have a black roof, you may not have those parts in that color. Red or blue slopes work just as well, and you can change the colors of the walls to match. In real life, old buildings are often repainted in colors other than those they were originally. LEGO models are no different; don't feel restricted to what a book or an instruction manual suggests. Experiment with different combinations of colors based on what you have in your collection or even just the mood you're in while you're building.

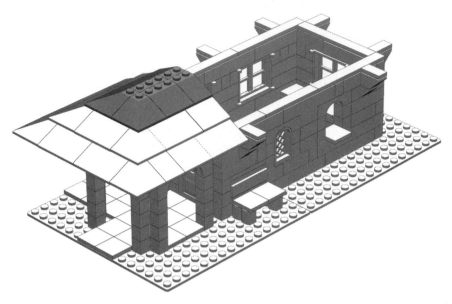

Figure 3-16: Nearly there. The graceful pagoda-style roof takes shape—at least some of it!

Figure 3-17 shows the completed main model. What follows in the next section is a submodel—one that helps complete the main building.

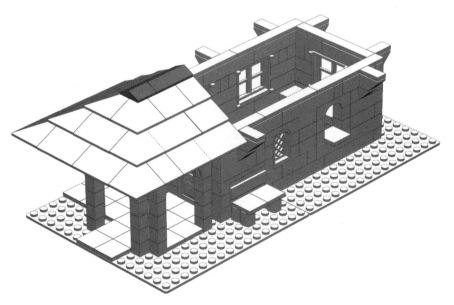

Figure 3-17: Peak elements cap this section of the roof.

A *submodel* is a group of pieces that you assemble apart from the main model. For example, you may build the wings of an airplane separately and attach them to the body at the end of the building process. Or you might put together some pieces that then become the engine for a car. Once you have completed the body of the car, you add the submodel (in this case, the engine) as a single unit, made up of the group of parts you have used to assemble it. In the case of your train station, I'm going to build the larger section of the roof as a submodel.

As you may have guessed by now, the larger part of the roof will be removable. Sometimes you will want to have access to the inside of your LEGO buildings so that you can help your minifigs go about their business. One way to achieve this is to have a building that splits in half and opens up like a dollhouse. In such a case, you can get to the interior of the building from the open sides. The design I'm using here allows you to pull off part of the roof and see the insides from above instead. So watch as I build the rest of the roof and see how it's going to look.

Submodel: The Train Station Roof

Another reason you may want to occasionally use submodels is to eliminate the need to include them in the main instructions.

This roof submodel is a perfect example. The first step in making this submodel involves starting off with some pieces flipped upside down (Figure 3-18). Having that step included in the main instructions may have lead to a bit of confusion, so it's better to handle this part of the roof as a separate unit—a submodel.

Step 1

The roof submodel is exactly the same width as the portion of the roof we already build on one end of the main model. The length of the roof submodel is the same as the opening we left above the main part of the railway station. In other words, when it's finished it will perfectly match up with the main model and form a complete roof. In Figure 3-18, I start with some plates facing studs down.

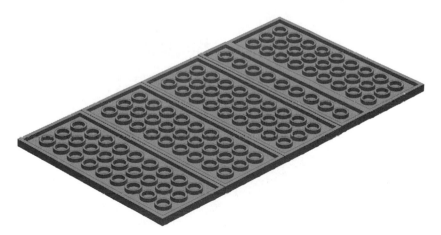

Figure 3-18: No, your book isn't upside down; the plates are turned studs down.

Step 2

In Figure 3-19, it's easy to see the positioning of the next course of plates (now shown in dark gray). If I'd put these plates down first, it would have been trickier for me to properly show you how to position the next layer.

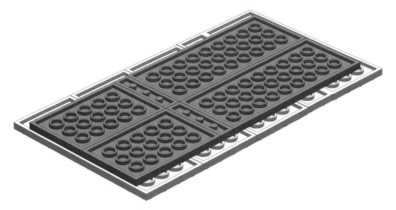

Figure 3-19: By starting out with the plates studs down, it's easier to place the first course of plates.

Step 3

Once I get through the first two steps, I turn the plates right side up. Notice the direction that each layer of plates is turned. The two layers should have the long sides of the plates placed perpendicular to one another. This is another form of the overlapping technique, where long pieces are placed at right angles to each other. In the case of 4×N plates such as those shown in Figure 3-19, this type of overlapping creates a very strong base upon which to build another part of the model.

In Figure 3-20, you can see that I begin adding the slopes to form the angled part of the roof.

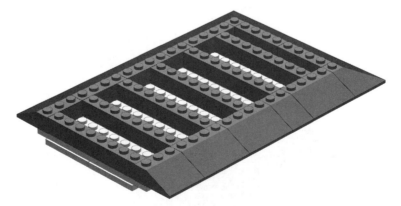

Figure 3-20: Flip the plates over, and then start adding slopes around the edges. The 1×8 bricks in the middle set the stage for the next layer.

One idea I hit upon earlier in this build is that of planning ahead. In Figure 3-20, you can see that I'm already thinking of the next layer of slopes and how they will connect. They will overlap not only the bottom layer of slopes, but also the 1×8 bricks running through the middle. As always, this adds strength to the model. These 1×8's provide another form of bracing. Also, by not making the inside of the roof a solid mass of bricks, I save weight and, of course, bricks!

NOTE   *The inner five 1×8 bricks can be any color you have handy. You won't see them once you're finished.*

Step 4

In Figure 3-21, I add a second layer of roof bricks. Notice the 1×4 standard bricks in the middle. I'm using them, like the 1×8's below them, as a support system for the layer that will be added above them.

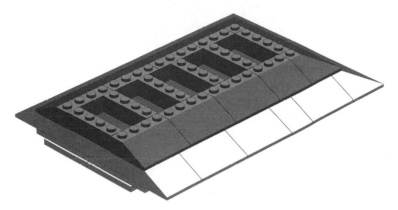

Figure 3-21: 1×4 bricks play the same role as the 1×8's below them.

Step 5

One big part of a successful LEGO model is that every layer or substructure works together to produce the final result. In Figure 3-22, you can see a 2×3 brick that seems to stick out among the slope bricks in the layer. This isn't a mistake; it sets the stage for pieces I will add in the next step. This example shows one layer working together with another to create the effective model I've been talking about.

Step 6

As promised, Figure 3-23 shows you why I added that 2×3 brick in the last step. This becomes a solid platform upon which to build the remainder of the chimney. The peak elements, also added in this step, cover up part of the 2×3 brick and make it appear to simply rise from the inside of the building, just like a real chimney would.

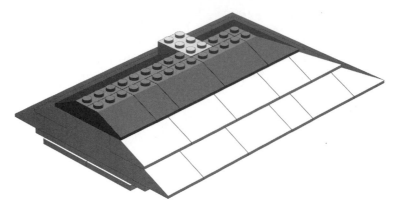

Figure 3-22: Prepare a place for the chimney.

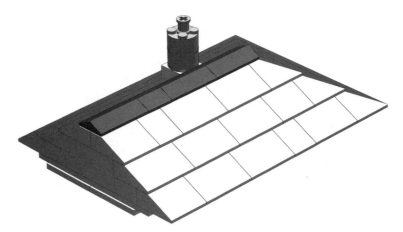

Figure 3-23: The submodel is now complete. Try placing this roof section onto the rest of the model. The result should look just like Figure 3-4.

Don't forget that if you don't want to use this building as a train station, it can serve many other functions. In addition, you can apply the building techniques you used throughout this chapter to any other model you create.

Substitution: When Other Parts Will Do

By this point, you might be saying to yourself, "I'd like to build a station like that, but I don't have all those special pieces." Don't worry! You can replace certain specific pieces with other more common pieces. This is a design technique known as *substitution.* It has nothing to do with replacing French fries with mashed potatoes, but it has everything to do with making the best use of your existing LEGO pieces.

Although you might not be able to make an exact copy of this model with your own collection, you can come close by substituting pieces where needed.

Substitute Walls

Even if your collection comes mostly from assorted buckets, you should have enough basic bricks to make the walls the way they appear in the first model. You may not have exactly the right number of pieces in the same colors, though, so don't be afraid to change colors. Gray, brown, or even white would all be reasonably realistic colors.

Substitute Arches

It's often possible to build an arch from inverse slopes. To do this, you first need to determine the slope, or curvature, you are trying to imitate. To get the slope, you use a combination of the rise and the span.

Imagine the *span* as the length of an imaginary line that runs from the bottom inside edge of one side of the arch to the opposite side. Then, imagine the *rise* as the distance from this line to the center underside of the arch itself (also known as the *soffit*), as shown in Figure 3-24.

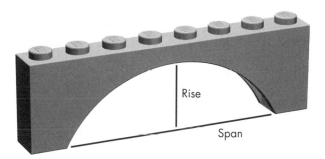

Figure 3-24: The two most important parts of an arch

It's easy to see that by increasing the span of your arch, you are stretching it out sideways, and therefore, you're lowering the angle at which the curve of the arch extends across the other side. This can be a useful shape for things like bridge construction.

Similarly, you can visualize that if you increase the rise of the arch, the angle from the base of one side to the point at which the arch peaks will increase as well. High narrow arches are commonly found in doorways or as part of building facades.

Typically, when I am trying to replicate an arch with slopes, I use a photo or a sketch of the structure as a guide. I then hold up inverse slopes to the picture and try to match the angle of the arch with the angle of the bricks. You can see in Figure 3-25 that by choosing carefully and sometimes mixing different angles of slopes, you can make some handsome arches without using a single arch brick.

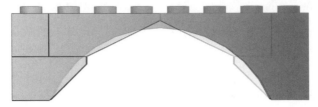

Figure 3-25: A standard 1×8×2 arch is shown superimposed over top of a composite arch made up of 1×2 and 1×3 inverse slopes. The result is nearly the same shape.

Additionally, you may wish to insert standard bricks or plates between the layers of the slopes to increase the rise of the arch without affecting its span.

Substitute Windows

Windows can sometimes prove frustrating, because they aren't always as easy to come by as one would hope. By using some simple tricks, however, you can give your station its own characteristic windows. Figure 3-26 shows that by simulating a small arch (replacing a 1×4 arch element), I've created a look similar to the original train station model in Figure 3-4.

To replace the windows on the side and end of the station, try the trick shown in Figure 3-27. It's not perfect, but it's better than no windows at all.

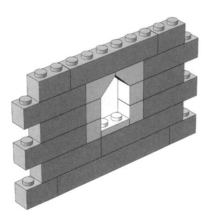

Figure 3-26: You can replace the 1×4 arches used in the original design with inverse 1×2 slopes.

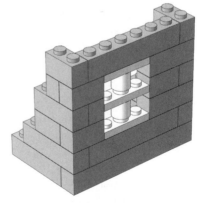

Figure 3-27: Substitutions won't look exactly like the pieces they're replacing, but searching for combinations that work is half the fun.

In Figure 3-27, you can see that the thickness of a standard plate has again been put to good use. Here I use three 1×3 plates separated by two 1×1 cylinders. The result is a window that is three bricks high and that fits perfectly where I need it.

Substitute Roofs

Finally, you might need another way to create a roof. What you may find when you search your collection is that you have sloped roof bricks, but they aren't the black color shown in the first version of the model. If this is the case, you can easily substitute red or blue slopes for the black ones and still maintain the same style of roof. Or, you may find you just don't have enough slope bricks of any color and need another way to make your roof.

In the next example, I use common 2×N bricks to create the illusion of a sloped, though somewhat jagged, roof. I do this by setting down a layer of bricks that mimics the length and width of the sloped roof. As with the original, I am sure to include internal bracing in the form of longer bricks that run from side to side. (These are not unlike the ceiling joists found in real buildings.)

Next, I carefully add the second layer, making sure to overlap any point at which two lower-level bricks come together. By moving each layer inward by three studs, I come close to simulating the slope originally created by the 33-degree roof bricks. I am effectively combining the overlapping and staggering techniques in this process.

You can use this example (shown in Figures 3-28 through 3-33) to replace the steps shown in Figures 3-13 through 3-17.

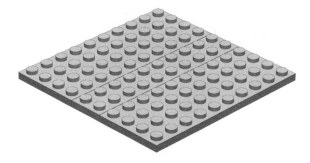

Figure 3-28: These are the same plates you see in Step 8 of the main model (Figure 3-13). Begin building your substitute roof from that point forward.

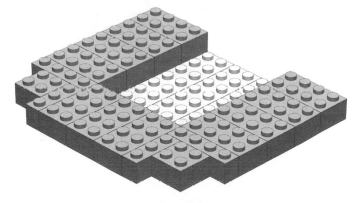

Figure 3-29: Instead of slopes, I used standard bricks.

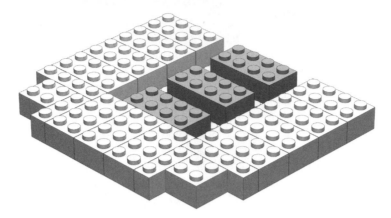

Figure 3-30: The three 2×4 bricks in the middle will help support the next layer.

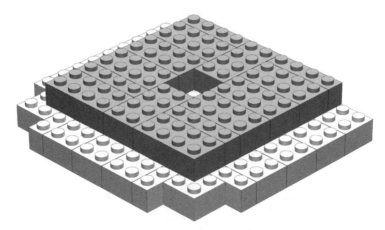

Figure 3-31: The second layer is staggered from the first. This provides the imitation slope for the roof.

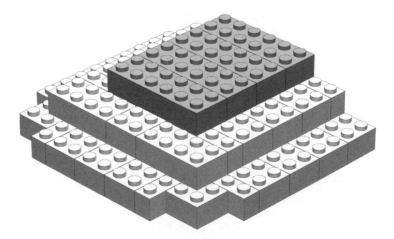

Figure 3-32: 2×6 bricks hold everything together at the top.

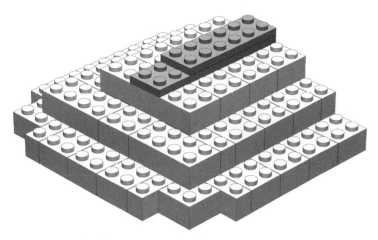

Figure 3-33: The plates overlap, and help hold together, the 2×6 bricks from the previous step.

You can create the larger part of the roof (the submodel) using this same technique.

Another way to create simple sloped-roof structures is to attach ordinary plates (4×N, 6×N, and so on) to hinged elements and then angle them as you like. Figure 3-34 shows a simple example of this technique.

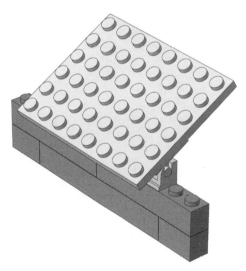

Figure 3-34: Roofs made from hinged plates can be angled at any pitch you need.

The brick hinge is a wonderfully useful element. It comes in two varieties. The version shown in Figure 3-35 has a 2×2 plate as the hinged portion. It is also available with a 1×2 plate on top.

Pieces like the brick hinge allow you to add varying angles to your models that wouldn't be possible with just standard bricks and plates.

Figure 3-35: The brick hinge

If you want to use the brick hinge and plate technique, it's important to plan ahead and build the hinges into the top of the wall. The spaces between them are filled with two plates (shown in Figure 3-36) because a full-height brick would hit the underside of the roof plate.

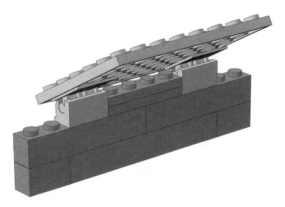

Figure 3-36: A hinged roof can be easily opened so that you can peek inside your building if need be.

Review: Building Techniques and Alternatives

The train station model presented in this chapter helped us look at some very basic building techniques as they apply to a minifig-scale structure. It showed that the overlap technique, which I first demonstrated in Chapter 2, is one of the most fundamental principles when it comes to successful LEGO models. You will use it time and again throughout just about every model you build. Although stacking and staggering are important also, it is the overlap method that best creates strong bonds between LEGO elements.

The main model in this chapter also demonstrated substitution on a couple of different levels. The building itself, as I pointed out early in this chapter, can be used for any number of different roles; it doesn't have to just be a train station.

The various sections of the building also provided examples of substitution. And although the alternate roofs, windows, and arches don't look quite as realistic as the "official" version, they do offer some flexibility. For example, a proper arch brick can only ever be a certain size and shape. On the other hand, your slope-derived versions can grow or shrink as you need them to. So although the improvised version of the train station might not win awards for its looks, you can certainly use it to add character to a LEGO town with just the bricks you have at hand.

This principle—substituting one technique for another—is something I'll hit on again throughout this book. Remember that substitution isn't a single technique. Rather, it's a way of looking at a problem and (in the case of LEGO models) finding an alternative part or bunch of parts that can provide you with a solution when the "right" parts just aren't available. It serves to remind you just how flexible and creative the LEGO system can be. You are never stuck with just one way of doing things or just one particular element that you need to use. Your imagination and alternative pieces are all you need to solve most building problems.

4

MINILAND SCALE: THE WHOLE WORLD IN MINIATURE

In 1968, something spectacular happened in Denmark: an entire new world was created. That was the year the LEGO company opened a very unique theme park, called LEGOLAND, not far from its headquarters.

NOTE *Denmark is a small Scandinavian country located north of Germany and Poland, bordered by both the Baltic and the North Seas. It is the country in which LEGO was founded in 1932, and it remains home to the company's corporate headquarters.*

Along with rides and snack shops, LEGOLAND also contained an incredible group of LEGO structures. This part of the park became known as *Miniland*. In the early days of the park, these Miniland creations replicated—at scale, of course—many famous Danish landmarks and buildings. Later, as the company opened other theme parks in more countries, new Miniland structures were built, modeled after other cities and structures from around the world. In Figure 4-1 you can see an interesting scene captured at LEGOLAND in Carlsbad, California.

Figure 4-1: Don't worry: things aren't as bad as they seem. This fire truck is only a couple of feet long, its ladder is just under 3 feet tall, and the people in the scene are each less than 4 inches high. The details are what make it look very real. (Photo by Tim Strutt, Ottawa, Ontario, Canada. Used with permission.)

Interestingly, even though miniland scale is used extensively in the LEGO parks, you won't really find any official LEGO sets that contain miniland-scale characters. Equally notable is that unlike the very specialized pieces that make up any given minifig, miniland people are most often created from a variety of reasonably common LEGO elements. They may have parts such as inverted slopes for legs, plates for arms, or even 1×1 cylinder plates for eyes.

Miniland Scale: Bigger but Still Small

In the last chapter, I talked extensively about the idea of scale and how it related to minifig models. I had you work out that minifig scale is around 1:48. However, the concept of scale doesn't go away when you're talking about miniland models; instead, the numbers just change.

Most of the miniland-sized models at the LEGOLAND theme parks are built to a 1:20 scale. This means that an average character (such as the fireman shown in Figure 4-2) is about 3.5 inches tall. Hopefully, this explanation helps you understand an important point about scale. As the number on the right (the scale value) gets smaller, the model you are making gets bigger. Therefore, the 1:48 minifig characters are about 1.5 inches high, whereas the 1:20 miniland figures are more than twice as tall.

Although miniland figures may be a bit blockier looking than their minifig counterparts, you can build them with more interesting costumes and poses, as you'll see later in this chapter.

When building with minifigs, you mix and match their torsos with various legs or you give them different hairpieces and accessories. In the end, however, most minifigs end up looking somewhat similar. When you build your own miniland figures, the range of characters you can create is virtually unlimited. They will never be exact replicas of minifigs and will end up with their own unique features.

Figure 4-2: A minifig fireman and a miniland version of a similar character. The miniland man is two and one-half times as tall as his smiling minifig counterpart.

Creating a Basic Miniland Figure

You can build miniland figures in an almost endless variety of poses and outfits. Before you go crazy trying to accomplish all those possibilities, however, let me first show you a no-frills figure (see Figure 4-3) so you can get a sense of how these little folk are constructed.

This figure's outfit (or lack thereof) doesn't really tell you what he does for a living, and he's not in any sort of action pose that lets you know what he might be doing. For now, just study his simple form so that you can get an idea of what building techniques I used to create him. I'll give you instructions to build your own miniland character a little later in this chapter.

Figure 4-3: Like a department store mannequin, this figure is just waiting to be attired in any number of outfits.

First of all, take a look at his head. The head is square and a bit boring, as you can see, but don't worry: I'll show you how to add details later that take away some of that blocky feeling. Notice that the head is centered over the shoulders using a very simple technique; I'll also describe this technique in a bit.

Now take a look at the torso, which is essentially two studs by three studs in size, though it is made up of several smaller pieces. After all, you need to make sure you have somewhere to attach the arms, and you also need to allow yourself the ability to create costumes by varying the colors of bricks and plates.

The arms, attached at their normal location, are just 2×2 hinge plates, and in this example, there are not really any parts that represent hands.

Here, the legs are perhaps the simplest part of all. They are really nothing more than standard 1×1 bricks with inverted 1×2 45-degree slopes for the hips.

The Best Bits: Useful Pieces for Miniland People

Although no LEGO element should ever be considered useless, it's also true to say that, in some circumstances, some pieces are more useful than others. Tables 4-1 through 4-3 list parts I used to create the basic miniland figure in the previous section. You might find that these are the most handy to start out with. Think of the contents of these three tables as your toolkit for creating these little people. You may not use each piece in every figure you build, but these do give you a sense of the types of pieces you might want to gather before you start working on this type of model.

Small plates, like the ones shown in Table 4-1, are the key to creating the details of the head and neck.

Table 4-1: Small Plates for Making Miniland-sized Heads

1×1 plates	2×2 plates
1×2 plates	Offset plates

Technic bricks, like those shown in Table 4-2, are used to create the mechanism by which the arms are attached. The clip plates—used as hands—are optional.

Table 4-2: Assorted Pieces for Making Miniland-sized Torsos

2×3 plates	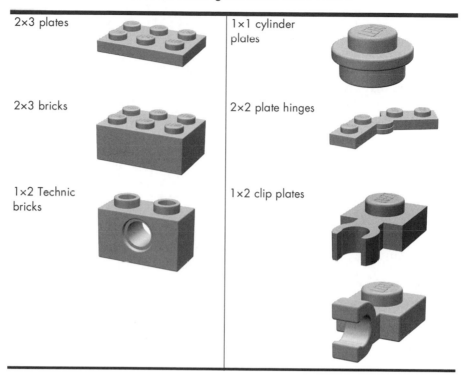	1×1 cylinder plates	
2×3 bricks		2×2 plate hinges	
1×2 Technic bricks		1×2 clip plates	

Changing the slopes and bricks you use for the legs can help create different costumes for your characters. The examples in Table 4-3 are good choices.

Table 4-3: Various Pieces for Making Miniland-sized Legs

1×1 cylinder plates		1×2 plates	
1×1 cylinders		1×2 inverted 45-degree slopes	
1×1 bricks		2×1×3 standard and inverted 75-degree slopes	

As you begin to blend the basic techniques with your own flair, you will undoubtedly find that you are mixing up how the head attaches to the body and how the legs are connected and positioned. Much like other such lists in this book, this list just gives you guidelines that are only intended as a jumping-off point for your own creativity.

Basic Miniland Figure

You saw a picture of a basic miniland-scale character in Figure 4-3. Then, in the last section, you saw some of the most useful LEGO elements for creating these whimsical people. To get you started building your own cast of characters, I'll show you six easy steps you can use to make a basic version of this type of model. From there, you can explore the variations on hair, outfits, and poses that I'll talk about in the following pages.

Figure 4-4 shows you the first three steps to follow. I haven't included a Bill of Materials for this model, but by looking at the toolkit I provided for you in Tables 4-1 through 4-3 and the steps themselves, you should easily be able to figure out which pieces you need.

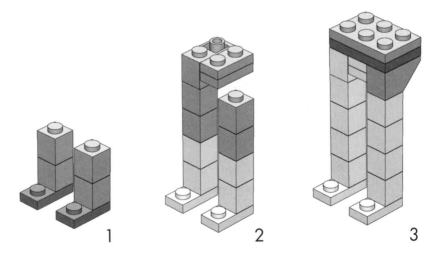

Figure 4-4: Steps 1, 2, and 3 for creating a basic miniland character

Notice that in steps 1 through 3 (Figure 4-4), I have added more than one layer of parts per step. Because this is such a small model, it's easy to understand instructions like this. They help save steps by instructing you to add several pieces, at different layers, all at once. I use this same technique with steps 4 through 6 (Figure 4-5).

One interesting feature of this basic miniland figure is that you can pose the arms at any angle you like. Note in Figure 4-5 (steps 4 and 5) that the hinge element, representing the arm, simply sticks into a 1×1 cylinder plate that itself is stuck into a 1×2 Technic brick. There is just enough friction between the stud (on the hinge) and the cylinder plate to hold the arm up just a little or even straight up in the air! The head, as you can see in steps 4 and 5, is centered on the torso thanks to a single offset plate.

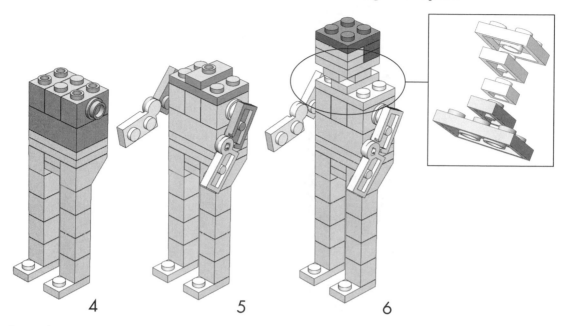

Figure 4-5: Steps 4, 5, and 6 for creating a basic miniland figure

Mix-and-Match Parts

You just saw how to create a very basic version of a miniland person. Now it's time to make that character come alive by adding some additional details. In this section, you'll examine various ways to create not only heads, arms, and legs, but also clothing and accessories to match. The following categories are similar to the toolkit I detailed earlier, but they differ slightly in how the figure is broken down.

Once you get the hang of building these parts separately, you can use different combinations of them to create your own world of miniland-sized people, each with a unique personality. Where possible, I'll try to draw on pieces I included in the toolkit I provided earlier (Tables 4-1 through 4-3).

Heads and Hats

By now, you may have noticed that the faces of miniland people are somewhat abstract; they have no eyes or nose to speak of. In fact, their entire composition is really just representations of a person, not the hands, movable arms, and detailed faces that you see in the minifig world.

Therefore, creating a "face" for your miniland person becomes a matter of trying to suggest where the skin is located and where things like hair and hats begin. In Figure 4-6, I isolated the elements used to create the impression of a face and neck. Use whatever color plates you like in these locations to make each character unique.

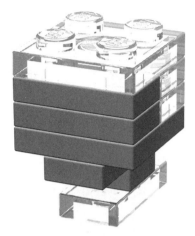

Figure 4-6: The solid elements represent the character's face in this figure; the clear elements represent the character's hair or hat, and perhaps its neck. Use different colors of plates to create realistic skin tones for your miniland folk.

You can also experiment with combinations of plates, cylindrical plates, and other parts, like the 1×1 plate with studs to create items like hats and hair for your miniland people. In Figure 4-7, you can see that the head in the middle appears to be wearing a baseball cap, whereas the head on the far right looks like someone who's good with a curling iron.

Figure 4-7: A basic head on the left, a capped head in the middle, and a head full of curls to the right

Shirts and Skirts

In the toolkit I provided earlier in this chapter (Tables 4-1 through 4-3), I broke down each figure into its head, torso, and legs. Of course, in reality, you might be building an astronaut who wears a suit that covers the entire body. Or, your figure might be a lovely lady in a dress where again, you would want to consider the torso and the upper-leg design together. This section looks at how to dress a character.

You give the impression of a miniland person's career or hobby by combining the parts you use and the colors in which you select them. For example, in Figure 4-8, you see three very different outfits that you could use to help populate your miniland world. On the far left is a soccer referee's uniform, in the middle is a classy cocktail dress, and on the right is the plain gray suit of a businessman.

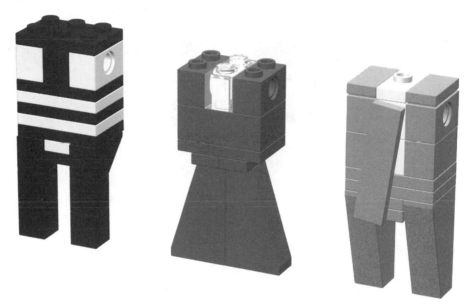

Figure 4-8: Clothes do make the miniland person. Remember that little details and careful color choices can add a great deal of realism and charm.

How do you know that the outfit on the left in Figure 4-8 is that of a referee? The striped appearance of the shirt and black pants are pretty good clues. You might finish this particular character off by adding a cap, such as the one you saw in Figure 4-7 and perhaps something to represent a whistle or flag that the character might be holding.

The dress in the middle of Figure 4-8 shows how you can use things like the 2×1×3 75-degree slopes to create a very feminine look. These slopes are centered under two offset plates, which help give this character a more slender waist. In addition, the 1×2 at the very top center can be matched to the figure's facial color, thereby giving the illusion that the dress has an open neckline.

Lastly, on the very right of Figure 4-8, you see the clothes of a hurried businessman. Don't be afraid to use little tricks like attaching his tie off center in order to let the white of his shirt show a bit and to give the impression that he has just rushed off a busy subway car. It's these little details that add *character* to your characters.

Lots of Legs

Heads and clothing are important, but then so are the legs and feet upon which your characters stand. Figure 4-9 shows some simple and subtle variations on the basic leg/shoe design you first saw in the standard figure earlier in this chapter (see Figure 4-3).

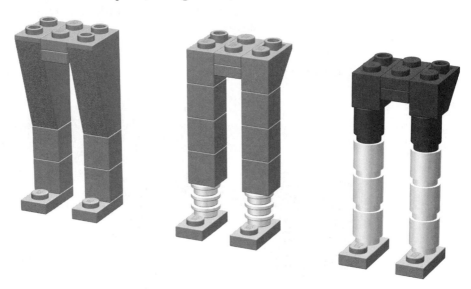

Figure 4-9: Most leg designs eventually create the two stud by three stud base upon which you then build the torso.

You can use the design on the left of Figure 4-9 for just about any character who is wearing long pants. To add a little fun to a figure, put him (or her) in pants that are too short (such as those in the middle image of Figure 4-9). Maybe your person is a nerdy scientist who has trouble picking properly fitting clothes. The more shapely arrangement of elements on the right of Figure 4-9 might suggest the legs and cycling shorts of an athletic character who just got off a mountain bike. Here again, match the lower 1×1 cylinder bricks with the flesh color you chose for the face and arms.

Arms and Accessories

Part of what makes miniland figures so interesting is that the pieces you use to create certain parts of them will vary from character to character. For example, in the basic figure in Figure 4-3, you saw that a simple 2×2 hinge plate was enough to suggest the presence of arms. But they didn't portray any particular action or suggest any occupation that this figure might have.

Simple part substitutions and setting the arms at different angles can indicate a wide variety of actions or gestures. Figure 4-10 illustrates some ideas on how to add some life to your characters by simply adding flair to their arms and hands.

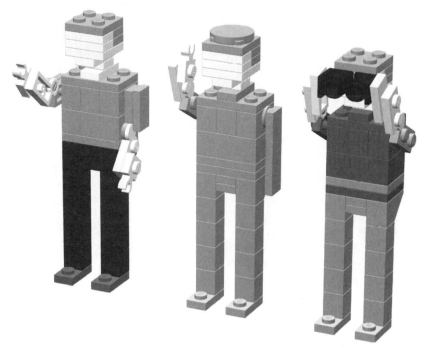

Figure 4-10: Hailing a taxi, saluting an officer, or watching birds—miniland folk can do just about anything you can dream up for them.

One interesting thing to note in Figure 4-10 is that the two leftmost characters both have hands made from 1×1 plates with clips on the side. The character to the right, however, has no hands at all. Rather, I've used offset plates to extend the arms so they hold the binoculars. This helps illustrate the idea that it's more important to achieve the look and feel of the thing you are trying to create as opposed to fretting over how to model every last detail. The basic miniland character, as shown in Figure 4-3, has no hands either. But it looks like a person nonetheless. Keep that goal in mind as you build.

On The Run: Making Miniland Figures Come to Life

Now you know how to model miniland figures and even how to dress them in various outfits. The next step is to give them the feeling of motion or action. They can't all just stand there at attention with their legs perfectly straight. But unlike minifigs, miniland figures have no hinges on their legs. Thus, making it appear as if they are moving or doing something is a matter of selecting elements that once again give the *appearance* of something that isn't really there.

As you can see in following examples, the action being undertaken is implied by the position in which you, the builder, pose the figure.

The character shown in Figure 4-11 appears to be in motion rather than just standing still.

With her arms swinging out from her body, the woman in Figure 4-11 looks like she may be walking. Notice the 75-degree outside corner slopes that I used to create the illusion that her long dress is moving with her legs. Rearranging the elements you used to create the legs and/or substituting other pieces is all that it takes to add some life to an otherwise motionless figure.

Now take a look at the person in Figure 4-12.

Figure 4-11: You can make a character appear to be walking by simply moving the arms and legs slightly ahead and behind the body, as shown in this illustration.

Figure 4-12: A few subtle changes (different pieces or just pieces in different positions) can give the impression of lots of action.

This fellow is crouched down, perhaps calling to a pet dog or watching as his bowling ball rolls down the lane. What you may notice is that he's really not all that different from the very first character you saw back in Figure 4-3. In fact, to make him bend down, you only have to change or move a few pieces. In Figure 4-13, I colored those pieces in black so you can see which ones are different than those in Figure 4-3.

Figure 4-13: Pieces shown in black (as part of the figure on the left) are the only ones different than the pieces I used to build the figure on the right. Changing just a few elements changes the entire impression of what this character may be doing.

Miniland Buildings

Perhaps the only drawback to miniland-style creations is that buildings for these characters need to be quite a bit larger than those you might make for minifigs. Such models can be taxing on even some larger collections of bricks. That doesn't mean that you shouldn't try to make them, just that you might have to look at smaller structures for inspiration. In other words, a miniland-scale Empire State Building is probably much too ambitious for most builders to undertake.

Creating a Scene: Combining Figures and Buildings

Working at miniland scale is a good way to practice creating facades of small buildings rather than the entire structure. A *facade* is the detailed front face of a building that might have plain sides or sometimes no walls or back at all. Movie studios have used facades for many years to re-create things like suburban street scenes or the main street of an old-west town.

You can create a small scene by combining your miniland figures and the facade of a building or two. These works are sometimes called *vignettes* or *dioramas*. The focus is on just what can be seen from the front; the side and/or back of the buildings are *not* intended to be part of the snapshot. Think of these scenes as three-dimensional photographs that capture a moment in time.

Facades work well in miniland scale for two reasons. First, they allow you to explore greater detail than you would capture if you were creating a similar minifig scale building. Second, they allow you to create a taller and wider model without having to worry about the sides, back, or even the roof of the building; thus they require fewer elements than a complete structure. To illustrate this technique, I'll focus on a single vignette, exploring the components that you need use to help bring it to life.

Street Life: A Simple Downtown Scene in Miniland Scale

Figure 4-14 shows you the scene we'll be discussing. It's a simple street setting in front of a small cafe or shop that is located on a busy downtown corner. Along with the customer using the bank machine on the right, you also see a person about to mail a letter. As noted earlier, the larger scale of miniland construction allows you to include more detail than you normally see in minifig scale.

Figure 4-14: A typical downtown scene. Everyday objects and actions make scenes look realistic.

The People in Your Neighborhood

Let's look more closely at the individual ingredients that make up this scene, starting with the characters that populate our street.

In the close-up shown in Figure 4-15, notice the child figure that is standing next to the adult using the automated banking machine. Creating smaller characters is really just a matter of reducing each of the main features (head, body, arms, and legs) proportionately. In the end, it's really most important that the figure look right. If you build a child chracter and the legs look too long, then they probably are. Simply shorten them until things start to look the way you expect.

Figure 4-15: Characters doing realistic things will add a sense of life to your dioramas.

The bank machine itself is built into the exterior wall of the building. Although at first it may appear out of place in the context of the older-style building, it represents the type of modern changes that are sometimes applied to structures that are decades old.

The character shown in Figure 4-16 clearly has a letter in her hand that she is about to deposit in the mailbox. Notice as well that she's wearing a variation on the dress that we first saw back in Figure 4-8.

Figure 4-16: Mailing a letter is another everyday activity that you'd see on a real street.

NOTE *Your characters may stand up best when you firmly anchor them to a baseplate, as shown in the Figures 4-15 and 4-16. You might find them a bit wobbly if you just place them on a tabletop or another flat surface.*

Building the Buildings

Now let's look at some close-ups of the architecture I used to construct the building itself. Figure 4-17 shows that the corner of the building was built as a *quoin*. This is a technique where you use bricks of different color, size, or texture to form a pattern much like the one you see in this illustration. It looks sort of like a zipper running up the corner of the building.

Figure 4-17: This architectural technique can be found on many real life buildings. Capturing such details in your LEGO creations gives them a more realistic feel.

In the example shown here, the quoin is mostly decorative. It is built from different colored bricks than the rest of the wall. Although it is an important part of the building—the corner—it is not structurally different than the two walls it connects.

Sometimes repetition of a single piece can add interest to an otherwise boring feature. The area above the large second-story windows could just as easily have been built with plain bricks. But as you can see in Figure 4-18, by using a number of 1×4 arches side by side, I've created a more attractive visual pattern. Like the quoin, these arches are purely decorative.

The larger 1×8×2 arches that are above the windows are a dramatic feature that adds flair to the model. To say they are above the windows is actually not quite correct. As you can see, they are positioned just in front of the many 1×2×2 windows, but they also hide a portion of them. This is very common in buildings of this design.

Perhaps the most important thing you can try to do when you are assembling a vignette like the one shown in Figure 4-14 is to copy whatever details you can from real life buildings. Also, remember that building evolve over time as they are renovated or restored. Don't be afraid to incorporate modern items in a building that looks like it was built in the last century.

Figure 4-18: The arches above the large windows could easily be created with inverse slopes if you don't have the actual arch pieces you need. See Chapter 3, Figure 3-25.

Behind the Scenes

Remember earlier when I talked about facades being used by moviemakers to create the illusion of buildings? Figure 4-19 shows our street scene example as it would appear from behind.

Figure 4-19: A behind-the-scenes peek at the diorama

Despite appearances, the building is essentially just two walls and a support column. You can clearly see there is no roof and no second floor, and the walls are far from complete. This is the point I made earlier—a facade allows you to concentrate on just how things look from the front and not worry about interior details or even walls.

Figure 4-19 also shows the support column from a better angle since you are now viewing the facade from the back. I'm using the column to support the end of the wall that contains the bank machine (see Figure 4-14 for a front view). A sturdy column, linked to the end of the wall, makes an excellent substitute for the side walls you *don't* build for a model like this. (Refer to Figures 2-24 through 2-27 in Chapter 2 for pictures of different types of columns.)

In the close-up in Figure 4-20, you can see that the column is *tied* to the wall with a simple beam. This is another way of saying it's built into the wall. Connecting (or tying) the two is really just a matter of using a 2×8 or 2×10 brick or even a composite beam like the one you saw in Figure 2-21 in Chapter 2. The beam is built into the column and extended out until it also becomes part of the wall. The second illustration in Figure 4-20 shows both the wall and the column with a few bricks removed from each. This better illustrates how the 2×10 brick joins the two structures together.

Figure 4-20: A close-up of the column and part of the main wall on the left. The image on the right shows the same two structures with bricks removed to reveal how the 2×10 connects them.

Using a single column, instead of an entire wall, can help you to save bricks. For instance, if you are short on the color of bricks being used for the front of the building, you can use a different color to build the column. If you place the column behind a solid part of the facade, rather than sitting it behind a window, it is reasonably well hidden. Therefore the bricks you use to build the column can be any color or combination of colors you have at hand.

Review: Miniland Scale, Big Possibilities

You've seen how very unique miniland scale figures can be created from mostly basic bricks, plates, and slopes. The other technique you looked at—creating a vignette of a scene—gives you a little world in which to put your new figures. As a follow-up project, you might want to try creating a larger street scene with more building facades and a larger cast of characters going about their business. Or, you may wish to try working on a miniland-scale car or even a boat for your figures to travel in.

5

JUMBO ELEMENTS:
BUILDING BIGGER BRICKS

In Chapter 3, I talked at length about scale and how it relates to building LEGO models. The discussion lead you through the steps to create a small-scale train station to add to a small-scale LEGO town. In this chapter, you're going to go the other way. You're going to build a model that is larger, not smaller, than the real life object it represents.

One great way to demonstrate this idea is by taking advantage of an interesting characteristic of LEGO bricks; you can use them to make other LEGO bricks. No, I'm not suggesting that you melt down your bricks and remold them. Rather, I'm talking about the technique whereby you use individual bricks to construct a *jumbo brick* that looks exactly like the small version, just many times larger.

When you go to build a jumbo brick, you use a technique called *scaling up*. This is the idea that you take the dimensions of the real life object and multiply them by some number. That number is the scale factor that you first saw in Chapter 3.

In your first encounter with scale, I suggested that a minifig world might be built to a scale of around 1:48. In other words, a model building or vehicle would be 48 times smaller than the same object in the real world. In this chapter, you'll explore macro building, or making the model larger than the real life object.

Macro building involves reversing the relationship of the numbers in your scale. For example, the model in Figure 5-1 is ten times bigger than the real brick it represents. That means it was built to a scale of 10:1.

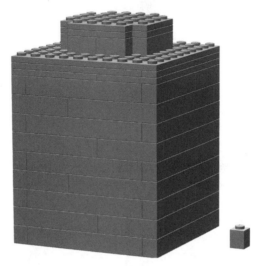

Figure 5-1: This jumbo model of a 1×1 brick dwarfs the real 1×1 that served as inspiration. It is ten times larger and stands nearly 4 1/2 inches tall.

NOTE   *Remember from Chapter 3 that the number on the left signifies the number of real objects you are talking about and the number on the right represents the model version.*

For the example shown in Figure 5-1, you would say that you are building a brick to *ten times scale*—also sometimes written as 10X.

It's important to note that the ten times scale is applied to each of the three dimensions. Take the length and multiply it by ten, then multiply the width by ten, and finally do the same to the height. This gives you the final size you are aiming to build. So in the example in Figure 5-1, your 1×1 brick has sides that are 10 studs wide, by 10 studs deep, by 10 bricks or courses high.

NOTE   *You can also describe this process as building to a "factor of" something. Keeping with the current example, you can say that you are building jumbo bricks to a factor of 10. This is an expression you may hear from time to time, and it's an effective way of describing the scale to which you are building something.*

Figure 5-2 shows a 1×1 brick scaled up to a factor of 4. This might make it a little easier to see the relationship between the two numbers that make up the scale.

At first glance, you might think that Figure 5-2 is a visual representation of 1:4 scale. In fact, it is just the opposite. It shows 4:1 scale. You can see that it would take four of the actual brick (shown on the left) to equal the height of the macro model (shown on the right). Don't forget that the length and width are also four times larger in the jumbo version.

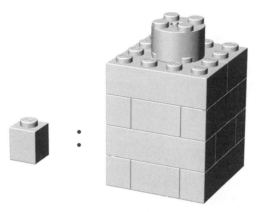

Figure 5-2: 4:1 scale demonstrated

NOTE *As I discuss the scale of models and objects, I am talking about only one dimension at a time. For instance, I say that the jumbo is four times as high or four times as wide as the real thing. If I was to talk about all three dimensions (length, width, and height) at the same time, I'd be discussing the* volume *of the object. That would tell you how many of the real objects it would take to occupy the same amount of space as the jumbo. For example, for a 4X model, you would multiply 4×4×4. Put another way, a 4X scale 1×1 brick takes up as much space as 64 normal sized 1×1's!*

There isn't much to building a 4X jumbo 1×1 like the one in Figures 5-3 through 5-5. In fact, it's as easy as one, two, three.

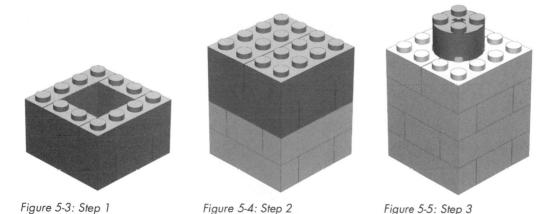

Figure 5-3: Step 1   Figure 5-4: Step 2   Figure 5-5: Step 3

In step 1, I actually show you two courses of bricks because this construction technique should be familiar to you by now. You'll recognize the arrangements of 1×2 and 1×4 bricks as the chimney pattern from Chapter 2.

Step 2 isn't much more complicated. You add a third layer of 1×2's and 1×4's and then cap the model off with two 2×4 bricks. To appreciate the true effect of macro-sized bricks, always construct them using the same color elements.

In step 3, a 2×2 cylinder brick finishes our jumbo-sized 1×1 model. Although it's possible to cover the studs using tiles, I've avoided this technique for two reasons. First, it adds to the number of pieces you need to make each brick. Second, if you leave exposed studs on the top of each jumbo brick, you can later build with them very much like you use the real versions at normal size. I'll discuss this later in this chapter.

Scaling Up: How It's Done

Now you're ready to build your own jumbo brick. To begin, take a different-sized brick and build it to 4X scale. The classic 2×4 brick should provide a good example of how the same scale can be applied to different sized models.

When you're scaling up a simple object like a LEGO brick, it's really just a matter of multiplying each of the original dimensions by the factor you're using—in this case, 4. In Table 5-1, I show you the actual dimensions of a 2×4 brick and the dimensions of the jumbo version at 4X scale.

Table 5-1: Dimensions for Building a 2×4 Brick to 4X Scale Size

	Real Brick	**Jumbo Brick Model**
Width	2 studs	8 studs
Length	4 studs	16 studs
Height	1 brick	4 bricks

The calculations here are really fairly simple. You know that your actual model will be 8 studs wide, 16 studs long, and 4 bricks high. Begin building this example by laying down a foundation layer that is 8×16 studs. (The example shown here, beginning with Figure 5-6, uses 1×8 and 1×6 bricks, but you can use whatever pieces you have available as long as the end result is the same.)

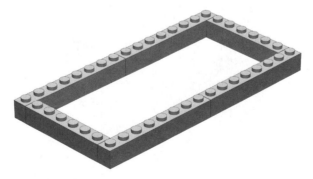

Figure 5-6: Step 1

Next, as shown in Figure 5-7, you need to build another course on top of the initial one you set down. (Don't forget to always overlap as much as possible.) The third layer, shown in Figure 5-8, is just more of the same.

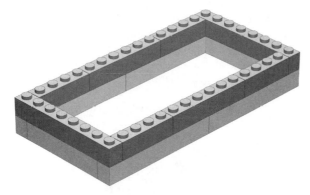

Figure 5-7: Step 2

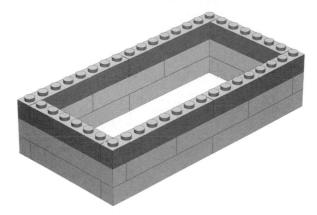

Figure 5-8: Step 3

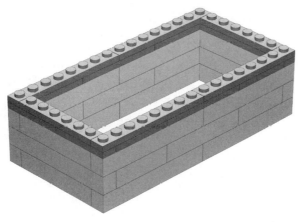

Figure 5-9: Step 4

For the fourth and final layer, begin to finish the jumbo by covering the top completely, not just with another outside course of bricks. You can do this in one of two ways: either by using two layers of 1×N plates around the top of the model (as shown in Figure 5-9), and then topping things off with some 2×8 and 4×8 plates (as shown in Figure 5-10); or by building the final course using just 2×8 bricks and no plates at all.

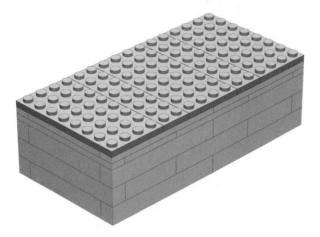

Figure 5-10: Step 5. In place of plates as the top layer(s) you can use 2×8 bricks if you have them.

NOTE   *For simplicity's sake, I've not included the tubes (inside the brick) with these instructions. However, a simple solution to creating them will be shown later in this chapter when you build a jumbo version of a 2×2 45-degree slope.*

Finally, you need some studs on top of this jumbo. But where do they go? The 1×1 you looked at earlier was easy since the stud went right in the middle.

For this example, you need to add the eight studs found on the top of every standard 2×4 brick. Look carefully at an actual 2×4 brick. You'll see that the studs are evenly spaced and that they are closer to the edge of the brick than to each other. In fact, in Figure 5-11, you can see that A is only about half the width of the distance indicated by B.

Figure 5-11: By studying actual elements, you learn facts that will help you make your jumbo models look more realistic.

When you look at the top of the finished jumbo brick in Figure 5-12, you will see that the 2×2 cylinder bricks, used to represent studs, should be placed one stud away from the edge of the brick. At 4X scale, they will also always be two studs away from the next nearest 2×2 cylinder.

In other words, the cylinders are placed twice as far from each other as from the edge of the brick, just as you saw in Figure 5-11.

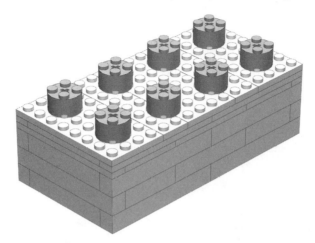

Figure 5-12: Step 6. The finished model of a 4X jumbo 2×4 brick.

If you look carefully at Figure 5-12, you will see that the studs feel right. Although the calculations for their placement may not be precise enough to land a man on the moon, they are more than sufficient to build jumbo bricks.

The Walls Are Closing In!

Because you only scaled up the 2×4 brick by a factor of 4 in the preceding example, you again used 1×N bricks to represent the side walls of the brick. The reason for this is that even though the scaled-up 2×4 brick is bigger than the previous 1×1 example (see Figure 5-5), the thickness of the walls is the same on both bricks. Scaling them up by the same factor means the jumbo models should have walls that are equally thick.

The thickness of the outer wall of a real 1×N brick (or a 2×N brick) is just about 1/16 of an inch. The width of the brick itself, as seen in Figure 5-13, is just over 1/4 of an inch.

Figure 5-13: Standard LEGO bricks have walls that are approximately 1/16 of an inch thick.

If we take 1/16 of an inch and multiply it by a factor of 4, you get 4/16 or 1/4 inch—almost the same as the actual brick.

This means that a real 1×N brick is just about the right width to duplicate the outer wall of a jumbo brick built to 4X scale.

For the 10X example shown in Figure 5-1, you need to use 2×N bricks to simulate the thickness of the brick walls. For the 4X version, those would probably have looked unnecessarily chunky and out of proportion. You can see what I mean in Figure 5-14. Here, you use 1×4 bricks used for the jumbo on the left, which allows it to have walls that are the correct proportion. The example on the far right uses 2×N bricks and, as you can see, the walls are much too thick. In fact, there's no opening for a stud, so this is obviously a bad choice.

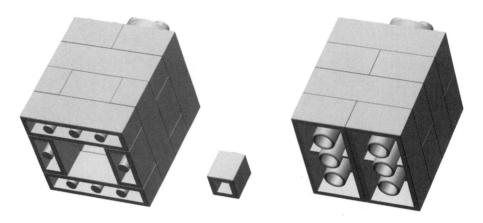

Figure 5-14: One of these things is not like the others, and it might not be the one you think! The version on the right was built with the wrong bricks and lacks the open core of the jumbo version (far left) and the real 1×1 (center).

The decision about what size bricks to use to construct any model is most often made on a case-by-case basis, so it's nearly impossible to devise or apply a single rule that applies to every situation. Given enough other knowledge, however, it is reasonable to assume that you can work out many of these small details as they present themselves.

Sometimes you need a test build to see if a particular solution holds water. In the instance just described, it would be sensible to set out the first layer of bricks in both sizes (2×N and 1×N) and compare them. Right away you would see that with 2×N bricks, the resulting scaled brick would have a hollow underside that would be too small (or even nonexistent) in relation to its overall size. Conversely, you would see that if you made the model of 1×N bricks, it would look more like your original.

NOTE   *A test build is like sticking your foot in a pool to find out the temperature of the water. Instead of jumping in completely, you just go partway in to see if things are what you expect—that the water isn't freezing cold. When you are building with LEGO bricks,* *you can do something similar. Build a section of a large model to see if a certain technique is working. Or try building a small-scale version of something to see if it translates well into LEGO bricks. If it does, then build a larger version.*

By tinkering and experimenting during a test build, you can save yourself a great deal of frustration later on. Although it may be easy to spot the correct approach in the example of the 1×1 built to 4X scale, imagine instead that you were trying to build a 10X scale 2×4 brick. Take it one step further and imagine you made the wrong choice and tried to build the side walls from 1×N bricks instead of 2×N bricks. You could easily have put together two or three hundred bricks before you realized the mistake in your selection of materials. However, if you had done a test build of even a layer or two and then evaluated the results, you would likely have corrected yourself early on. In fact, it may not have even been necessary to build an entire course of the 2×4 jumbo brick. You would likely have spotted the problem by just building a few layers of one or two corners.

Other Parts, Same Technique

You might be wondering, "Are there other parts, besides standard bricks, that make good jumbos?" The answer is "yes." You can scale up many other elements from within the LEGO system just like the basic bricks I've already shown you. Standard slopes and plates are relatively easy since their geometry is simple to copy. Other elements, such as arches, Technic pieces, or some of the specialized elements are also possible to scale though they might require a bit more planning and attention to detail.

Figure 5-15 shows a couple of example pieces to get you started.

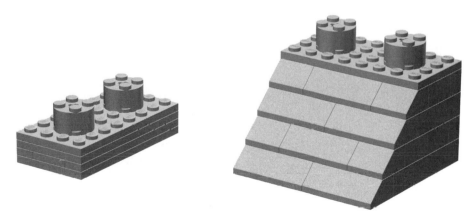

Figure 5-15: A 1×2 plate and a 2×2 45-degree slope

Both of the elements shown in Figure 5-15 make excellent subjects for macroscale building. Here's how to make your own versions of these common pieces.

1×2 Plate—Instructions for the Jumbo Version

If you're looking for a small but interesting element to get started with jumbo building, I strongly suggest a 1×2 plate. Once you've finished the larger-scale version, try holding it in one hand while you hold a real 1×2 plate in the other. The sense of scale should become quickly obvious when you realize that a tiny piece that you normally pinch between two fingers becomes big enough to nearly cover your palm!

As shown in Figures 5-16 through 5-19, constructing this element in 4X scale is pretty simple.

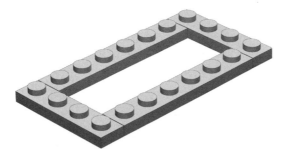

Figure 5-16: Step 1

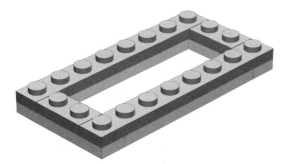

Figure 5-17: Step 2

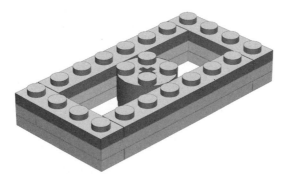

Figure 5-18: Step 3

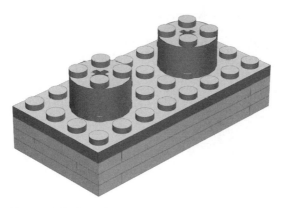

Figure 5-19: Step 4

The studs on the final model (Figure 5-19) appear a bit large, but they are built from a fairly common piece (the 2×2 cylinder brick). If you have 2×2 cylindrical plates, you can substitute two for each of the 2×2 cylinders I used here to make the size appear more accurate.

2×2 45-Degree Slope—Instructions for Jumbo Version

The 2×2 45-degree slope is another common element that's fun to re-create as a jumbo model. When you're choosing which elements to scale up, keep in mind that you may need large quantities of certain pieces. For example, the 2×2 45-degree slope uses a number of actual 45-degree slopes to re-create the angled side of the jumbo brick. Figures 5-20 through 5-24 show the steps you need to follow to build this element. As you can see, the model requires four 2×2 slopes and six 2×4 slopes. Building the same element to a larger scale (10X or 12X) requires even more actual 45-degree elements. Deciding which pieces to re-create as jumbo versions will, therefore, depend largely on whether or not you have enough of the actual-sized elements in your collection.

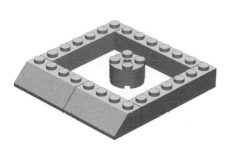

Figure 5-20: Step 1

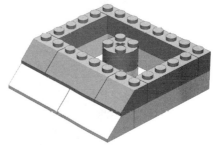

Figure 5-21: Step 2

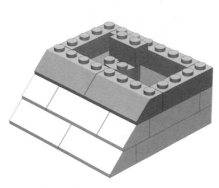

Figure 5-22: Step 3

Figure 5-23: Step 4

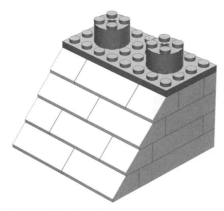

Figure 5-24: Step 5

Building with Jumbo Bricks

You'll find that the 1×2 plate and the 2×2 slope shown in the preceding pages can connect to each other in almost the same way at their regularly sized versions. The only real difference is the way in which they grip in order to stick together. Normal-sized bricks use the friction between the studs on top and the tubes inside other pieces to lock together, but jumbo elements lock together differently.

Remember when I mentioned earlier that you were leaving the small-sized studs exposed on the top of each of your jumbo elements? That was because the studs you built (the scaled-up versions) don't work to hold jumbo bricks together. Instead, you must rely on the normal-sized exposed studs to connect to the pieces of another jumbo brick. This means it's possible to build an entire LEGO set out of jumbo bricks.

This isn't unlike the idea of submodels that I talked about in Chapter 3. In the case of building an entire LEGO model out of jumbo elements, you could consider each of the jumbos to be a submodel. The main structure then is the model that you build from them. The building process is twofold. First, you need to re-create each individual piece in a jumbo size. Then you need to assemble the set exactly as you would the normal-sized version. In Figure 5-25, you can see that I've finished the first step, building jumbo versions of a number of different elements.

Figure 5-25: Once you've built each piece at 4X scale, you'll have a jumbo pile of bricks ready for the next step.

The jumbo elements in Figure 5-25 don't look like much. In fact, they just look like a pile of assorted LEGO pieces, though each of them is really a 4X jumbo model.

When you put them all together, just as you would normal-sized pieces, you end up building a complete LEGO model to jumbo scale. In Figure 5-26, you see the 4X model that arises from the pile of assorted jumbos shown in Figure 5-25. As well, in Figure 5-26 you see the original, much smaller, airplane model that I used as inspiration.

Figure 5-26: The inspiration for this jumbo plane is small enough to fit under its wing.

Bear in mind that this type of model—an entire set build of jumbo elements—can consume large quantities of bricks, so you might want to select to build a small set initially. In addition, you'll want to work at a reasonable scale, such as the 4X technique you used for the last few examples.

Best Solutions from the Simplest Plans

As you work through virtually any LEGO project, you will find yourself questioning the usefulness of this part or that part in this situation or that. You'll wrestle with choices between various techniques and, of course, at what scale to build something. It's all part of the art of LEGO building and part of the challenge that puts this building system at the top of its class. To that end, there is one principle that will help you no matter what you are constructing:

Make things only as complicated as they need be but no more.

Using the 2×2 cylinder brick to represent the stud on a 4X model (Figure 5-5) is an example of this kind of solution. It uses the minimum number of pieces required to complete the task and no more. When you're building or designing a new model, try always to focus on simple solutions like that.

Other Scales: What Scales Work, and Why

In theory, you can build a jumbo brick to just about any scale you like. In practice, some scales work better than others.

The smallest scale that works well is 4X. That's one reason I've used it several times throughout this chapter. In fact, most even-numbered scales work well, because it's much easier to center the studs on the tops of these elements. It's more complicated to put studs on top of a brick that has odd lengths for sides.

You should also keep two other issues to keep in mind when you're deciding what scale to build your jumbos. First, you'll probably want to build some plates, not just standard height bricks. Scales such as 4X, 6X, 10X, and 12X all offer easy solutions for making jumbo plates. For example, at 10X, the jumbo model of a standard brick is ten real bricks high. Therefore, a 10X scale plate is three real bricks and one real plate high.

NOTE   *A jumbo plate, regardless of which scale you choose, will always be one-third the height of a jumbo brick at the same scale.*

Similarly, at 12X, the jumbo model of a standard brick is twelve real bricks high, and a 12X scale plate is four real bricks high. You can see examples of the four scales I just mentioned, along with a standard 1×1 brick, in Figure 5-27.

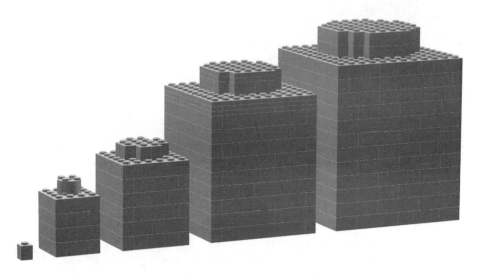

Figure 5-27: From left to right: a standard 1×1 brick, and the 4X, 6X, 10X, and 12X jumbo versions

The other tricky thing is dealing with the jumbo-sized studs that you'll need to finish off your jumbo size elements. You've already seen that at 4X scale, you can easily use 2×2 cylinder bricks as studs. However, at 6X scale, the 4×4 cylinder brick is the right shape but not quite tall enough. For 10X and 12X scales you will almost certainly find yourself creating studs out of square bricks rather than cylindrical ones. Later in this chapter, I'll discuss how best to handle studs scaled up to jumbo size.

Picking the Right Scale

For the first example in this chapter (Figure 5-1), you saw a 10X scale of a 1×1 brick. Then you learned how to scale some other pieces up by a factor of 4. Both of these scales worked just fine. In other words, the jumbo bricks you made looked just like the original regular-sized bricks, only bigger. Look carefully though at the detail needed to fashion the hole in the middle of the 10X Technic brick shown in Figure 5-28.

Would it be possible to have achieved this level of detail (Figure 5-28) if you tried it in 4X scale? No, probably not. The hole through the brick is a complex shape that benefits from being built to a larger scale where you can better define the curves.

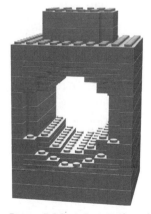

Figure 5-28: A 1×1 Technic brick offers an interesting challenge when you are building a jumbo version. Creating the hole in the middle is best achieved using larger scales.

Examine the way in which you were able to create a fairly realistic-looking stud on top of your 4X 1×1 brick in Figure 5-5. Would that same technique have worked for a 10X brick? No, not at all. The 2×2 cylinder brick simply wouldn't be big enough to represent a stud at 10X scale. Instead, you need to build the stud out of several smaller elements to make it appear correctly sized.

NOTE *You can find complete instructions for building the 10X Technic brick shown in Figure 5-28 at www.apotome.com/instructions.html.*

It's easy to see that just as it is important to use the right parts for the right job, you must also choose the right scale at which to build. This idea applies to just about any LEGO model you may try to build. Trying to build a 6-inch-long Titanic might result in a ship so small it is hard to determine what inspired it. Starting with such a large inspiration can be hard, unless you are willing to work toward an equally large model. Looking at it another way, it is probably easier to build a 6-inch-long fire engine and have it contain a few essential details that help capture the feeling of the original than it is to do this for the Titanic. Think about matching your building scale with the item you are trying to build.

Approximation

Building a model out of LEGO bricks requires you to make many decisions. You need to figure out how large a model to build, what color bricks to use and, very often, how to handle the tiny details that may not be possible to replicate exactly. To make your model look as realistic as possible, you will find that you need to *approximate* certain features to at least give you the look of the original. Sometimes just coming close is close enough. Where else in life do you get a great deal like that?

Jumbo bricks are no exception. Almost all have a tiny feature that can be hard to replicate. I'm talking about the studs on each element.

Let me use a 10X-scale stud to easily demonstrate this problem. First, refer to Appendix B of this book. There you will find information about printing out one of the model design grids you will use throughout this book. Print out a copy of Design Grid #1. It looks very similar to traditional graph paper. On that paper, draw a circle with the correct diameter to represent the stud. Imagine you're looking down at the top of a 10X jumbo 1×1 brick, like the one shown in Figure 5-1.

Now start shading in squares until you almost fill the circle without really going outside of it. You should find that your drawing looks like Figure 5-29; the shaded squares don't quite fill the circle. This means that this example of a jumbo stud will be just a bit smaller than if you could make it perfectly cylindrical.

Now shade in additional squares until your drawing looks like Figure 5-30. This version of the stud is slightly larger than if you could model it to be exactly cylindrical. Neither technique produces a perfect jumbo copy of the original. These are both examples of a shape being approximated with LEGO bricks.

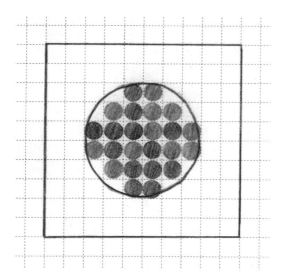

Figure 5-29: The small shaded circles within the larger circle represent the tops of actual bricks that will be used to re-create the jumbo stud.

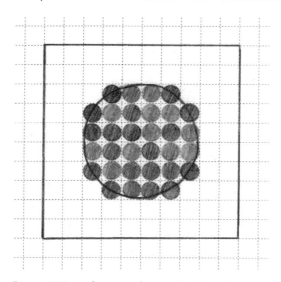

Figure 5-30: In the second example, shown here, more real bricks are added. This makes the jumbo stud appear larger than in Figure 5-29. You can use either version depending on your preference.

Figures 5-31 and 5-32 show how the two different studs appear when built of actual bricks.

Both techniques work, and two 10X macro bricks will connect together with either size, so it's a matter of which one you like best. Approximation is as much about what you *feel* looks best for your particular model than it is about what is correct from the most technical point of view.

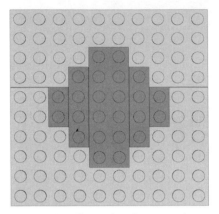

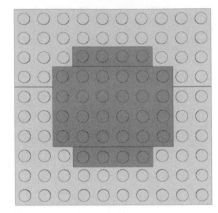

Figure 5-31: The stud in this example is a bit smaller than the relative diameter of a real one, but it will work just fine.

Figure 5-32: The stud in this example is slightly larger than the correct diameter, but it will also suffice as a jumbo stud.

Review: Jumbo Bricks Are Just the Start

So you've built a few jumbo bricks and you understand the concept of macro building. Now you're looking for other projects to build using the same technique. There is really only one rule that applies when you choose subject matter for macro models:

Start small and don't build too big.

First, try re-creating *other* elements you have in your collection. You may want to tackle a 1×1 headlight brick or maybe see if you can find a way to build the texture on the face of a 1×2 grille brick. (See Appendix A for illustrations of these and many other pieces.) Pick pieces that you already find interesting and know you'll enjoy seeing in large scale. And remember, try smaller elements first. For instance, don't try building a 1×16 Technic brick right off the bat. Try a 1×1 first to see if you can figure out the geometry you need to make the hole appear round.

Then, why not try building an entire set out of jumbo bricks, as you saw in Figure 5-25? Again, select a set that is already very small. Start with a set that has perhaps 10 or 12 pieces at most. Then, as you get more comfortable with the technique, you might want to try something bigger. Remember, the larger the set you are trying to build from jumbo elements, the smaller scale you will want to use. In other words, you might be able to build a 10-piece set at 10X scale, but if you were building a 25- or 30-piece set, you might want to stick to 4X scale.

Regardless of the scale or subject matter you choose, I think you'll find that jumbo bricks are fun to build and will catch the eye of anyone who happens to see them.

6

MICROSCALE BUILDING:
MORE THAN MEETS THE EYE

In the last chapter, I showed you several *macroscale* building techniques; there you learned to make models much larger than the objects they represent. This chapter focuses on the opposite technique, something called *microscale* building. As the word *micro* indicates, this scale is very small. Keep reading to find out just how small. If you are someone with a limited supply of LEGO bricks, or perhaps you do your building in a confined space, then the microscale route might work well for you. You can still create interesting models no matter how limited your palette of pieces might be.

Figure 6-1 shows an example of the type of subject matter you might explore when building at this scale.

Though only 7 inches long, this microscale cargo ship captures many of the details of the real thing, including shipping containers, the bridge, and the always necessary smokestack.

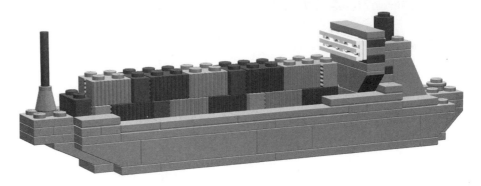

Figure 6-1: Microscale works well when the real life inspiration is huge.

Now that you know that *micro* is yet another scale at which you can build models, you probably want to know how to define micro. How small is small? Let's back up a couple chapters and think about the train station (shown in Figure 3-4).

In Chapter 3, I showed you how to build the walls, doors, and windows of that building to accommodate the standard-sized LEGO minifigs. However, suppose you wanted to build the train station smaller, maybe only one-half or even one-third the size. In such a case, the features of the building would no longer be properly sized for minifigs. What label then would you apply to the scale of the building? In a word: micro. In this book, the term *micro* or *microscale* applies to models of objects that are built much smaller than is suitable for minifigs to live or travel in.

So far in this book, I've talked about several different scales to which you can build models. To put them all in perspective, take a look at Table 6-1, which describes each one.

Table 6-1: Comparison of Various Scales Used to Build LEGO Models, from Largest to Smallest

Scale	Description
Macro	Discussed in Chapter 5. When you are working at this scale, the model ends up being many times larger than the original object.
Lifesize	As the name suggests, models you create at this scale will be exactly the same size as the original object. These could be sculptures (as seen in Chapter 7) or just about any faithful reproduction of a real life object.
Miniland	Models and figures built to miniland scale are roughly twice the size of minifig scale constructions. This is the scale used to create the miniland displays at the LEGO theme parks.
Minifig	The train station we built in Chapter 3 was created at minifig scale. Buildings, cars, and other objects are all built in proportion to the minifig characters.
Micro	I'll show you microscale in this chapter. The models built this way are typically even smaller than those built using the minifig scale.

NOTE   *In order to standardize microscale building for the purposes of group displays, some LEGO builders have decided to use a 1×1 cylinder brick to represent the size of a person within the microsized world. In other words, in such cases, one brick in model height is equal to roughly 6 feet in the real world. This should give you a good idea of the scale of the micro world.*

Of course, there are any number of scales upon which you can base your models. For instance, you may decide to build a 1:3 replica of the grandfather clock that sits in your living room. That certainly wouldn't be minifig scale. The model isn't larger than the original, so you know it's not macro. In fact, it really doesn't match any of the major scales noted above. That's okay. The scales I laid out in Table 6-1 are just guidelines, not rules.

These scales are, however, useful if you want to understand the scale at which you are making your models. For instance, suppose you are building a model that you want to display alongside one built by a friend or a member of the LEGO builders group to which you belong. If you both (or all) agree to build something to minifig scale, you each know what that means. The minifig label provides a reference to a particular size of building. That way you don't arrive with a 1-foot-tall warehouse that's supposed to go next to your friend's 3-foot-tall ice cream stand. That could be embarrassing!

Microscale: Small Scale with Big Possibilities

When we looked at minifigs back in Chapter 3, I helped you figure out that structures or vehicles intended for those little folks should be built to about 1:48 scale. However, microscale models aren't locked into one set of numbers, much like the macroscale bricks back in Chapter 5 that weren't all built to the same scale. For example, a 1-foot-tall model of the Empire State Building in New York would be approximately 1:1250 scale, because the actual building is 1,250 feet tall. On the other hand, a 1-foot-tall model of the Great Pyramid in Egypt would be approximately 1:480, because the actual pyramid is about 480 feet tall.

This might seem a bit confusing because earlier I mentioned that some builders use a 1×1 cylinder brick to represent the height of a microscale person. The examples of the Empire State Building and the Great Pyramid are obviously not built to the same 1-brick-equals-6-feet specification. In fact, they aren't even built to the same scale as each other! But they are microscale examples nonetheless. These examples demonstrate that the actual scale can vary within the micro world, but models still hold to the same principle; they are extremely small versions of very large things. Just as you did in Chapter 5, where you learned to build 4X and 10X versions of the same brick, you can use different numbers to achieve the dimensions for a microscale model.

It's also worth noting that neither of these two models would be classified as minifig scale since even minifigs would look like giants next to the LEGO version of either structure. Instead, both of these models are definitely considered microscale for the reasons I've already mentioned.

Getting Started: Ignore the Details

Okay, you don't really want to throw out every detail, but many smaller features on large objects are just not going to be included in your final work. In Chapter 5, I talked about a technique called *approximation*. This is the building method where you try to give things the look and feel of their real life counterpart without necessarily duplicating every last detail.

That same principle can also be applied to microscale models. The easiest way to do this is simply to look at the thing you are modeling and try to see only the characteristics that stand out the most. How does that work? To find out, let's go back to the Empire State Building as an example of how to create a model at this scale. If you tried to create a minifig-scale version of that building, it would still have to be more than 26 feet tall! Remember that in Chapter 3 you discovered that minifig scale is about 1:48. Because the real building is 1,250 feet tall, you would divide that number by 48 and end up with 26.04 feet as the height of your model.

Most people don't have enough LEGO bricks to tackle a project of that size. A microscale version of such a large building makes much more sense. But in choosing microscale, you need to recognize that smaller details such as window sills, decorative statues, or signs may have to be left out so that you can capture the essence of the building in something less than 26 feet.

The Empire State Building has a unique shape that is easily recognized. Bringing it to life in microscale involves trying to re-create that shape with as few elements as possible. All you are trying to achieve is the *feeling* that your model is this building not that it is an exact replica.

Start by sketching the shape of the building on some graph paper.

NOTE *For this next example, I've used one of the model Design Grids. This is special graph paper that has lines drawn to the same size and shape as real LEGO elements. Refer to Appendix B of this book for more information on the Design Grids. For now, just follow along with the example shown here.*

I found some images of the actual building on the Internet and used them to come up with the drawing you see in Figure 6-2.

Notice that I've only drawn the outline of the building in this first illustration. The silhouette is the most important thing I want to achieve in making this model. As previously noted, I've essentially left out all the details at this point. Seeing only the shape of your subject helps you see the big picture of the model you are attempting to produce. Because microscale building is often about creating the illusion of a larger object, it's very important that the model look right at first glance.

How did I know how big to draw it? I didn't. I just guessed, though I obviously wanted to make it fit on a single page or less. You may find that your first few drawings are too large or too small or that they don't capture the profile the way you want. Don't give up. Making a second or third sketch doesn't take that long, and your plan will likely improve each time. Note that at this point, I'm not even worrying about designing to a particular scale, I'm just focusing on finding a design that captures my subject.

Next, I begin to add the major details (see Figure 6-3).

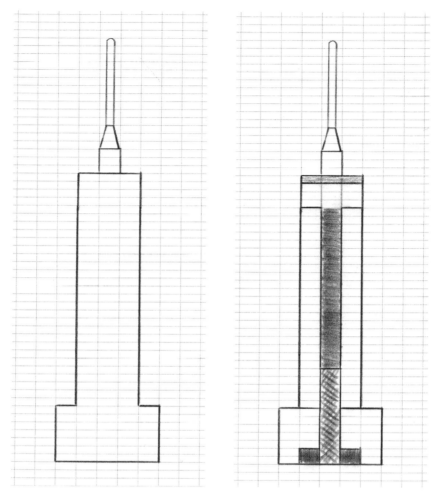

Figure 6-2: A rough outline of the building

Figure 6-3: I've sketched in the main features of the building.

As you can see in Figure 6-3, I've drawn in the main entrance, shaded an indent near the top of the tower, and added the shape of the channel that runs vertically up the center of the building. Notice that in this drawing, I've tried to use different shades of pencil to represent different parts of the building. In some cases, this is to remind myself that even though this is a two-dimensional drawing, it is the plan for a three-dimensional model. By shading some areas darker, I'm leaving a visual clue for myself that these will be closer to the back of the model rather than right up front. The center channel, which runs most of the height of the building, is a perfect example of this technique. It is recessed from the face of the famous skyscraper, and I want to try and duplicate that look if I can.

It's also worth pointing out that I'm not being too careful with how my lines meet or how each area is colored in. This is just a sketch and isn't meant to be perfect. Perfection is boring; have fun with your design sessions!

Lastly (as shown in Figure 6-4), I've added some boxes to represent the windows. The key word in this last sentence is *represent*. As noted above, microscale models will never capture every last detail and often, with a very large subject, we can't even depict things as large as windows. You can, however, add some plates of a different color to give the sense of where windows are located.

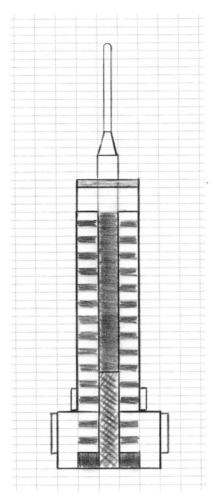

Figure 6-4: The blueprint for my micro marvel

Interestingly, this is one model that really does look good in light and dark gray. Although many of the ideas presented in this book would benefit from a splash of color, this model is one that doesn't. The simple two-tone effect, offered by the two shades of gray, is exactly what I'm looking for.

Translating Ideas into Bricks

Now I have a plan. How does this become a LEGO model? Look at the drawing I've made and remember that the main idea of microscale building is to make something as small as possible and yet have it remain recognizable. Keep in mind that each of the boxes (or cells) on the design grid is the same height as a standard 1×1 plate. Therefore three cells equal the same height as a standard 1×1 brick (see Figure 6-5).

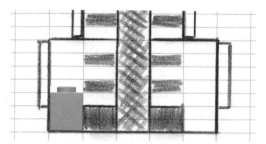

Figure 6-5: A portion of the blueprint showing how a 1×1 brick compares to the design I've laid out

To my eye, the bottom left and right corners of my sketch (shown in Figure 6-5) look very much like 1×1 LEGO bricks. Based on that assumption, I can quickly figure out what bricks and plates might work best to construct the rest of the building. In Figure 6-6, I added in some light and dark gray plates to suggest what elements I will use to build the real model.

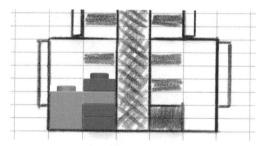

Figure 6-6: A more direct comparison between actual elements and the partial plan for the model

Although these may not be the exact pieces I end up using, they give me a sense of what *types* of elements I'll need.

You can see (in Figure 6-6) that I have only represented some of the windows and even then, they are only represented by dark gray plates that I intended to give the feel of windows. As I continue to match the sketch with appropriate sized elements (based on the 1×1's I started with) it doesn't take long for a little building like this to come together as the finished model you see in Figure 6-7.

Figure 6-7: Real life brought down to size—micro size!

In the final version, I've included a foundation made from standard plates, though how you choose to do this (in your own version) is entirely up to you. For instance, if you were using this building as part of a larger micro-scale exhibit, you might need it to sit on something different—perhaps a waffled baseplate.

You'll find that if you look carefully at this model, you can see that it's constructed almost entirely of plates. Not every micro model will be like this but, in many cases, the smaller size of plates offers you greater creative control over your work. Of course, you may not have the right number of light and dark gray plates to make this exact replica of the Empire State Building, but don't let that stop you from making one anyway. Try building one from just bricks to see if you can match the shape. Or try using other colors to come up with your own version. You could use white, tan, or even yellow bricks and plates to make something that at least resembles this famous landmark. Remember that was the goal—to make something that resembled this building but didn't necessarily duplicate every last detail.

NOTE *You can find complete instructions for both the cargo ship in Figure 6-1 and the Empire State Building in Figure 6-7 at www.apotome.com/instructions.html.*

Recap the Technique

You've now seen that building microscale models is as easy as following three simple steps:

1. **Sketch out the edges.** Identify the outline of the object you're building, ignore any other details. This gives you the essential shape to use as a starting point.
2. **Find the features.** Look for major features, especially interesting shapes or patterns that help define the basic look of the object.
3. **Discover the details.** Pick some of the smaller details to model. Be careful to select only things that are critical to the overall feel of the object.

It's not really necessary to use paper and pencil to work out the design of your model, though you may find it very useful. Sometimes part of the fun is just digging through your LEGO bricks and working through the steps with the real elements in your hands. You can simply take apart mistakes and rebuild that portion. Some mistakes become happy accidents that end up being better solutions than the ones you originally had in mind. Either way, the benefit is that you are thinking in three dimensions and solving problems as you go.

How Do I Know What Scale I'm Using?

There are two ways to determine the scale of your micro model:

1. Decide on a scale *before* you begin building.
2. Figure out the scale *after* you're done building.

Let's look at each method separately.

Decide on a scale before you begin building.

Pretend for the moment that you're building a model to go along with something a friend is building. Perhaps you're putting together a microscale town. The two of you agree to a scale of about 1:100. This ensures that no matter what subject matter you use for inspiration (real buildings, photos, drawings, and so on), the structures you build will have similar proportions.

Picking a scale for a project like this is really arbitrary. You want to select a scale with a fairly large difference between the two numbers. In this example, you've picked 1:100, but you might also find success with other scales. If you're both building gigantic sky-scrapers for a microscale city, you might want to build at an even smaller scale like 1:200 or 1:300. Remember, the bigger the second number is, the smaller the model will actually be.

Deciding upon a scale prior to building means that you will use the scale factor to know how big your model should be. For example, a real life 100-foot tall water tower would become just over a foot tall when built as a 1:100 scale LEGO model. A 25-foot corner store would be only 3 inches tall when modeled in LEGO bricks. Put together on a table, these two models would look as though they belonged to the same scene. Building to a specific scale helps you make sure such elements look right together.

Figure out the scale after you're done building.

The second method, for determining scale, works exactly opposite to what I've just described. I used the second technique for the earlier Empire State Building example. I decided on the overall shape of my structure and then found LEGO elements that matched a particular part of it. Then I decided what other pieces to use based on how big they needed to be compared to those first parts I picked out. In the end, my model was about 7 inches high. Because I know that the real structure is 1,250 feet tall, I can figure out the scale using some more simple math:

```
1250 × 12 = 15000
```

(This converts the building's height from feet into inches, since I used inches to measure my model.)

```
15000 ÷ 7 = 2143
```

(This divides the real height by the height of my model. The result is my scale factor.)

It's easy to see that the Empire State Building I described above was built to a scale of 1:2143. Now that's micro!

Replacing Full-Size Parts with Microscale Stand-Ins

In many ways, microscale building is just as challenging as any other scale. You are forced to make decisions about which parts to use in what situations. Often, you might know that a particular LEGO piece exists, but you can't use it since it's much too big for this scale. Let's look at two different classes of parts (wheels and windows) and see how you can simulate them at microscale without using elements actually designed to fill those rolls.

Microscale Wheels

Take, for example, most of the LEGO wheels. Many are the appropriate size for minifig or miniland scale, but they are much too large to be used as wheels for vehicles built to microscale. That doesn't mean they can't be used to represent something else, but you probably won't use them as wheels. Instead you may find yourself using 1×1 cylinder plates turned so that they are sitting on edge (see Figure 6-8).

Figure 6-8: Simple microscale truck with 1×1 cylindrical plates for wheels

The transport truck shown in Figure 6-8 gives you an idea not only for microscale wheels, but also provides an example of how to turn bricks on their sides to create certain shapes or patterns.

The trailer portion of the truck is created by stacking 1×2 bricks on top of each other. Those stacks are then sandwiched between 2×3 plates. The entire trailer section is then turned so that the studs are facing to the back of the vehicle.

NOTE   *For complete instructions on building the transport truck, please visit www.apotome.com/instructions.html.*

Microscale Windows

As with the wheels, many of the actual LEGO window elements will not look right when you use them as windows for buildings at this scale. You can use plates as I did in the Empire State Building earlier in this chapter, however. Or, for models based on smaller buildings, you can use something like the 1×1 headlight brick with its side stud facing inward. Several of them, when grouped together, create the impression of a picture window for the house shown in Figure 6-9.

Figure 6-9: This house is much too small for minifigs but just right for a microscale suburbia.

Notice that the door to the house is merely suggested by the recessed darker area to the right of the windows. This is really just another example of the technique I used to suggest the windows for the Empire State Building. Sometimes a change in brick color or depth is all it takes to give the illusion that a particular feature exists when it really doesn't.

Instructions for Microscale House

The little house shown in Figure 6-9 is a simple model you can probably build from pieces you already have in your collection. Figure 6-10 shows the Bill of Materials for this mini-mansion. This is followed by a series of figures (Figures 6-11 through 6-16) that show the steps you need to follow to build the house.

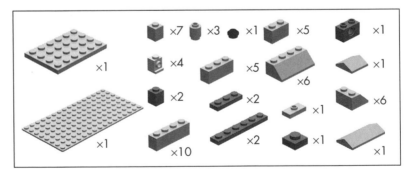

Figure 6-10: The Bill of Materials for the microscale house

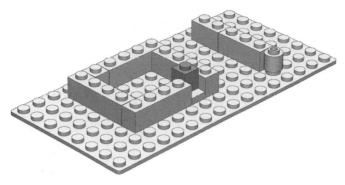

Figure 6-11: Step 1. Place the dark gray 1×1 on an offset plate.

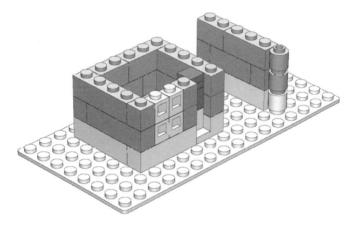

Figure 6-12: Step 2. Install the front windows, which are just 1×1 headlight bricks facing backward.

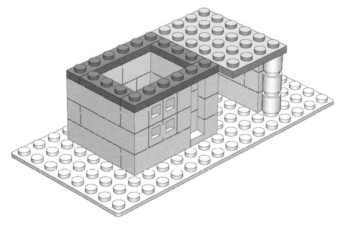

Figure 6-13: Step 3. Place a 1×6 plate near the top front to help hold the windows in place.

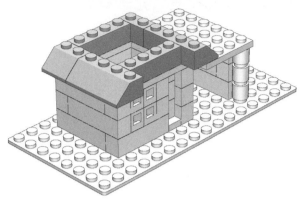

Figure 6-14: Step 4. Start the roof. The slopes on the left should hang over the edge of the wall.

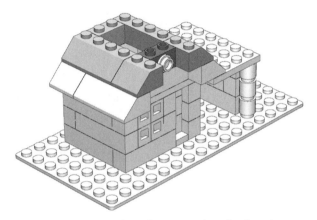

Figure 6-15: Step 5. Place the 1×2 Technic brick in the top center and attach a transparent 1×1 cylinder plate.

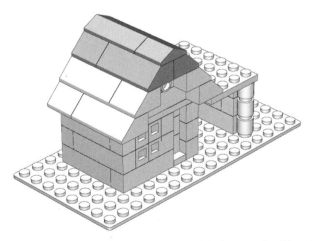

Figure 6-16: Step 6. Complete the roof with a couple of handy peak elements.

Recap of Replacement Parts

Part of the beauty of microscale models is that you don't always need to use specialized parts to finish off your models. Simple bricks, plates, and slopes can become windows, doors, wheels, wings, trees, and so on. Use your imagination.

On the other hand, when you have specialized elements you want to use, you have many opportunities to do so with microscale models. Often, you will need a quick change of direction like that junction elements can offer. Other times, you will want interesting shapes such as macaroni bricks or interesting patterns such as grille bricks. The trick is to see the piece not just as another LEGO element but as the front end of a semi rig (as shown in Figure 6-8) or the windows of a tiny house (as shown in Figure 6-9).

Review and Suggested Subject Matter

In Chapter 5, I showed you macroscale models—the extra large versions of real life objects. I indicated that when you were looking for ideas for macro models, you might want to pick things that are very small. That way, your jumbo version wouldn't be impossibly large.

In microscale building, the opposite theory applies. Because your goal is to build a model that is much, much smaller than the real life version, you can pick things that are naturally very large. This could mean something as large as a car, or it could mean something enormous, such as a skyscraper or an aircraft carrier.

The following is a short list of things that might make good subjects for microscale building:

Automobiles	Houses
Trucks	Apartment buildings
Buses	Dinosaurs
Locomotives	Zoo animals
Train cars	Amusement park rides
Spaceships from movies	Skyscrapers
Stores or a mall	Pyramids
Construction equipment	Ships
Hotels	Aircraft carriers
Castles	Bridges
	Monuments

Of course, these are just suggestions, and like everything else in the LEGO system, there are no limits to how you apply your own imagination and creativity. Microscale models are an excellent technique to explore when your collection of LEGO elements might be limited in size, though as you've seen, this restriction does not have to limit the scope of your microsized LEGO world.

7

SCULPTURES: THE SHAPE OF THINGS TO BUILD

How can you make a bunch of square bricks look round? Or oval for that matter? And how exactly do you make them to look like a dinosaur or the face of your favorite uncle? Does this ever happen? Well, hardly ever if you look at them one at a time. The trick is using them in just the right combinations to make them appear to take on rounded, oval, or other more organic shapes. That is the idea behind sculpting with LEGO bricks.

Sculpting is different from other forms of building with LEGO bricks, in that your primary goal is often to simply re-create a specific shape or series of shapes in the most realistic way possible. You can argue that the macro bricks in Chapter 5 are sculptures, and you aren't wrong. But in those cases, the models are based on simple geometry and mathematics. *Sculptured* models also use those things, but they require a little more of your eye and judgment to make them successful. A sculptured model can be something as obvious as a sphere (perhaps a globe of the earth) or a sphere-like shape that you work into a larger model. You can take the techniques you learn from making spheres and use them to create the head of a large-scale minifig, an animal figure, or even part of a certain building or vehicle.

In this chapter, I'll first walk you through the principles behind creating a basic sphere like the one shown in Figure 7-1. Then, I'll take those lessons and apply them to another situation where the curved natural shapes proved useful.

The first sphere you build doesn't need to be enormous in order for you to learn the techniques necessary to create it. The one shown in Figure 7-1 is only 16 studs wide and 13 bricks high. It's just a little larger than a typical softball.

Figure 7-1: This sphere is modeled in three different colors. You can pick a color scheme like this, use just a single color, or change colors at each layer.

Spheres: Round and Round They Go

In this section, you'll build a very basic sphere. You can create one using nothing more than standard bricks—no plates, slopes, or other special elements are required.

A *sphere* is really just another word for a ball-shaped object. One of the best things about a basic sphere is that you can build one with just the bricks you'll find in a bucket of assorted bricks. You can also make your first sphere just about any size you want, depending on how many bricks you want to use. *The method for producing the rounded look of the sphere remains the same if you're building one the size of a softball or one as big as a basketball.*

The degree to which you can make a LEGO globe or ball appear spherical depends mostly upon how big you build it and how many small plates you add to the mixture of parts. The larger it is, the more rounded it is likely to appear. By using more plates, to fill some of the square corners, you can also add to the circular appearance. For the example in this chapter, I'm going on the assumption that you don't have a huge number of small plates, so you're going to build a sphere using *just* bricks. It will end up looking like Figure 7-2.

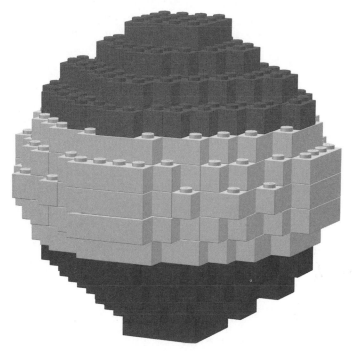

Figure 7-2: The goal. This simple sphere contains only 220 bricks, but you can use the same technique to make ones that are much larger.

As you can see, using full-height bricks alone gives you a somewhat blocky looking sphere. For this example, however, the goal isn't to create a perfectly smooth ball, but rather to demonstrate the technique. First, take a look at the Bill of Materials for this project (Figure 7-3).

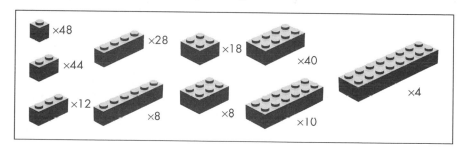

Figure 7-3: Bill of Materials for a basic sphere. This design uses common bricks and not even a lot of them!

The pieces you need to make a small sphere, like the one you're creating in this chapter, are very common and should be within the reach of even a modest-sized LEGO collection.

Divide and Build: Two Sections Means Twice the Fun

One of the most common ways to approach a sphere is to divide the building process into two pieces: the top half and the bottom half of the model. What makes this interesting is that you start at the middle and work up to the top and then go back to the middle and build down to the bottom. Is that confusing? Take a look at Figure 7-4 to see what I mean about starting in the middle.

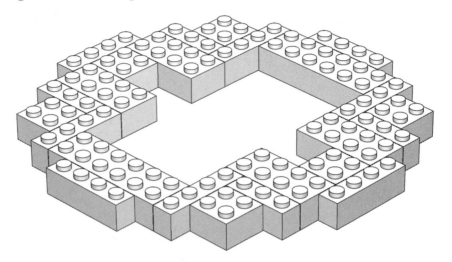

Figure 7-4: Step 1. The first layer of bricks is really the middle of the sphere.

You start building at what is essentially the equator of the sphere (if you think in terms of a planet). You lay down a jagged ring of bricks (as in Figure 7-4) that is as big around as the model will ever get. Note that for the first few steps, the model appears uneven and not very round; that changes as you get further along.

NOTE   *You may wish to arrange the first layer of bricks on a piece of fabric such as felt; this allows you to create the design shown in the first step without having the bricks slide around as they would on a smooth table. Once you have the second layer in place, you can remove the cloth.*

Begin the second layer by using the stagger technique I discussed in Chapter 2. Remember that *staggering* sets one layer of bricks back from the front edge of an adjoining layer of bricks to produce a stair-step pattern.

As you see in Figure 7-5, the sphere begins to evolve very slowly at first. It doesn't look like much right now. In fact, the second layer isn't all that much different from the first. However, if you look carefully at the bottom of Figure 7-5, you can see *some* studs from the first layer that aren't covered by the second layer. By using the stagger technique, you have begun the sculpting process, which is even more noticeable in the next step (Figure 7-6).

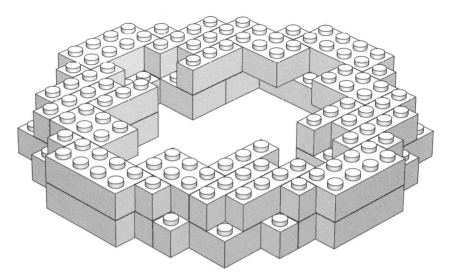

Figure 7-5: Step 2. The second layer is staggered, leaving studs of the first layer exposed.

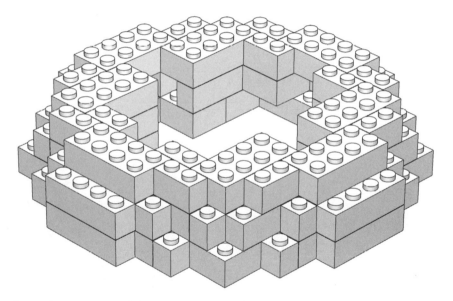

Figure 7-6: Step 3. Each layer requires fewer bricks and continues to recede from the layer beneath it.

In step three, you again leave studs of the previous layer exposed. Although the model still doesn't look much like a sphere at this stage, it's important, as always, that you plan ahead and keep staggering the layers as you build. Note that you don't leave the same studs exposed each time you add a layer. By changing which studs get covered and which ones don't, you add to the natural round shape you're hoping to achieve. You'll see more of this in the next three steps (Figures 7-7 through 7-9).

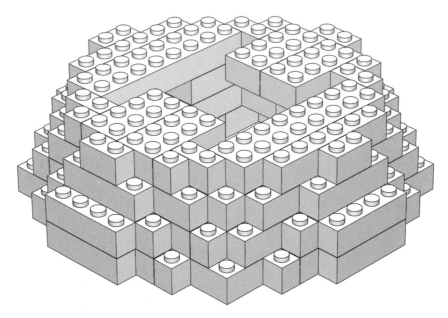

Figure 7-7: Step 4. Here you're beginning to close in the top of the sphere.

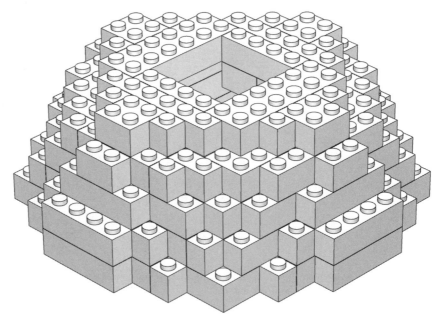

Figure 7-8: Step 5. Although the sphere is comprised entirely of standard rectangular bricks, it is beginning to seem a bit more rounded overall.

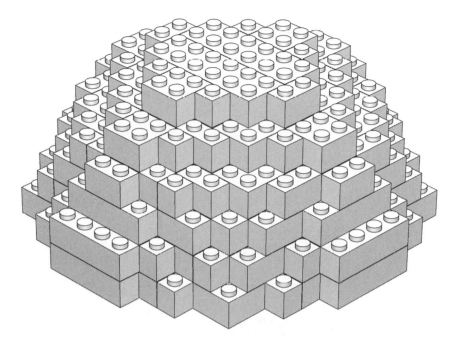

Figure 7-9: Step 6. The sphere is closed in but you're not quite to the top yet.

As you reach the last layer of the top half of the sphere, you'll notice something interesting (see Figure 7-10).

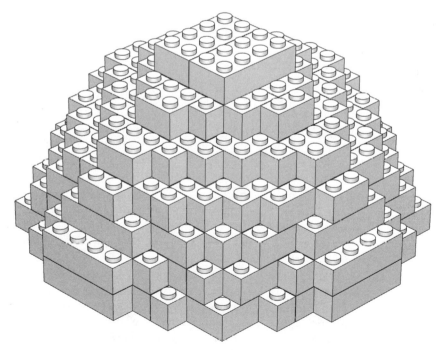

Figure 7-10: Step 7. Two 2×4 bricks are all you need to cap off the top of the sphere.

In step 7 (Figure 7-10), you can see that the last two pieces you add are just 2×4 bricks. Keep those bricks in the back of your mind for a moment because I will discuss them again once you've completed the sphere.

Step 8 doesn't add any bricks to the model but just changes the orientation of the sphere. This is called a *rotation step*, and that's exactly what you do. Take the sphere and rotate it 180 degrees until it looks like Figure 7-11.

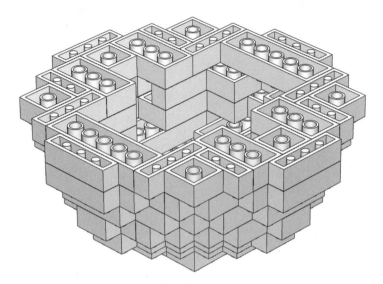

Figure 7-11: Step 8. Before you start the second half of the model, turn the whole thing so that the tubes are facing up.

You are now looking at the underside of the first layer of bricks that you placed back in step 1 (see Figure 7-4). Again, it's important to note that you didn't add any bricks during this process; you just flipped the sphere upside down.

For a small version of a sphere, as in this example, flipping it over is the easiest way to build the bottom half. In other words, we add to what we've already built, we just do it with the bricks facing studs down. When building a larger version—perhaps a globe of the earth or a life-sized soccer ball—you may wish to try another technique; build the two halves completely separate from each other. When each of the two halves is complete, you can set the upper half on top of the lower half and carefully press the two together. The example we're building here is small enough that you can simply work on the whole thing as one unit.

In the next five steps (Figures 7-12 through 7-16), you can see that you follow a pattern similar to what you've already been doing, except now, instead of leaving studs exposed on each layer, you leave portions of the bottom of bricks uncovered. It's also interesting to note that as you build the bottom half of the sphere, you are placing the bricks on upside down as well. It's not that this technique is dramatically more difficult, but because the orientation is different, you may find that each brick requires just a little more thought to place it on the model.

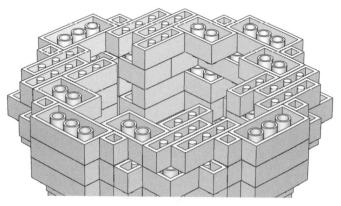

Figure 7-12: Step 9. You're still staggering bricks; it's just that you're now doing it upside down. But don't worry: it'll all work out in the end.

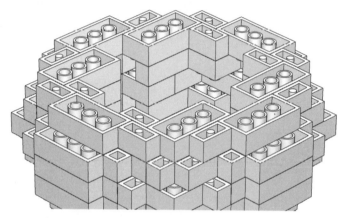

Figure 7-13: Step 10. In Chapter 2, I noted that staggering also involves a bit of overlapping. The same holds true here.

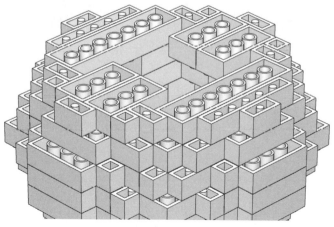

Figure 7-14: Step 11. Watch the placement of your layers carefully on a model like this. The way in which you're staggering is exactly what's giving the sphere its shape.

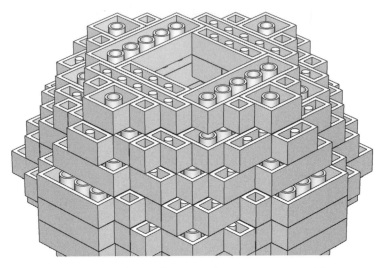

Figure 7-15: Step 12. The small opening that remains is certainly square, but the next step helps solve that problem.

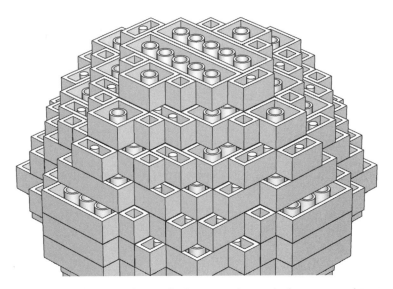

Figure 7-16: Step 13. Close in the bottom with exactly the same combination of pieces you used back in step 6.

You add the final two pieces in step 14 (Figure 7-17).

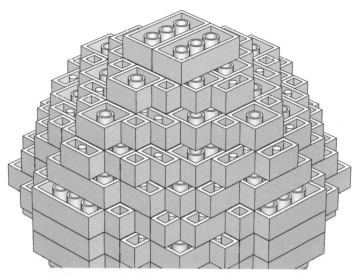

Figure 7-17: Step 14. 2×4 bricks once again give you the finishing touch you are looking for.

Just as with the two pieces on top of the sphere, the last pieces of the bottom are two 2×4 bricks. Remember I asked you to keep those in mind? Here's what I want you to notice. Compare the two 2×4's on top (Figure 7-10) with the two 2×4's on the bottom (Figure 7-17). Exactly the same, right? Now compare those bricks with the flat areas found on the "sides" of the sphere. In Figure 7-18, I've tried to highlight this in a close-up.

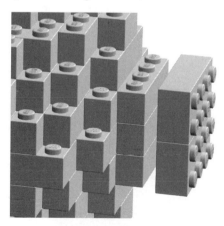

Figure 7-18: Matching the size of your top with the smallest areas on the sides of the sphere will help you get a sense of just how "round" you've been able to make your sculpture.

You can see that two 2×4's are *almost* the same size as those flat areas along the equator. This is what helps you to know that your sphere is the right size and shape. Remember that the top and bottom of your sphere are represented by two 2×4 bricks—all facing studs up. The four "sides" of your sphere (where the sides round off to their smallest face) are made up of three layers of bricks, but it's the portion of their sides that is flat that is most important. Those outward facing sides (as seen in Figure 7-18) should be just about the size of the outward facing surfaces of the two 2×4 bricks on the top and bottom. Having them nearly the same is what helps to give the sphere its rounded appearance even though it's built entirely of bricks that are not round at all.

Beyond Spheres: Sculpting Other Subjects

In both Chapters 3 and 5 we looked at things that had very straight sides and were primarily constructed using the overlap technique. Sculpting, on the other hand, relies more on the stagger technique you have been using so far in this chapter. The example you built to learn about sculpting was a simple sphere. But there are only so many times you would ever need to build something so plain. More likely, you'll want to sculpt an animal, a statue, a cartoon character, or perhaps some extraterrestrial being born in your imagination.

Choosing a Subject

For this section, I tried to find a subject that would be familiar and yet still offer interesting ways in which to build it as a LEGO brick sculpture. I chose the famous Great Sphinx of Giza. It has overlooked the sands of Egypt for thousands of years. The real Sphinx is itself a sculpture, so this model is then a sculpture of a sculpture. You can see the model I created in Figure 7-19.

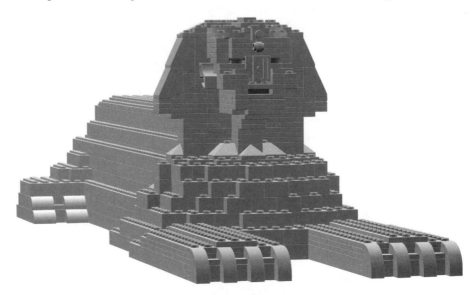

Figure 7-19: The Sphinx combines the head of a pharaoh with the body of a lion.

As with the Empire State Building example from Chapter 6, the first thing I did was look on the Internet to find pictures of the Sphinx. Unlike what I did with that micro model, I did not use the design grids for planning the construction of the Sphinx. Rather, I went on the look and feel of the work as it progressed. Remember, there is no right way or wrong way to tackle a project like this. If you prefer to use the grids to help plot your design, that is perfectly acceptable.

Aside from the fact that it's so well known, I picked the Sphinx for two other reasons. First, it is a relatively simple shape to attempt to copy in LEGO elements. By contrast, a sculpture of a knight riding a horse would have presented much greater challenges due to the larger number of shapes, curves, and angles required.

Second, it is essentially just one color and therefore allowed me to concentrate on shape alone, rather than having to also select proper colors as I went. What color should the Sphinx be, though? To make it look very accurate, I modeled it in tan colored bricks. If you want to build your own but don't have enough of those elements, you might want to think of an alternate color such as white or yellow. Although not as realistic as tan, these colors would be less cartoonish than if you build it out of red or blue.

Getting Started on the Sphinx

In Chapter 6, I talked about finding a unique feature on the object you are using for inspiration. In the case of the Sphinx, most people recognize the human-like head with a Pharaoh's headdress. This is the starting point I selected. If you were building the model on your own, you might decide you'd rather build the body of the statue first (a form based on a lion at rest) and work your way up.

NOTE   *For complete instructions to build the Sphinx model, visit www.apotome.com/ instructions.html.*

For the example in this book, I built the head until it looked right and then created a body to match. I made this decision because I was more concerned about capturing the look of the head than I was about getting the body exactly correct. After all, if people don't recognize the head, then the rest of the sculpture may not matter anyway.

Analyzing the Angles: Building the Head

In an attempt to copy the head of the statue, I first looked at the angles that make up the headdress. It is the headdress that helps define the shape of this part of the Sphinx, and getting it to look realistic was important to the success of my sculpture.

The sides of the headdress slope at an angle of around 55 degrees. That's a little less than a 65-degree standard LEGO slope, but it's pretty close. (For more about this slope piece, refer to Appendix A, the Brickopedia.) After I selected these pieces to start with, I began building the head.

You can see the Sphinx's head starting to take shape in Figure 7-20. As the sides of the head began to rise, I also wanted to build outward to capture the face. Remember, a sculpture needs to look right in all three directions: length, width, and height. I couldn't just build a flat face because the sculpture also needs to appear accurate when viewed from the front or the side.

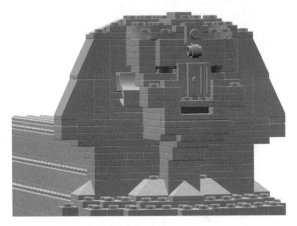

Figure 7-20: The head and headdress of the ancient statue

In Figure 7-21, I've shown the head rotated 90 degrees so that you can see the face coming to life. Does it have to be perfect? No, not at all. This was a relatively small model, so trying to duplicate every last detail would have been very difficult. It is important, however, to capture the overall appearance of the object and let the mind of the viewer fill in the remaining details.

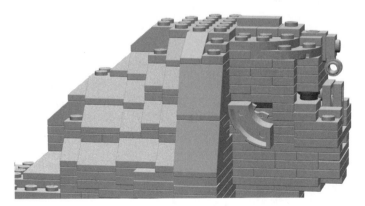

Figure 7-21: Sculptures of faces challenge you to think in three dimensions.

Special Features: Special Techniques

The actual Sphinx has several unique features that I wanted to capture. Each presented its own challenges with regard to parts selection and building techniques.

The Nose

One of the features I did simulate was the missing nose on the real Sphinx. Notice in Figure 7-22 how I used plates with their undersides facing outward to give the impression of uneven stone where the nose was once attached.

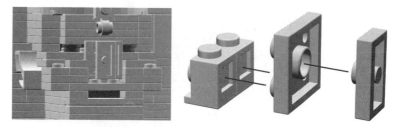

Figure 7-22: Note the unique ways each piece connects to the others. The three pieces on the right join together to become the nose, as you can see on the left side of this illustration.

You can see in Figure 7-22 that I took advantage of the unique geometry of LEGO studs and tubes. The offset plate (to the far right of Figure 7-22) fits perfectly into the tube of the 2×2 plate next to it. The plate, in turn, fits snuggly into the open sides of the headlight bricks next to it.

The Ears

The ears, like the nose, are another example of how you can turn LEGO elements in directions other than with their studs pointed upward.

In Figure 7-23, you can see a 2×2 macaroni brick with its underside facing away from the side of the head. The more natural curved shape of this element helped add some character to the face of my Sphinx model.

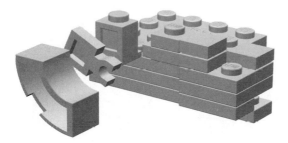

Figure 7-23: A blown-up view of the ear so that you can see how the pieces attach to the side of the head.

The Paws

The large paws, stretching out from the Sphinx, are mostly rectangular but do have some curved toes at the end.

To create these more natural shapes, I tucked a 1×2 half-arch piece under a 1×3×2 half-arch (Figure 7-24) to represent each toe. As you can see, the smaller of the two parts nests perfectly under the larger half-arch, creating a less blocky appearance.

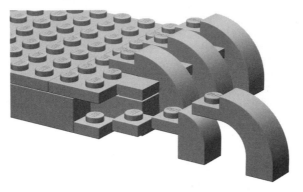

Figure 7-24: Curved pieces like these half-arch elements are naturally pleasing to the eye and add character to this otherwise rectangular section of the model.

The Headdress

In Figure 7-25, I've turned the head yet again so that you can see the back of the Sphinx's headdress.

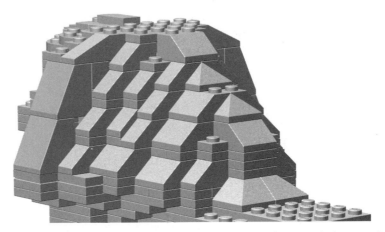

Figure 7-25: The back of the headdress was an exercise in sculpting with slopes. I didn't follow any hard-and-fast rule. I just kept adding and removing slopes, changing the type of slope I was using, and generally just working at it until I had the natural look I wanted.

When you actually sit down to build any sculpture from real bricks, you will also find yourself turning it to various angles to make sure it looks right from every direction. In the case of my Sphinx, standard slope elements, in several different variations, proved immensely useful for sculpting the back of the headdress.

Figure 7-25 shows the headdress blending into the body. It's important to point out that I didn't get the look I wanted on the first attempt. You probably won't either when working on your own sculptures. Don't be afraid to take parts off the model, move them around, or swap in new parts until you have sculpted the shape you want.

Building the Foundation Last

There are certainly many times when you will want to start at the bottom of a model and work your way up. For example, you'd probably apply this approach to most buildings. In such cases, you will find it much easier to build successfully if you build a solid foundation and work your way up, building the walls next and finally the roof.

In the case of my Sphinx model, I chose to go the opposite route, but for a reason. I built the head first to make sure my replica looked the part—that it looked like the head of the Sphinx. Then I built a body to match the head.

Once the head was completed, it was easiest to work on the shoulders next, then the back, and finally the legs. When building downward from the neck, it was easier to make the body match the scale at which I built the head. Since I wasn't overly concerned with making a perfect representation—I settled for reduced detail at this small size—it wasn't critical that I work out the exact scale like we did for the train station back in Chapter 3. Instead, this was more an exercise in eyeballing the model to make sure it has the look I was after.

The shoulders and neck of the Sphinx are primarily a combination of standard bricks, plates, and slopes too. Never overlook the inherent flexibility of these basic pieces; this is one reason that they have long been the heart of the LEGO building system.

As I continued to build the lower body and legs (see Figure 7-26), I also continued to go back to the pictures of the Sphinx I found on the Internet. Images of real life objects, buildings, vehicles, and so on can be enormously beneficial when you're building LEGO models. If you are ever able to see, in person, the thing it is you wish to build, then be sure to take some photographs while you are there. Capture the subject in a wide shot, to get its overall size and shape, but also be sure to get close-ups of details and features that you want to replicate. This research technique is used by Master Builders who work for the LEGO company. Why not use it to make your work more realistic and natural?

The completed Sphinx model is shown in Figure 7-26. Notice that I made a conscious decision to leave some areas of the model uneven; not every edge is perfectly square. This was an attempt to reproduce some of the wear and tear that time has taken on the actual Sphinx.

Figure 7-26: The body of my Sphinx is basically a box shape with staggered sides. It's the head and face that really brings the sculpture alive.

Review: Sculptures—In the Eye of the Builder

When sculpting real life objects, look for edges that can be rounded by either staggering some bricks (as in the sphere example) or by using slopes. Also keep in mind that things like faces, statues, or mountains may not be completely symmetrical. That is to say, one side or another may be shaped slightly differently than the others. If you can reproduce some of that organic quality, it will add a great deal of depth to your creations. The stagger technique will help you greatly when trying to reproduce more natural shapes.

Remember also that I built the Sphinx model using trial and error and worried more about overall *look* and *feel* than about strictly following a blueprint. On the other hand, the sphere, required some careful planning to make sure that the shape was very precise. You will want to use a bit of both techniques to build sculptures. How much of each you use will depend on your subject. In the end, it comes down to how the model looks to your eye; this is what decides whether or not it has been a successful build.

8

MOSAICS: PATTERNS AND PICTURES IN BRICKS

You might be wondering, "Just what is a mosaic?" The title of this chapter offers a clue. The term *mosaic* is used to describe artwork consisting of patterns or pictures created on a surface using stones, tiles, bricks, or even glass. You've probably seen an area above a kitchen sink that displays a pattern made up of small ceramic tiles glued to the wall. That is a mosaic.

Since the core of the LEGO system consists of small bricks and plates that you can easily use to form patterns or illustrations, LEGO is an ideal medium for creating mosaics.

Two Types of Mosaics

LEGO elements offer you two different ways in which to create mosaics. The first style, known as *studs-out*, is formed by attaching smaller bricks or plates (often 1×1's or 1×2's) to a baseplate with their studs exposed, or "out," where you can see them. Figure 8-1 shows a mosaic pattern created in this manner.

Figure 8-1: The elements that make up the main image are facing studs-out, whereas the border of this small mosaic is made up of standard tiles.

In Figure 8-1, you can see that the studs on each piece face out toward the viewer. Studs-out mosaics tend to be blocky in appearance but are fairly easy to plan and build. Later in this chapter, I'll show you a couple simple ways to turn an image into a mosaic.

The second way to make a LEGO mosaic is to use something known as the *studs-up* approach. In this case (shown in Figure 8-2), the pattern is created by viewing the bricks and plates from the side so that their studs are all pointed up toward the top of the picture.

Figure 8-2: You can use studs-up mosaics alone to create interesting, stand-alone, artistic pieces, or as part of a larger model to add lettering or other images.

A more advanced version of this technique involves turning some of the plates (and sometimes tiles) by 90 degrees to allow for more subtle shapes. In this chapter, we'll look at the basic technique but also create a more complicated pattern.

What Can You Do with Mosaics?

The *mosaic technique* is very much like other building methods I've already shown you such as overlapping, stacking, and staggering. On its own, it's just another way of putting LEGO bricks together. It's *where* you decide to use the technique that makes it truly effective.

When you use it alone, the mosaic technique can help you make interesting and artistic panels that you can display just as you do paintings or photographs. Such mosaics may be repeating patterns or may be images you have copied from real life. In these types of mosaic, the end result stands alone and does not require anything else to make it complete.

Another way to use this form of building is to incorporate a mosaic section into a larger model. For example, you may want to spell out the name of a company on the side of a cargo truck or a locomotive. Or, you might want to simulate a painted mural on the side of a downtown building. In other words, you would use the mosaic technique to *enhance* another model, the remainder of which would be built with the other techniques you already know.

How Big Should a Mosaic Be?

The size of your mosaic depends on what you intend to do with it. As noted earlier, the technique can have several applications. You might build a mosaic that you just want to be a display piece (such as an image of your pet or favorite car) on a 32×32 stud baseplate or perhaps on the larger 48×48 stud version.

On the other hand, you may want the mosaic portion of a larger model only to be a small section of a wall or the side of a vehicle. I'll show you examples of both uses in this chapter.

What You Need to Make a Mosaic

As noted earlier, a LEGO mosaic can be any size you like. If it is an image you want to display that you've made with the studs-out technique, it is likely to be the size of whatever baseplates you have available. Figure 8-3 shows a picture of the two most common large waffle-bottom baseplates that LEGO makes.

The smaller, darker baseplate is 32×32 studs, whereas the larger one is 48×48 studs. For the remainder of this section, you'll focus on creating works assembled on the 32×32 version.

In addition to a baseplate, you need lots of 1×1 elements to make a mosaic. If you can obtain enough standard plates in this size, then you can create a very thin picture. Otherwise, you'll more often build your studs-out mosaic using 1×1 standard bricks. Although it will be thicker from front to back, the resulting image, as it appears to the viewer, will be just the same when viewed from the front. You may also want to use other standard bricks, or even peak elements, to create a frame around your image.

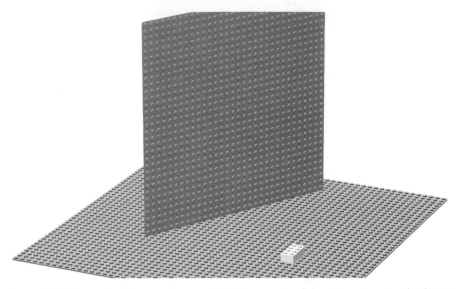

Figure 8-3: The small white square near the bottom center of the picture is a standard 2×4 brick. This gives you a sense of the size of the 48×48 baseplate.

To create a studs-up mosaic, you again need lots of small elements (1×1 bricks and plates), but you also need whatever other pieces are required to fit the mosaic section into the larger model you're building.

Designing a Studs-Out Mosaic

In Appendix B of this book, you will find information regarding model Design Grids. Take a moment now to visit the website for this book (www .apotome.com/grids.html) and print out at least one copy of Design Grid #1.

You'll find that this grid looks very similar to traditional graph paper, except that each square is exactly the size of a standard 1×1 LEGO element as seen from above, looking down on the stud. To plot the location of different colored bricks, simply shade in the squares, much like I did when planning the Empire State Building model in Chapter 6.

For the examples in this chapter, I'll be using only the colors gray, black, and white. For your own models you can, of course, use any colors at your disposal.

Geometric Patterns

As a simple way to get started with mosaics, you might want to try a geometric pattern. Like the tiles above a kitchen sink, this technique involves repeating one or more designs to create a pleasing image.

The Design Grids can be used to plan this type of mosaic or you can just build one freehand, developing the pattern as you go. You may wish to try a repeating pattern at first. Outline a small set of squares (perhaps 6×6, 8×8, or 10×10) such as those shown in Figure 8-4. Then use this small area to create a patterned tile.

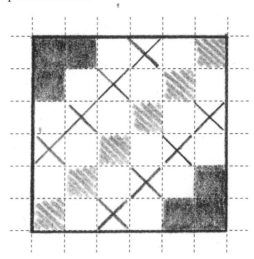

Figure 8-4: Planning a mosaic tile doesn't need to be complicated. This rough sketch took only a couple of minutes, but it gave me a good idea of what the final product would look like.

The next step is to use your sketch as a pattern to create the actual mosaic out of LEGO pieces. As noted earlier, you can use a 32×32 stud baseplate if you have one, or you can even use smaller waffleplates and simply join them together.

In both Figures 8-5 and 8-6, you can see there's really nothing complicated about actually building the mosaic. It's simply a matter of attaching your 1×1 elements to a baseplate.

Figure 8-5: If you have enough 1×1 plates, you can make a very thin mosaic. If not, you can always use 1×1 bricks instead.

The mosaic in Figure 8-5 was made using 1×1 standard plates. Compare that to Figure 8-6, which was made using 1×1 standard bricks instead. From this point forward, I will refer to 1×1 bricks when discussing this technique, since they are much more common and inexpensive than 1×1 plates.

Figure 8-6: 1×1 bricks work just as well as plates when you are creating a studs-out mosaic. Your art is a bit thicker, but in the end, it looks just the same when viewed from the front.

When you're done setting down the elements onto the baseplate, your first tile might look something like the pattern shown in Figure 8-7. This isn't a complete work of art (yet!) but rather one of many sections that can work with others to form a final presentation.

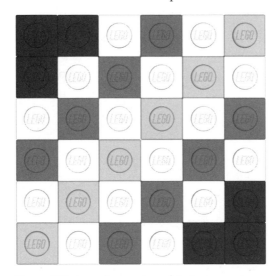

Figure 8-7: A small grouping of 1×1 pieces gives you a tile that you can then repeat to make even more complex patterns.

Compare the sketch in Figure 8-4 to Figure 8-7, and you'll see that I've replaced the different shaded squares with various colors of LEGO pieces; I've worked with black, white, and two different shades of gray. Of course, when you're creating your own mosaics, you can use any of the brighter colors you have in your collection of elements.

Remember earlier I mentioned using repeating patterns (like tiles above a kitchen sink) to create larger mosaics? Take a look at Figure 8-8, and you'll see what happens when I repeat the 6×6 pattern I just created.

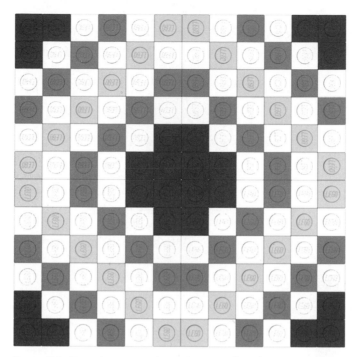

Figure 8-8: Four tiles grouped together to make a larger mosaic.
This pattern can then be repeated to make even bigger images.

Figure 8-8 is a mosaic made up of four copies of my 6×6 tile from Figure 8-7. Notice that I've rotated a couple of the tiles to make the black corners meet in the middle. This helps create a more pleasing pattern and also one that can be repeated as many times as you like. I can in turn create four more copies of the 6×6 pattern and place them next to the first four (see Figure 8-9).

Figure 8-9: Eight copies of my original 6×6 tile are aligned to create a repeating pattern.

In Figure 8-9, you can see that the pattern continues to match and repeat. This could become the ballroom floor for a minifig-scale hotel. Or, as noted earlier, you can simply repeat it until it fills a large waffleplate and becomes a pleasing image of nothing but patterns. Try designing your own tile pattern. Then see what it looks like when you put multiple copies side by side.

Copies of Pictures

If you want to try something a bit more complicated, you can tackle a photo mosaic. These, as the name suggests, are LEGO pieces arranged to look as much like an actual photograph as possible. There are a couple of interesting ways to create this type of mosaic. The first, print and trace, is a fairly low-tech approach that also gives you a bit of room to add your own artistic flair to the project. The second, converting to pixels using a computer, is a more sophisticated approach, but it can still result in natural and interesting results.

Print and Trace

To make this technique work, you'll need two things.

1. **A decent picture of what you want to turn into a mosaic.** If it's a digital picture, make sure it's loaded into your computer. If it's an actual printed photograph, first scan it in so that you can manipulate it digitally. You'll also need to print the picture you've decided upon, but before you do that, there are two more things you'll want to do first.

    a. Crop the image so that the picture is more or less square on all sides.

    b. Resize the image so that the length and width are as close to 6 1/2 inches (162 millimeters) as you can get. This assumes you are attempting to make a 32×32 stud mosaic.

2. **A copy of Design Grid #2 (see Appendix B).** Preferably, this should be printed on paper that is not too thick or opaque.

To create the pattern for your mosaic, just place your printed image under the copy of the Design Grid that you printed out. You may wish to staple or paperclip the two sheets together so that they don't slide apart. Now simply shade in the squares on the Design Grid to match the light and dark patterns you see through the grid. In Figure 8-10, you can see that I've applied this technique to an image of a fish that I found on the Internet.

Although the studs-out technique tends to be a bit blocky looking, it does work reasonably well for subjects with strong shapes, outlines, or patterns. When selecting a picture to use, try to make sure that the important part of the image fills as much of the space as possible. In other words, a close-up of a friend's face will work better than a picture of a car driving on a bridge far off in the distance.

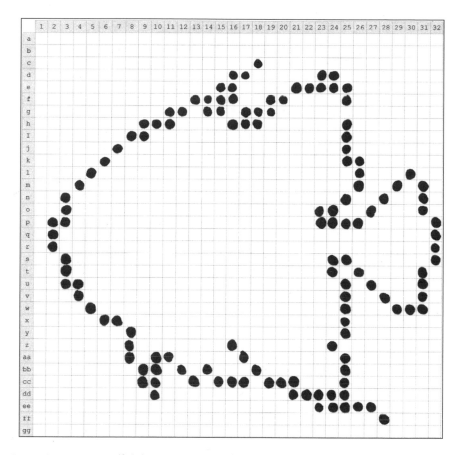

Figure 8-10: An angelfish begins to emerge from the design grid. Preplanning gives you some sense of what the final mosaic will look like.

In Figure 8-10, you can see that the illustration of the fish I used mostly fills the 32×32 grid. That gives me as much space as possible to use when defining the outline of the object in the image. Keep in mind that with a studs-out mosaic, you are not going to end up with smooth, flowing lines. For certain, your mosaic image will end up being a bit rough. The challenge then is to see just how natural you can make your design despite the handicap of doing it all with square pieces.

NOTE *You may notice the numbers along the top side of the Design Grid and the letters along the left side. Refer to Appendix B for more information about these markings.*

In Figure 8-11, I've begun to add some of the details within the outline of the fish. I've used different shades of pencil and even different ways of shading the squares to suggest differences in color.

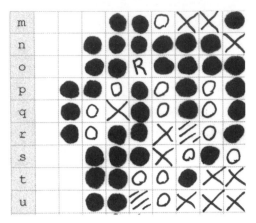

Figure 8-11: A close-up of just the face and mouth of the angelfish. Coloring within the lines is optional.

You may wish to use the legend printed at the bottom of the Design Grid to remind yourself which symbol represents which color. As you can see in Figure 8-12, it's easy to put it to use. Simply draw a symbol (or shading pattern) in a box and then write the name of the color next to the symbol it represents.

Figure 8-12: It takes only a minute to jot down the legend to go along with your design. This helps make the actual building process of your mosaic much more enjoyable.

It's worth pointing out that it really doesn't matter how neat your design looks on paper. By that, I mean don't worry if you don't shade in each of the boxes with computer-like precision. The Design Grid version is just a rough sketch of what your final LEGO mosaic will look like. The only important thing is that you can tell what color you intended to go in each square. No one will see the paper version, so be as messy as you like.

NOTE *It can sometimes be a challenge to see through the Design Grid to know which boxes to shade. If you're having trouble, try holding the original image up to a window; then place the Design Grid on top of it. The light shining through should help you see where you want to sketch in your mosaic. Need a similar trick you can use when the sun's not shining? Try finding a translucent plastic storage container—like the one in which you might store LEGO bricks—and turn it upside down. Then, as before, put the original image, with the Design Grid on top. There should be enough light filtering up from below to help you see what the original image looks like.*

Finally, in Figure 8-13 you can see how my angelfish design turned out. Although it's far from photorealistic, it's a reasonable representation of my subject matter.

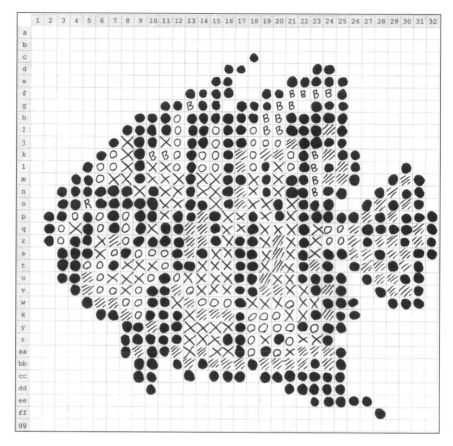

Figure 8-13: Although a bit rough around the edges, the blueprint for my fish mosaic still gives me a good starting point.

As you translate your paper design into actual LEGO elements, be sure to make changes as needed. The pattern you've drawn on the Design Grid should provide you with an excellent starting point, but you don't need to follow it exactly. Sometimes seeing the actual pieces on the baseplate will trigger the desire to make changes; make as many as you feel you need to until the picture feels right.

If you're having trouble seeing what the mosaic looks like before it's complete, try one of two things:

1. **Set your semifinished work on edge and step away from it.** Most mosaics are best viewed from at least a short distance away. It will help some of the lines and rough edges blur together and form a smoother image.

2. **Squint your eyes just a bit.** This reproduces that blurring effect without requiring you to get up and walk away from your build area. Don't spend hours with your eyes this way, but a few seconds now and then should help you to see how the work is progressing.

Converting to Pixels Using a Computer

The second (more high-tech) approach to creating the blueprint for your mosaic is to use computer software to apply a mosaic effect directly to your digital image. I've created an example using a picture of one of my own cats. In this case, the original image of Izzy was taken when she was just a kitten.

Figure 8-14 shows both the original unaltered image and the version that has had a mosaic effect applied to it.

Figure 8-14: The real Izzy meets the digital Izzy. A side-by-side comparison of an actual photo and what it looks like after applying a mosaic filter.

As you can see, the original image on the left fills as much of the square as possible, just as I suggested earlier in this chapter. You can also see the same image on the right but with a bit of computer processing added. I used a program called Paint Shop Pro to add something called a *mosaic filter*. This special effect, appropriately enough, turns an ordinary image into a series of square blocks of color—in this case black, white, and grays.

To get the exact level of filtering that I wanted, I played around with the size of the blocks that the program uses to create the effect. When I was done, the image on the right had exactly 32 squares across and down—just like the LEGO waffleplate I've mentioned previously. You may be able to achieve similar results using a program that you have on your own computer. The filter itself may not necessarily be called mosaic, but look through the effects menus in your image-processing programs until you find something similar.

Once you've doctored the original image, the only thing left to do is to print out the mosaic version. This then becomes the blueprint for your building process. You can simply use it like a map; it will show you which squares should be which colors. Of course by using a color image and a color printer, you can create a more exciting mosaic that puts to use LEGO elements of all the colors of the rainbow.

Figure 8-15 shows the Izzy mosaic on my build table at the beginning of construction.

Because the digitized image doesn't have the row and column labels that you find on Design Grid #2, you have to do something else to keep track of where you are on the baseplate versus the printout. One way to do that is simply to cut your image into quarters. You can see in Figure 8-16 that I've drawn a line vertically through the center of the image and another horizontally.

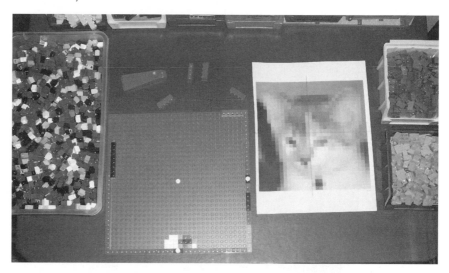

Figure 8-15: Everything you need to build a mosaic. Be sure you have lots of small elements like 1×1's and 1×2's handy.

Use each quarter on the printout to represent each quarter on the actual LEGO baseplate. In other words, if there is a light gray square in the very bottom left corner of the quartered section on the image, then make sure the bottom left corner of the baseplate gets a light gray element. Then look to see what color goes next to that piece and build up the mosaic accordingly.

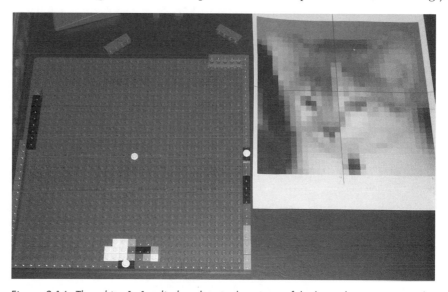

Figure 8-16: The white 1×1 cylinder plate in the center of the baseplate represents the point on the photo printout at which the four quarter sections meet.

You may want to break your mosaic plan down into even smaller sections. You might try dividing each of the four sections into four more, for a total of sixteen. That way you aren't trying to re-create the entire mosaic at once, but instead, you are working on small, manageable areas.

The result, when all the bricks are affixed to the baseplate, is a real life mosaic that looks more or less like the plan I started out with. And, as you can see in Figure 8-17, it looks pretty much like my original subject as well.

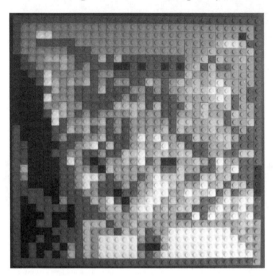

Figure 8-17: Izzy the kitten becomes Izzy the LEGO mosaic. Remember to step back a few feet and let your eyes see the bricks as one image and not as individual elements.

If your actual brick version of the mosaic doesn't look as you intended it, don't give up. Try setting it upright and stepping back. Look at the entire image and try to see what parts of it don't seem to be sitting right with you. Then, go back and replace a few bricks at a time until the problem areas disappear.

Designing a Studs-Up Mosaic

As you saw earlier, a studs-up mosaic offers some subtleties that studs-out mosaics do not. Because you are using plates as seen from their side, rather than full-height bricks, you are obviously dealing with smaller changes in color and shape. Take another look at a studs-out versus a studs-up mosaic in Figure 8-18.

Although there's nothing wrong with the letters in the studs-out mosaic, it's also clear that the word LEGO is a little more natural looking in the studs-up version. Being able to incorporate simple shading or highlighting techniques (such as seen above the letters on the studs-up version in Figure 8-18) gives you more control as a builder.

Figure 8-18: A side-by-side comparison of the two basic mosaic techniques. The studs-up version (on the right) offers some advantages when it comes to lettering.

Designing mosaics from a studs-up perspective isn't really that much different than what you've already seen, but it does add more depth to the skills you are developing.

Design Grids for the Studs-Up Technique

Before you start this section, again refer to Appendix B of this book. This time, look for Design Grids #3 and #4. Both of these grids present LEGO elements from the side, as you would see them if you were holding a standard plate element between your fingers, like in Figure 8-19.

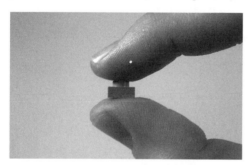

Figure 8-19: The plate view grids approach design work as though you are looking at a model from the side of the elements.

These *plate view* versions of the Design Grids take a different approach to planning LEGO models. For most models, they allow you to plan your work as seen from the side to help establish shapes and angles. When you use them to prepare a mosaic, they give you the ability to sketch out more subtle patterns than are typically possible with a studs-out approach. Take, for example, the simple sketch of the letter B shown in Figure 8-20.

It's easy to see that the studs-up mosaic technique offers you the chance to include finer details on such things as letters. When used in a larger mosaic and viewed from a short distance, this letter will begin to appear almost hand drawn. You can compare that with the chunky lettering you saw back in Figure 8-1 when we were looking at the studs-out technique.

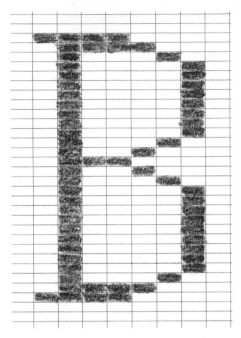

Figure 8-20: Serifs and gentle curving loops make this letter B an excellent subject for a studs-up mosaic.

Mosaics on Edge

Mosaic is a technique that lends itself to being turned on edge from time to time. Especially in those cases where you've used a plate view mosaic to spell out letters or even complete words, you may find things look better if you turn your work 90 degrees. For example, take a look at the small mosaic in Figure 8-21.

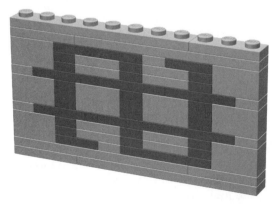

Figure 8-21: Alien writing? It could be, but keep reading to find out what it really is.

It may not look like much. In fact, when you first look at Figure 8-21 it's hard to even tell what letter, if any, it's supposed to be. Turn it 90 degrees and look at again. You're likely to recognize the character now (see Figure 8-22).

The dollar sign, with its thin vertical lines, is much more recognizable when turned upright. But now there's a problem. What do you do with a small mosaic like this when its studs are turned the wrong way? Rather than having to build an entire model turned on its side like this, you can easily incorporate this submodel into a larger work.

Let's say you want a bank, or maybe even a casino, to add to your LEGO town. The dollar sign mosaic could be used to help indicate the nature of the building you're constructing. In fact, with just a bit of planning, you could make the dollar sign part of the wall of the building, as you see in Figure 8-23.

You can see that I've built a portion of the wall surrounding the dollar sign mosaic to give you an idea what the final model might look like. Of course, you're probably wondering, "What makes it stay in like that?" The answer is a bit of geometric trickery that is surprisingly easy to accomplish.

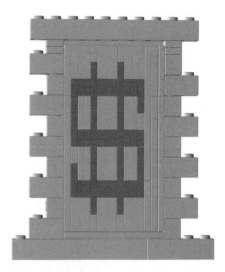

Figure 8-22: Turning a letter or symbol the right way makes it easier to read. But how do you add it to a model where the other bricks are pointing in different directions?

Figure 8-23: At close range, you will be able to see the different orientations of the bricks and plates. From a short distance away, however, your model takes on a more uniform and realistic look.

What you don't see in Figure 8-23 are the two 1×1 Technic bricks, one on either side that are helping to hold the mosaic section in place. To give you a better idea of what's really going on, I have created some close-up images of this wall example. In Figure 8-24, you can see that the right side of the mosaic is supported by a 1×1 plate (shown in black) that fits perfectly into one of the two Technic bricks. The plate is oriented vertically, like the rest of the mosaic, whereas the Technic brick is oriented with its stud up, just like the rest of the main wall.

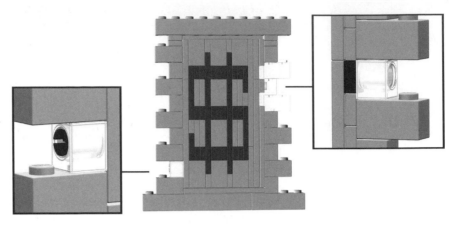

Figure 8-24: Mixing Technic bricks with regular system parts offers some amazing construction possibilities.

The left side of the mosaic (as seen in Figure 8-24) is supported by a Technic pin (shown in black) coming out of the other Technic brick and into the bottom of the plate next to it. Once again, the Technic brick is oriented with its stud facing up, whereas the plate to its right is turned 90 degrees just like the rest of the mosaic-related pieces. The result, when viewed from even a short distance, is that the mosaic section is really just part of the wall. The delicate lines that form the dollar sign become natural looking and easy for the eye to read.

Review: Mosaics of All Sizes and Shapes

As I noted earlier in the chapter, there is no one right size or shape for a mosaic. Instead, the technique can be applied to complete pictures (like the one of Izzy shown in Figure 8-17) or can be a much smaller arrangement of pieces that you use to embellish a model (like the dollar sign example just discussed).

If you add a mosaic section to a larger model, the work will display itself. If you decide to try your hand at an image, be sure to show it off once you're done, like in Figure 8-25. Let people know what interests you, and show them how you've captured that in LEGO pieces.

Figure 8-25: Of course, if you haven't noticed already, it's worth pointing out that the LEGO name itself makes for a great mosaic subject.

There is no one rule to guide you in determining how large a mosaic should be or which of the two basic techniques you should use. Let the requirements guide your decisions. If you need to spell out a company name on the side of a building, then build your mosaic letters to an appropriate size. If, on the other hand, you're creating a portrait of a favorite relative, be sure to make it large enough to capture their entire personality.

9

TECHNIC: NOT AS TECHNICAL AS IT MAY SEEM

The last chapter began by asking the question, "What is a mosaic?" To kick off this chapter, you might find yourself asking a similar question, "What is Technic?" In order to find that answer, let's first look at a little bit of LEGO history.

In 1977, the LEGO company released an exciting new line of products known then as the *Technical Sets*. The name soon changed to the *Expert Builder series* and then morphed yet again to become known simply as *Technic*. These sets contained the standard bricks and plates with which we are still familiar, but in addition, they also contained things like gears, axles, and bricks with holes that you could lock together with pins. For the remainder of the chapter, I simply refer to this genre as Technic in keeping with its current name.

Figure 9-1 shows one of the first models to be released that premier year in the Technic sets series.

Figure 9-1: This Technic go-kart was one of the very first in a series of more complicated sets that introduced gears and other new elements to the LEGO system.

Set #948 (#854 in Canada and Europe) was a rugged little go-kart with a one-cylinder motor. It was not a working engine, but rather a collection of plates and other parts arranged to resemble a motor. The steering on the kart did work though. In Figure 9-1, you can see that the wheels on the front of the vehicle are turned slightly. This is thanks to the rack-and-pinion steering made up from some of the new Technic parts that were introduced. The set design shows what you could do with just 200 pieces and a little imagination.

Part of what made these new models even more exciting—beyond the new types of LEGO elements they contained—was the fact that they were still compatible with traditional bricks, plates, and slopes.

That compatibility of standard system parts with basic Technic pieces is the main focus of this chapter. You'll start by examining some of the Technic parts in greater detail. I'll follow this with an explanation of some simple assembly tips. Finally, you'll see how some of these techniques can be incorporated into a small Technic model.

It's important to point out, however, that this chapter is really just an overview of the Technic system. The nature of the parts and the ways in which you can use them offer you the ability to create complicated models and projects that are beyond the scope of this book. If you're planning on getting heavily into Technic building, I suggest that you look at other books that are available; specifically those related to building LEGO Mindstorms models. The Mindstorms system is an enhancement to traditional Technic that LEGO introduced in 1998. It includes a programmable brick that can interact with your home computer allowing you to build robots and other sophisticated machines. Also, books about Mindstorms typically include lots of good techniques and ideas that can apply to Technic models that don't use the programmable element.

NOTE *For a list of links to books about the Mindstorms system that may also contain advanced Technic building techniques, visit www.apotome.com/links.html.*

Technic: A System Within a System

I first discussed the idea of a *system* back in Chapter 1. I described a system as a collection of different bits and pieces, and also the ways in which they connect with each other to become a larger object or series of objects. For the purposes of this book, think of Technic pieces as a *subset* of the larger LEGO system you've already studied. A subset is just a smaller group of something set apart from a larger group by one or more differences.

In the case of Technic, the difference is that these elements are primarily oriented toward creating machines, and the smaller components within them, or structures—not in using the standard brick connections you're used to. For instance, you could use Technic pieces to help you build a crane (an example of a machine), or you could use them to build a bridge (an example of a structure).

Technic Pieces: An Overview

To give you a better idea of what Technic pieces look like, I've included illustrations of some of the most common elements from this category. A separate complete overview of the Technic subset appears in Appendix A (the Brickopedia). The pieces shown in this chapter give you an overview of the types of elements described as being Technic pieces.

NOTE *You may find that your own LEGO collection doesn't include a large number of the parts described in the following pages. That might lead you to wonder, "Where can I get more Technic parts if I need them?" There is no one perfect answer, but here are a couple of suggestions. First, go to the official LEGO website (www.lego.com) and look for sets that carry the Technic label. Or, you can look on the website for this book (www.apotome.com/ links.html) and find up-to-date links to current sets that also contain some Technic-style parts. Building up a stock of Technic parts can take time, but the added flexibility they bring to your models is worth the effort.*

The images that follow show the range of sizes in which LEGO Technic pieces have been made. I've included images for many of the most common Technic elements, though many more exist that I've not recorded here. An explanation of the cataloging technique used for these entries is available at the beginning of Appendix A.

Bricks

Technic bricks are very much like the standard 1×N bricks you first saw back in Chapter 1. The primary difference is that Technic bricks have holes running through them that allow you to connect them to gears or other bricks via pins or axles. You can see a Technic brick next to a standard brick in Figure 9-2.

Figure 9-2: A Technic 1×2 on the left compared to a standard 1×2 on the right. Note the hole running through the brick and the hollow studs. These help define the look of Technic brick elements.

Technic bricks, just like standard bricks, come in a variety of sizes from as small as 1×1 to as long as 1×16. A few samples are shown in Figure 9-3.

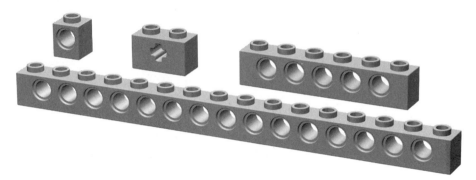

Figure 9-3: An assortment of various Technic bricks

It's interesting to note that most Technic bricks are designed with the holes centered between the studs on top. The most notable exceptions to that rule are the 1×1 and the 1×2 with two holes. You can see each of these pieces in Figure 9-4.

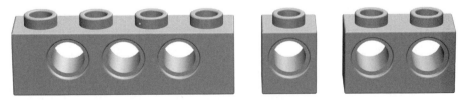

Figure 9-4: Compare the 1×4 with the other two parts shown here. The 1×1 and 1×2 have holes located directly below the studs rather than centered between them.

Studless Beams

It's easy to see the similarities between Technic bricks and beams. Both are long, thin elements with holes in the sides. There are, however, differences between them that make it worth differentiating between the two. Whereas bricks have traditional studs on top, beams do not.

Technic bricks come in only one width, whereas beams come in a square full-width variety and also a thinner half-width version. That means that while Technic bricks have the same geometry as standard 1×N bricks, full-width beams are a squarish shape when you view them from the end and half-width ones are significantly thinner. In Figure 9-5, you can see a brick sitting behind each of the two styles of beam.

Figure 9-5: A half-width beam sits in front of a full-width beam that in turn sits in front of a 1×4 Technic brick.

Beams began appearing in Technic sets in the late 1990s. They opened the door to models that used *studless building* techniques. This is a general term applied to any combination of parts that are held together in ways other than the traditional stud/tube connection. In the case of Technic beams, this usually means that they are attached to one another using pins or axles. I'll talk more about those pins in a minute, but for now you can see a simple example of studless construction in Figure 9-6.

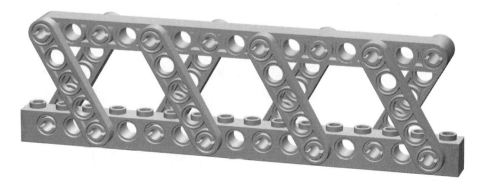

Figure 9-6: You could use a technique like this to produce part of a bridge or maybe the boom on a large crane.

The rounded look of studless construction adds a sense of realism, although some builders still prefer to work with the traditional studded Technic bricks instead of the newer beams.

Gears

In many ways, LEGO Technic gears are identical to gears you find in everyday objects such as bicycles, cars, or even old-fashioned grandfather clocks. The only real difference, of course, is that LEGO gears can be attached to and used with other LEGO pieces. Figure 9-7 shows a small sample of some of the many sizes of LEGO gears that are available.

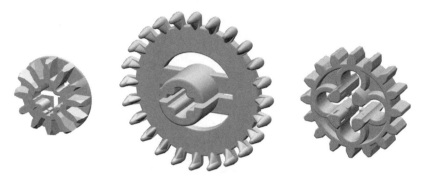

Figure 9-7: An assortment of various Technic gears

I'll talk more about how gears work later in the chapter when I discuss assembly ideas.

Pins/Axles

Earlier I noted that Technic bricks have holes that run through them. Those holes were obviously created for a reason—namely, to enable you to connect the bricks to each other and to other pieces (using pins) and to also allow you to attach things like gears or wheels to the bricks (using axles and/or pins). To allow for such a variety of connections, pins and axles come in an equal number of configurations, some of which are shown in Figure 9-8.

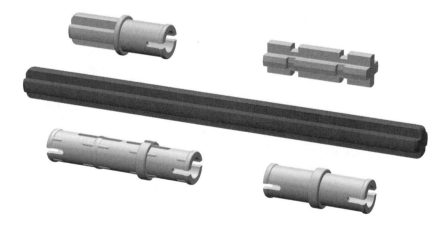

Figure 9-8: An assortment of various pins and axles

Bushings

Once you've inserted a Technic axle through the hole in another Technic element, you will most likely want to secure it with something. A *bushing* is a tight-fitting collar that slides onto an axle with enough friction to keep it from flying off when the axle spins. Although bushings don't lock completely tight (like nuts and bolts) they do go a long way toward keeping your axles in place.

You can see a simple example, showing a bushing in use, later in the chapter when we look at the helicopter model. For now, take a look at the half-width and full-width bushings versions in Figure 9-9.

Figure 9-9: Here are two fairly simple looking pieces, but don't let their plain looks fool you into thinking they're not important elements.

Couplers

There may be situations that arise where you want to connect Technic axles for aesthetic and/or functional reasons. *Coupler* elements allow you to join axles together at a variety of angles. They may have an opening that holds an axle firmly (like the opening facing front on the leftmost part in Figure 9-10), or they may have openings like Technic bricks that allow axles or pins to spin (like the opening on the bottom of the rightmost part in Figure 9-10).

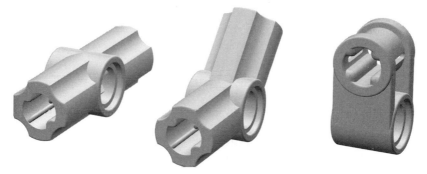

Figure 9-10: An assortment of various couplers

I mentioned features on most couplers that allow axles and/or pins to rotate or, by contrast, for axles to be held tightly and prevented from spinning. Figure 9-11 demonstrates the basic difference in these two attributes.

Figure 9-11: Rotating versus nonrotating openings in Technic couplers. The part on the left allows the axle to spin if needed, while the piece on the right keeps it from doing any spinning at all.

As noted in the part descriptions earlier, many pieces have one or both of these features. That is, some have an opening that allows an axle to rotate easily while that same piece may or may not also have an opening that fits an axle exactly and does not allow rotation. Finding the right coupler for the right task is always an interesting challenge when you are building with Technic parts.

Getting Started with Technic: Assembly Notes

As noted earlier, there are many wonderful books already on the market that deal with building complex Technic-style models, especially those incorporating the LEGO Mindstorms programmable brick system. Rather than try to re-create any of those advanced techniques in this book, I have decided instead to provide you with a handful of basic assembly tips and tricks that you can apply to almost any model regardless of the percentage of Technic pieces it contains.

Just as with regular system pieces, there are no right or wrong ways to assemble Technic elements. There are, however, some interesting combinations that might be worth pointing out.

In Chapter 2, we looked at three basic methods for assembling bricks: stacking, staggering, and overlapping. On their own, these techniques might not seem very interesting, but you learned that they are critical skills that can be used in combination to help you build models as complex as you wish them to be.

Gear Trains

Figure 9-12 showcases two very important assembly techniques. The first is what's known as a *gear train*.

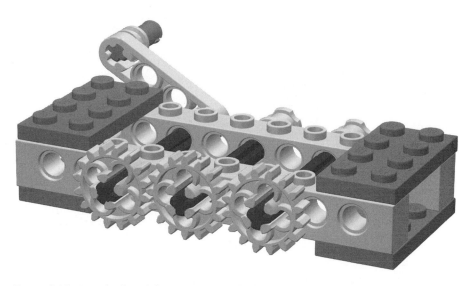

Figure 9-12: In order from left to right, you see the driver, the idler, and the driven gear.

The example shown here consists of three gears and a small handle or crank on the opposite side of the beams. Turning the handle (as shown in Figure 9-13) has the effect of causing the first gear (on the left) to rotate. That forces the gear in the middle (also known as an *idler* gear in this scenario) to turn as well. Lastly, the idler gear passes on its rotation to the gear on the right (called the *driven* gear).

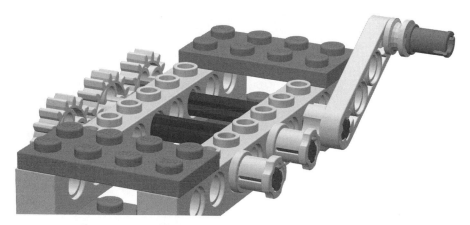

Figure 9-13: The gear set from the opposite side, showing the crank and also some full width bushing in action

The second technique demonstrated in Figure 9-12 is seen in the 2×4 plates that hold the Technic bricks together.

Look at what happens in Figure 9-14 when I replace those 2×4 plates with 1×4 plates. It is easy then for the 1×10 Technic bricks to shift out of alignment.

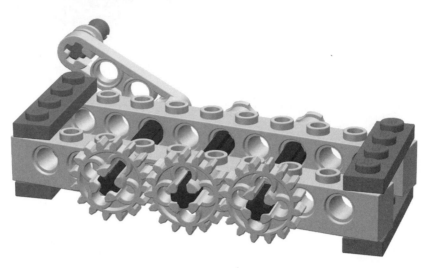

Figure 9-14: Looks can be deceiving. Although I only replaced the dark gray plates (both ends), the result is a major potential problem. See the next illustration to see what I mean.

Although at first things may not appear to be that bad, look at Figure 9-15 to see what can happen to the gears when the bricks become misaligned. It's quickly obvious why the 2×4 plates were so important. You'll want to make sure you use 2×N or even wider plates when creating frameworks within which Technic axles will need to spin smoothly so that the Technic bricks remain perfectly parallel to each other.

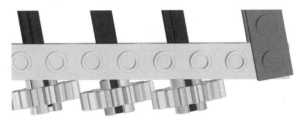

Figure 9-15: It takes only a minor misalignment to cause gears to no longer run smoothly. In the previous image, they appeared to be lined up, but in this top view, you can see that they clearly are not.

As you build any model containing Technic pieces, it's very likely that you'll spend at least some time making minor adjustments to the position of axles, pins, gears, and so on in order to make sure they line up as closely as possible.

Basics of Gear Ratios

If you've ever ridden a sleek 10-speed bicycle or a rugged mountain bike, you've probably already experienced the science of gear ratios. You know that when you are just getting the bike moving you want to be in a *low* gear. That is, you want to have a low ratio between the size of the chain ring in the front (attached to the pedals) and the cogs in the back (attached to the rear wheel). That means that you have to pedal a lot but that you have more power to get the bicycle in motion.

Then, as you gain speed, you know that the next step is to switch to a *higher* gear so that you are making fewer rotations of the pedals but getting much faster revolutions of the rear wheel. If you look down at this point, you see that the size of the chain ring you're using in the front is much larger than the cog you're using in the back. Take a look at some LEGO gears (in Figure 9-16) to see this further demonstrated.

Figure 9-16: In this example, assume that the gear on the left is the driver and the one on the right is the driven gear. This demonstrates a low gear ratio that is slow but powerful.

Imagine that in Figure 9-16 the small gear (with 8 teeth) on the left is toward the front of the bike and the larger one (with 16 teeth) is on the wheel at the back.

NOTE *I've left the chain out of this example to keep things as simple as possible.*

The gear on the left is only one-half the size of the one on the right. That means that every time you rotate the small gear, the larger one moves only one-half of a circle. That is an example of a low gear, just like when you're pulling away from the curb on your bike.

Switch gears, though, and you find that you're now using a high gear ratio, like the example shown in Figure 9-17.

Figure 9-17: In this example, assume that the gear on the left is the driver and the one on the right is the driven gear. This demonstrates a high gear ratio that is fast but less powerful.

With the larger (driver) gear now at the front, the smaller (driven) gear has to move much more quickly to catch up. This is just like what you do on your bike once you are moving along at a reasonable speed. This means you have to do less work (turn the driver gear fewer times) in order to make the wheel (attached to the driven gear) move quickly.

Deciding which gear ratios to use (low and powerful or high and faster) depends upon what function the gears in your model are trying to accomplish.

Going Vertical

Figure 9-18 showcases another classic Technic assembly trick. This one uses the inherent geometry of a standard Technic brick to allow one brick to be positioned perpendicular to the bricks around it.

The vertically aligned brick in Figure 9-18 may not, at first, appear to have much use. Keep in mind, though, that a piece like that may only set the stage for other more important pieces to be attached. Remember back in Chapter 3 I talked about alternative ways to assemble a roof? I showed you that with some standard plates and brick hinges you could create angled roofs that could take the place of slope elements. It's possible, in certain situations, to do the same sort of substitution for walls as well. Figure 9-19 shows just such an example.

Although a bare plate, mounted with studs facing out, may not be exactly the look you're after, you can use the piece as a base upon which to mount other elements, perhaps even a small mosaic or other decorative pieces.

Figure 9-18: The pins shown peaking out of the 1×2 Technic bricks are the key to holding the 1×8 brick in its vertical position.

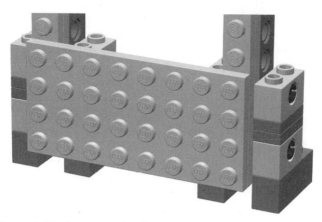

Figure 9-19: One example of a practical use for vertically positioned bricks.
They can be used to mount large standard plates, which can then be used
as walls or as mounting points for yet more elements.

Technic Meets Basic Elements

I've talked several times throughout this book about the built-in flexibility of
the LEGO system. Adding Technic elements to the mix does not change this
assessment. If anything, adding some Technic pieces to a model built primarily
of regular system pieces only enhances the creative possibilities. Now you can
have a car with working steering or a robot that has mechanical claws that
open and close. A subtle variation on this theme is when Technic pieces are
used to help system pieces interact in ways they wouldn't otherwise be able
to, but without turning the model into some sort of high-tech machine.

One interesting way to merge Technic and regular system parts is to use
a group of pieces that I call *pin-enabled* pieces. (Figure 9-20 shows you a few
samples.) You'll find more of these in Appendix A of this book.

Figure 9-20: An assortment of various pin-enabled elements

These pieces are a subcategory of the specialized elements category. Each of these pieces is a hybrid of a standard system element and a Technic piece. This combination results in elements that have Technic-style pins attached to them in one way or another. You can then use these pins to connect to the holes found in Technic bricks, beams, and so on.

Now that you know what pin-enabled pieces are, how can you put them to use? There's no one right answer to this question, so rather than try to list every possible scenario, I thought it might be best to just show you a simple example.

Back in Chapter 2 when I was discussing the stacking technique, I used a picture of an airplane tail to suggest a possible use for stacking bricks—to present different colored bricks as vertical stripes. Let's borrow the airplane tail again for this section and imagine for a moment that it's going to be part of a model that you want to take with you somewhere. Perhaps you're joining some friends for a group display of LEGO models, or maybe the plane is traveling with you to visit relatives on the other side of the country. You know that the tail end of the model will look something like Figure 9-21.

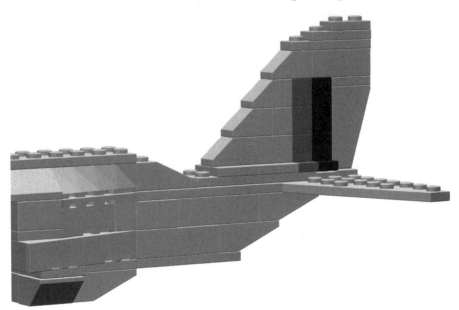

Figure 9-21: On the surface, this model may not look like it has any Technic pieces at all.

Regardless of where the model is going, you can envisage a scenario where you might want to remove the tail so that it does not get broken apart in transport. One simple way to do this is to build it as a submodel that you can remove from the body of the airplane. In Figure 9-22 you can see how this might be accomplished using pin-enabled elements and Technic pieces.

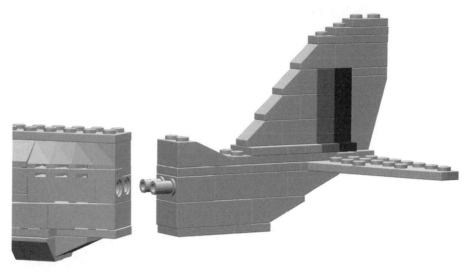

Figure 9-22: The tail can be easily removed so you can transport the model.

As demonstrated in Figure 9-22, you can remove the tail section as a complete unit from the rest of the airplane model. The close-up (in Figure 9-23) shows how each of the two key pieces is built into its respective section.

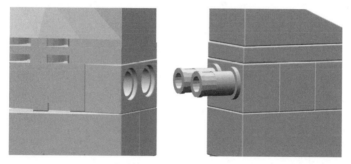

Figure 9-23: A close-up shows the secret hidden inside this model. A 1×2 Technic brick lines up perfectly with a 1×2 pin-enabled piece.

To accomplish this little trick, there are two things you want to keep in mind:

1. **Plan ahead and build the Technic bricks and pin-enabled elements into each of the two sections.** Obviously you want to build them so that they align with each other. In the example of the plane tail, I've built the pieces into the center of the fuselage.

2. **Be sure that your sections end up as the same size and shape at the joint where the model and submodel meet up with each other.** For the plane example, this means that when the tail is attached, it should look as though it is just a continuation of the rest of the aircraft.

Putting It All Together: Building a Technic Model

In the world of official LEGO sets, Technic models can sometimes rank among the largest and most complex designs. Some may be made up of 300 to 1,000 or more pieces. Some may have very few standard system parts in them, relying instead on large numbers of Technic bricks, beams, pins, and other parts I've talked about in this chapter. Your own Technic models need not be nearly this complex. You are, of course, free to incorporate as many or as few Technic pieces as you feel you need.

For the purposes of this book, in order to keep things a bit simpler, I've decided to present a Technic model that falls on the small side of the range. To illustrate how just a few Technic pieces can add interest and functions to an otherwise simple model, I designed the little helicopter you see in Figure 9-24.

Figure 9-24: Technic models don't have to be enormous or enormously complicated to be interesting.

At first glance, you might look at Figure 9-24 and wonder, "What makes this a Technic model?" That's a question worth asking, so let's take a closer look.

Right off the bat, a couple of things are obvious, and one thing might not be so obvious. If you look at the helicopter, it's easy to see that the landing gear and tail rotor are both made completely from what we've already identified as Technic pieces in this chapter. The landing gear (as seen in Figure 9-24) is made up of coupler elements and axles, attached to keyhole bricks that make up part of the helicopter's body.

Although the tail section may seem a bit oversized for the rest of the model, it is not without reason. Hidden behind the two 1×2 Technic bricks are two bevel gears. You can see them in Figure 9-25, which is taken from the rear of the model.

Figure 9-25: Two bevel gears meet at a right angle. This transfers motion from one axle to the other. Note the half-width bushing on the right, holding the axle in place.

You can see that the first of the two gears is mounted on the same axle as the tail rotor pieces (also made from Technic elements). That gear, in turn, mates with a second identical piece that attaches to the drive shaft that runs the length of the helicopter's tail. The shaft itself is much more visible in Figure 9-26.

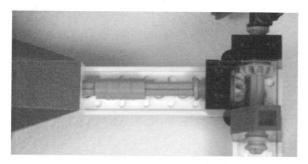

Figure 9-26: This shot might be disorienting at first. You're looking at the underside of the tail; the main body of the copter is at the left. This shows how the motion is transferred from the tail through to the main rotor.

The shaft then continues into the body of the copter where it ends in yet another bevel gear. This time the gear transfers its motion to a similar piece mounted vertically on the shaft connected to the main propellers. You can see both the gear inside the body and the one that drives the propellers in Figure 9-27.

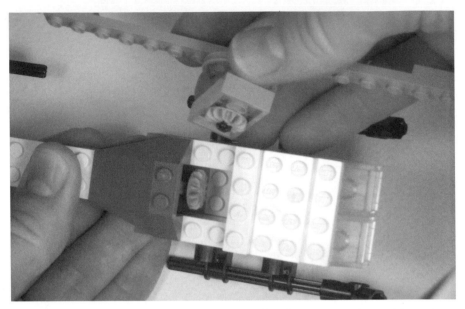

Figure 9-27: You can think of the rotor, including its bevel gear, as a subassembly, and you can build it separately from the model so it can be added last.

When fully assembled, the two bevel gears (inside the body of the helicopter) mate perfectly. If you've been following along, you'll know how the whole thing comes together. The small tail rotor acts like a handle that you can crank. The motion you put into the tail rotor is transferred along the main drive shaft into the helicopter body and then passed along again to the main rotor.

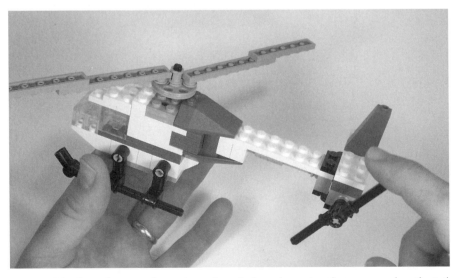

Figure 9-28: The still image shown here doesn't show the action that occurs when the tail rotor is moved. When you build your own, you'll see that.

The result, as demonstrated in Figure 9-28, is that by turning the tail, you cause the larger propellers to rotate. Any movement of the small tail rotor causes the larger blades to spin, and it is this special function that earns this little model the Technic moniker. This is a simple, yet effective, demonstration of a model that, without Technic pieces, would be far less interesting.

NOTE *Complete instructions for the helicopter example are included on the website that accompanies this book. Go to www.apotome.com/instructions.html to download full color steps to build your own version of this little model.*

Review: What Is Technic?

In this chapter, we sought to answer one simple question, "What is Technic?" You discovered that the answer really has two parts to it. First, you found out that Technic is a system within a system. It is a set of LEGO elements with unique and interesting features that can also work with the standard parts you've seen elsewhere in this book. Second, you saw that Technic is also a style of building with the specialized pieces that make up this class of parts. This could mean wheeled vehicles that have working steering or it could mean a small helicopter with rotor blades that turn when you give its tail a spin with your finger.

Defining Technic wasn't as easy as some of the other questions we've tackled in this text, but you shouldn't feel that Technic-style models are beyond your reach in terms of part selection or skills required. As you saw with the helicopter example, a Technic model doesn't need thousands of parts to make it interesting. It only needs one clever function that makes use of one or more Technic pieces. That's what makes it different than a model made from only standard system parts. And that's all you need to know to answer the question, "What is Technic?"

10

PUTTING IT ALL TOGETHER: WHERE IDEAS MEET BRICKS

We've covered a lot of topics up to this point. Through-out the various chapters, you've looked at basic building techniques, like overlapping and stacking; you've looked at different types of LEGO elements and how best to use them; and you've looked at ideas, like scale and color. Now it's time to put those skills to use. This chapter focuses on you, the builder, working toward designing the models you want to make. So, print out some Design Grids (see Appendix B), dump some bricks out onto your building table, and get to work!

Thinking Like a Model Designer

The role of designer is one you take on the minute you step away from existing sets and instructions for building LEGO models. Whether you are working from a real life inspiration or creating something from your imagination—something that has never existed before—you are *designing* the model of what will be the final result. Part of the joy of LEGO elements is that they allow nearly limitless combinations and patterns. Therefore you, as the designer, have hardly any boundaries.

If you are like some people, you may find the sense of being in complete control overwhelming. Although your head may be full of ideas, it may seem daunting to try and figure out how to turn those ideas into actual models. You may end up with a sketchpad that looks like Figure 10-1.

Figure 10-1: Freedom to create anything imaginable can leave some people wondering what to build.

Sometimes knowing what to leave out of your project makes as much difference as what you put in. That's where this chapter comes in.

Limit Your Scope

The term *scope* refers to the range of facets that your model is designed to encompass. In other words, scope seeks to help you answer these questions: "What is the purpose of this design?" and "How will I accomplish it?" It's quite easy to sit down at your build table with bricks at the ready and announce, "I'm going to build the Empire State Building!" You can then decide that this model will be 20 feet tall, include hundreds of windows, and be made entirely from light gray bricks. Such a model is possible. But is it out of your league right now? Probably so. Most likely, you've given it a scope that is far too large for you to accomplish at this time.

So, let's try again.

After you decide you want to build the Empire State Building, you look at your bricks and discover that you have a good number of dark gray, light gray, and white bricks. Why not use these colors to build your model? Perhaps changing colors at different layers of the building where the width or shape changes will help you make the shift look more natural. You also find that your supply of transparent bricks and/or windows is severely limited, so re-creating each window is out of scope and beyond your limits. Instead, you decide to use black bricks to simulate window openings. Lastly, you decide that a 2-or 3-foot-tall structure is probably more realistic than a 20-foot-tall one given the number of bricks in your collection.

You have just laid down a scope for your project that is much more feasible than your initial desires. Finding a suitable goal for building is not meant to be a limiting factor; rather, it's a guide that can help you be more successful in your endeavor and ultimately more satisfied with the time and effort you put into building.

Part of limiting your scope involves knowing what to leave out. In the Empire State Building example, one thing you left out was height. You reduced it to something more realistic. Quite simply, the idea for the first model was too big for the average builder. Second, you substituted a part for a specific detail on the real building that would have been difficult to accomplish otherwise. This was your black-bricks-for-windows solution.

You also decided to mix some colors so you could still build a reasonably tall model that didn't break the bank when it came to the number of bricks you needed in any single color. For most builders, the need to use more than one color (regardless of the actual color of the object being modeled) is a constant reality. As with size, though, your color limitations do not need to limit your creativity. Simply look at what you have and adjust your scope accordingly. For the Empire State Building example, the idea that your colors will include different grays, white, and black means that it might, in fact, be as visually interesting as if you had built it entirely in a single color. In this case, you might consider adding colors as a way to increase the scope, but it's actually adding clarity to the goal and materials you need to accomplish your model.

Having a well-defined scope also helps you decide the level of detail that you want to include. Ask yourself a question like this: "Am I striving for a high degree of realism in this model?" If you're doing a life-sized sculpture of a pet cat, then this is very possible. If you're doing a 3-foot-tall Empire State Building, the answer is quite different. You are forced to drop certain details to build to the reduced height you have chosen. Intricate detailing above windows may have to go, and you may have to represent the *feeling* of where windows would be, not each and every window. In addition, you might have to settle for simplified doors and other street-level accoutrements.

Learning to build within these types of boundaries is not as restrictive as it might first sound. In fact, it's an excellent way to improve your skills, hone your artistic eye, and maximize the enjoyment you get from your existing collection of LEGO bricks.

Getting Started: Pick Your Subject

Let's pick a subject for a model and follow it through from the first step to the last piece you need to complete it. Building with LEGO bricks is no at all fun if you don't like the subject matter you're working with. For that reason, be sure that you pick things to model that have some interest to you. Because you're just beginning to design your own models, you may want to pick subjects that challenge you on different levels. Pick tall thin models (like the Empire State Building) to practice your column building techniques. Choose realistic buildings (like a minifig-scale restaurant) to work on building to an exact scale.

In order to illustrate as many of the design and building principles as possible, I'm going to have you try to create your own original model of the NASA Space Shuttle. The reason for picking this subject is that it should offer a good mix of shape, color, and construction challenges.

Because this is an original model, why not give it an original name? The name *Triton* is appropriate for two reasons. First, it is the name of a real ship that once sailed as part of the British Royal Navy. Second, it is still the name of the largest moon that circles the planet Neptune. This model, then, is a fictional version of a real ship. That's okay because it adds some personal character to the original model. Figure 10-2 shows what Triton will look like when you're done designing and building it.

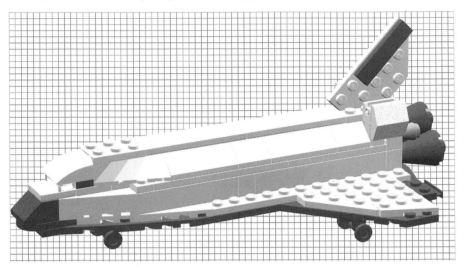

Figure 10-2: This is the goal of the design exercise.

While you're at it, why not give this project a set number? Because it's the first you're building using the techniques in this book, how about calling it set #0001. (It's not really necessary to give your models set numbers, but for the sake of this exercise, it adds a sense of authenticity.)

Of course, you won't have a picture of a finished model to work from, but you can gather pictures to help inspire you. Photos from books, the Internet, or even ones you might have taken yourself can all help give you ideas to work with.

Work from the Bottom Up

Where do you start when you want to build something like the shuttle? What section do you build first? You could start with the tail section, but if you did, how would you know if it is going to be the right size? You could begin constructing the cargo bay doors, but would you be able to easily attach them once the rest of the shuttle was done?

Rather than starting with either of those options, first look at what you're trying to duplicate. The shuttle has many distinctive features, but one stands out above all of the others: its unique wing design (as you can see in the drawing I've made in Figure 10-3 using Design Grid #1).

Because the wings are effectively the bottom of the shuttle, they are an excellent place to start modeling. This answers the question of what section you are going to build first. You can then decide how to attach and accurately scale other parts of the ship to match the wings. This is not unlike creating the ground floor of a building first so you know how wide and tall the remaining floors should be.

Design Grid #1 – 1:1 Scale
[Studs Up/Top Down Orientation]

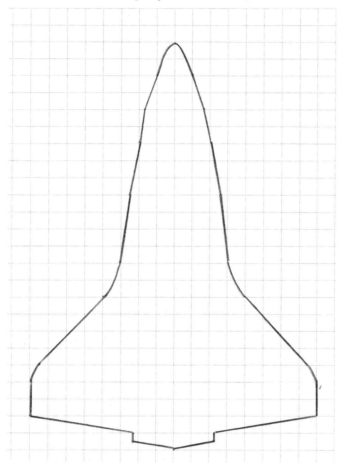

Figure 10-3: Copying the outline from a photo or drawing can help you achieve realistic results.

I created the outline you see in Figure 10-3 using the following very simple steps:

1. I searched the Internet until I found a diagram that showed the shape of the shuttle wings from below.

2. I printed this image onto a sheet of plain paper.

3. I printed out a copy of Design Grid #1 from Appendix B. This is the grid that gives you a *top-down* look at a model, as though you were seeing it from above looking down at the studs.

4. Finally, I put the image from the Internet under the Design Grid and traced the outline of the wings. This gave me a very accurate reproduction of the shape and a blueprint to help me find LEGO pieces that could match that outline.

The shuttle wings are far from the basic rectangles that formed the shape of the Wright brothers' flyer back at the beginning of the twentieth century. Therefore, to re-create their shape, you need parts that are more tapered. Wing plates and diamond-cut plates (see the Brickopedia, Appendix A, for sizes and shapes) should provide you with the geometric shapes you need.

Creating the wing using the Design Grid is just like putting together a jigsaw puzzle, except that instead of being given the pieces to assemble, you must find suitable pieces in your collection and get them to match the outline you've drawn on the grid.

You'll notice that in Figure 10-4, I used wing plates to form the outer shape but then standard plates for the space between. You can literally set real pieces on top of your penciled-in design because the squares on the Design Grid are exactly one stud by one stud in size.

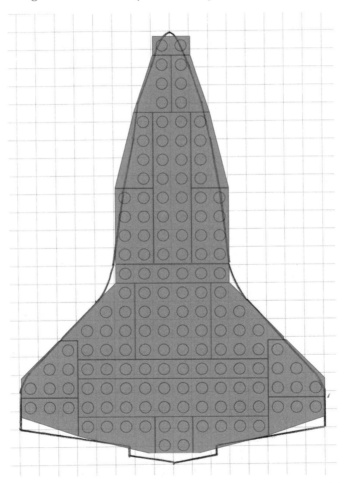

Figure 10-4: The LEGO elements are superimposed on a copy of the Design Grid with the outline of the wings drawn in.

Together these elements give you the foundation upon which to build the rest of the vehicle.

The size and quantity of these plates might vary if you are designing this model based on your own collection of parts. For instance, you might have to substitute standard plates in some cases where you don't have the exact wing plates I used here. But the goal always remains the same: regardless of whether your shuttle is 10 studs long or 100 studs long, you still want to try and make it look like the real thing.

Let Reality Guide Your Design Decisions

The idea illustrated earlier—finding one feature of an object upon which to base your model—is one that you can apply to nearly every creation you take from real life inspiration. It's as simply as following these three steps:

1. **Take a distinctive feature from the item being modeled.** In the shuttle example, you are using the unique wing as your guide. For a model of a train engine, you might select the crew cab. For a spaceship, you might decide upon the engines as your starting place. In all cases, you want to find something interesting you can use as a guide.

2. **Decide upon the types of elements that are best suited to represent that feature.** In the shuttle example, you pick out wing plates that help you match the shape, drawn on the Design Grids, based on the real wings. You don't pay much attention to size so much as you focus on duplicating the angles.

3. **Build the rest of the model by incorporating other elements that work with those in step 2.** As you finish the shuttle example, you'll see that the choices for each of the other sections, including the bricks used to make them, are driven by the base you set down in step 2. The wings provide a fixed reference upon which you build, both literally and figuratively, the rest of the model.

These steps provide you with a basic wing design, but right away you need to make a structural decision. How will you hold all these pieces together? Perhaps the easiest way to solve this dilemma is to follow the guide provided by the actual shuttle.

The portion of the wings you've created so far is most like the protective tiles that cover the underside of the ship. When you look at the real shuttle, you see that the upper layer of the wings is almost the same size and shape, but it is made from a different material than the tiles underneath. You can duplicate that look by adding a second layer of plates in a different color. As you can see in Figure 10-5, the second layer does not exactly match the shape of the first, but that's all part of the design. By working to re-create the parts seen on the actual shuttle, you end up solving the problem of holding your first layer of plates together.

If the second layer of plates was configured exactly the same as the first layer, nothing would hold them together. By selecting different sizes and shapes of plates, you make sure that the individual parts are arranged to take the best advantage of the overlap technique.

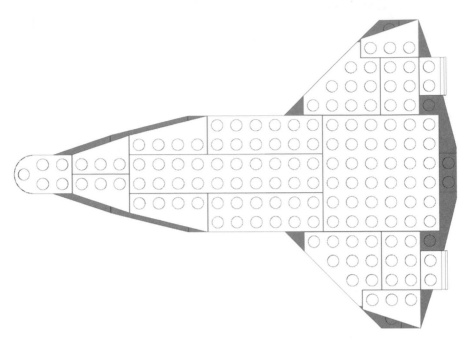

Figure 10-5: The second layer of plates doesn't quite match the first, but that's the way you want it.

A Different Perspective

So far, in this example, you've been using only Design Grid #1 from Appendix B. This grid looks down on a model from above, showing you only the tops of the bricks. It's good for estimating the length and width of the model as well as its overall shape, however, it does not allow you to see the height. That's why at this point, you want to begin using Design Grid #3 or #4 (Appendix B); they show a model from the side.

Each small rectangle on these grids represents a 1×1 plate as seen from the side. You can use this perspective to decide how many layers of bricks or plates you need to achieve your goal. You saw how you could apply this technique to planning a model back in Chapter 6 when you used the same grid to help plan the Empire State Building micro model. In that case, you used the *portrait* version (Design Grid #3) of the plate-view Design Grid. For the shuttle design work, you will use the *landscape* version (Design Grid #4) of the side-view grid. Because this sheet is longer than it is tall, it will accommodate a sketch of the shuttle as seen from the side.

NOTE   *See Appendix B for more information on how best to use the Design Grids.*

As you can see in Figure 10-6, by using the side-view grid paper, you can plan how tall the model will be (in this case, the body is roughly 3 bricks high) and also determine the location of key structures like the tail and engines.

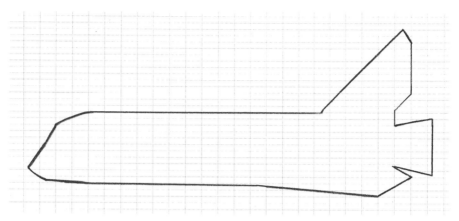

Figure 10-6: Sketches don't have to be perfect to be useful.

As you draw your plan, don't worry about making your sketch fit the lines on the Design Grids exactly. You will inevitably end up making compromises between what you draw and what you actually build. Rather than being a bad thing, compromise is often where the most inspired ideas come from. Sometimes *not* having what you think is the right piece leads you to using another piece (or pieces) that actually ends up providing a better solution.

Pick a Scale, Any Scale

Choosing a scale for any original model is one of the key decisions you'll make. We've talked about scale a number of times already in this book, especially in Chapters 3, 5, and 6. In the case of your shuttle model, you've let the design of the wing, and how it matches available wing plates, set the scale for you. In other cases, you might decide to pick a scale in advance and build everything to that exact size. The train station we built in Chapter 3 is an example of that style of design. The point here is that, since this is an original model, you have complete control over the scale you chose. If you're trying to match the size of another model for any reason, then you need to work to that scale. Otherwise, it's whatever scale you feel is best for the particular project you're working on.

Color Concerns

Like scale selection, selecting colors for your models is entirely up to you. And like scale, you may also have specific reasons for choosing one set of colors over another, based on what feeling you want your model to project. Color can change the way that people react to or feel about a model. For instance, a sculpture of a dog made out of blue bricks might make people think of a cartoon character rather than a real pet. A building made out of mostly gray bricks might make the structure feel more like a warehouse or a factory than a comfortable home.

Apart from the way a single color can affect the impression the model makes, *combinations* of colors can also have a dramatic effect on how people react to your work. For example, a helicopter built from primarily white bricks with red accent pieces will probably make most people think of an air ambulance. If you use the exact same design except you build it from black or dark gray bricks, you might lead people to think it is a military or police vehicle.

It's the fact that people have become accustomed to certain color combinations that makes them think of particular themes or settings. A model built of black and yellow bricks might give the feeling that it is somehow related to construction or industrial use because those are often colors used in those settings. Rides you find in amusement parks are often painted in bright primary colors like red, yellow, and blue. This gives them a feeling of fun that matches their purpose. The various color combinations go on and on. As you design your model, remember to look at the colors you are using to see if they represent the theme or the feeling you are trying to convey.

In the case of the shuttle model, you can let reality guide you. The real shuttle uses almost exclusively white and black pieces, reminiscent of the standard NASA color scheme for many of its rocket programs over the years. By sticking to the colors that people expect for the shuttle, you help add realism to your model despite its small size. As you can see in Figure 10-7, the black and white bricks create a dramatic contrast that brings out some of the main features on the ship.

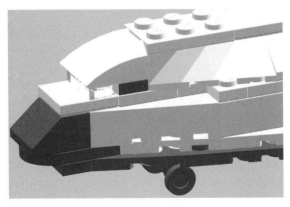

Figure 10-7: The contrasting black-and-white color scheme adds realism to your mini shuttle.

Elements of Design

There are certain ideas you need to keep in mind no matter what type of model you're planning to build. Although art courses may go into greater detail, this text focuses on only four major concepts of design theory: shape, color, proportion, and repetition.

Shape

What shape will your model be? There is a reason a car isn't shaped like a tree. Think about what form you are trying to create. For example, a plain flat wall can be boring. Don't forget to include curves, angles, indents, and other interesting surfaces in your model.

How shape relates to the shuttle model

In the case of the shuttle, you were trying to re-create the shape of the original ship (see Figure 10-8). This is one of your most important goals when you're working from a real life inspiration. Try your best to find the pieces in your collection that most accurately represent the shapes you are copying from the real object. In Figure 10-8, you can see that I selected certain plates for the wings and slopes for the top of the body, since those helped the most to re-create the shapes I wanted.

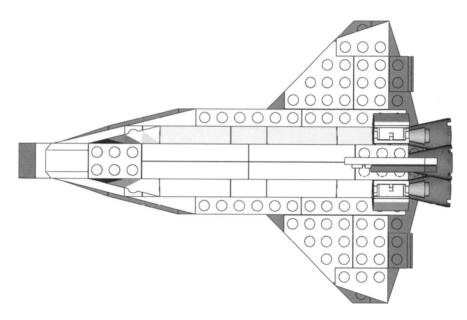

Figure 10-8: The shape of the shuttle is very distinctive, so matching that in your model is critical.

Color

Are you going to work with a couple of colors, or will you dig through your collection in order to use all the colors of the rainbow? Your choice of color can affect the overall impression the model makes, especially when combined with the shape(s) you have used.

How color relates to the shuttle model

Once again, you are led by reality when you select colors for the shuttle model. Black, white, and shades of gray are the most appropriate (see Figure 10-9). However, if you want to have some fun, you can build the same model in different color schemes. Perhaps a black and yellow version could be a construction shuttle, destined for a space station. Or, a red and white version could be a rescue shuttle, standing by in case of an emergency.

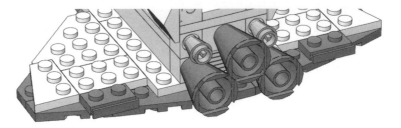

Figure 10-9: Wings made from black and white plates and differences in the colors of the engines help bring some details out on this otherwise monochromatic model.

Proportion

Are the substructures of the model the right size for each other? In other words, are they all the same scale? For example, building the doors to the same scale as the windows makes a building look more realistic.

How proportion relates to the shuttle model

The real shuttle is a complex flying machine. To make it so your model emulates this, you need to retain the correct balance between the length of the body and the width of the wings. You have to make sure the tail (shown in Figure 10-10) is tall enough, but not too tall and not too thick. You need to design the wings so that they are strong enough to serve as the base of the model but still thin enough to look like they are able to fly.

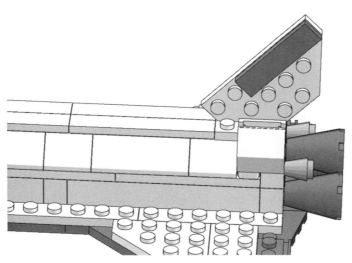

Figure 10-10: A single plate—mounted vertically between the studs below—offers the best solution to a tail that is tall and thin.

Repetition

Rows and rows of 2×4 bricks are boring. But a few rows of arches can be beautiful. Sometimes including the same shape over and over can add dimension to your model. Just be sure you select an *interesting* shape or LEGO element before you add too many to your creation.

How repetition relates to the shuttle model

The shuttle model uses repetition to good effect by employing 1×6 tiles (shown in Figure 10-11) along the top of the cargo bay doors, giving at least the *impression* that they might open. In fact, the doors themselves, made from 45-degree slopes, are also an example of where repetition can help add authenticity to a model.

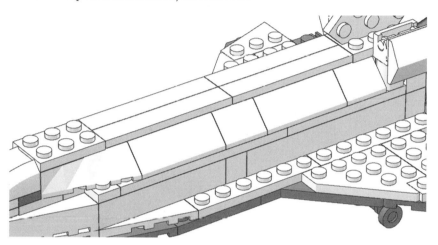

Figure 10-11: On this small model, you only repeated a few tiles and slopes to make the cargo bay doors. On a larger scale version of the shuttle, you will find yourself using much more repetition.

Bringing It All Together: The Final Design

I've talked about many aspects of design theory and how they apply to the model of the fictional Space Shuttle Triton. It's now time for you to become familiar with the instructions for building this creation.

I've included these instructions, along with build notes for each step. In Figure 10-12, you'll find the list of the pieces you need to make this model. As always, don't forget that substitution is a regular part of the building process when you're making original models. If you don't have every piece shown in the Bill of Materials, try to find a part or several parts that you can substitute for what is shown.

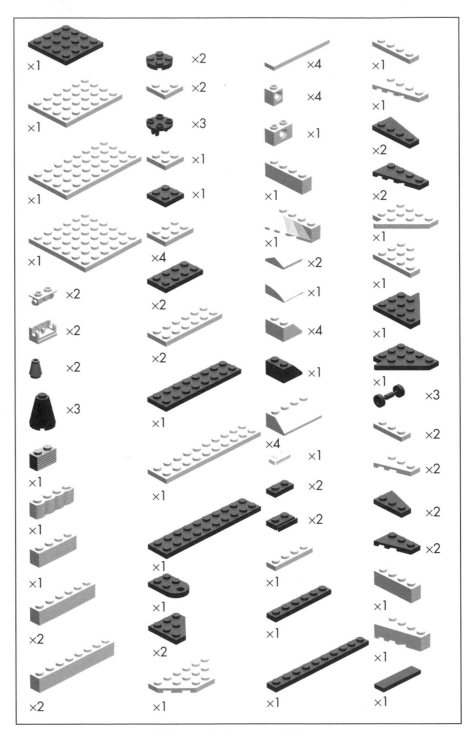

Figure 10-12: Bill of Materials for the shuttle Triton model

Step by Step: Shuttle Construction Details

As with many of the models featured in this book, I built a version of the shuttle using computer software. This allowed me to mark each building step as I went along so that the program could then create an image for each stage of the construction. I use a program called LeoCAD, but other such programs are available.

NOTE *For a complete list of software you can use to design LEGO models on your computer, visit my website: www.apotome.com/links.html.*

Step 1

Figure 10-13 shows you something similar to what you saw in Figure 10-4 earlier in the chapter.

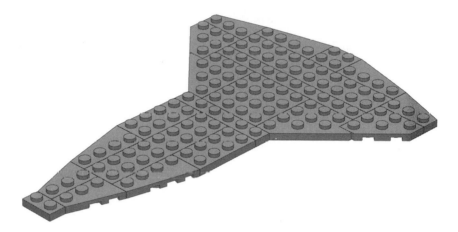

Figure 10-13: A combination of plates creates the unique shuttle wing shape.

This is the bottom layer of the wing structure. Look for a place within each model you design that makes sense as a starting point. In the case of the shuttle, the wings serve as an excellent base upon which to build the remainder of the craft.

Step 2

The second layer of plates (as seen in Figure 10-14) are *close* to following the outline of the lower layer, but they do not match it *exactly*. This slight mismatch is the result of a conscious design decision. If you look at the real shuttle's wings, you'll see some of the protective heat absorbing material lining the front edges. By leaving some of the lower layer exposed, you create the illusion of that material on the model. This is a slight variation on the staggering technique you first saw back in Chapter 2.

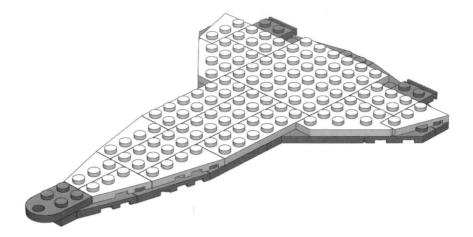

Figure 10-14: The second layer of plates helps hold the first layer together.

Step 3

The body of the shuttle model is very simple. At this scale, there isn't room for as much detail as perhaps you'd like. As you see in Figure 10-15, you've just concentrated on trying to create the basic outline for the cargo bay.

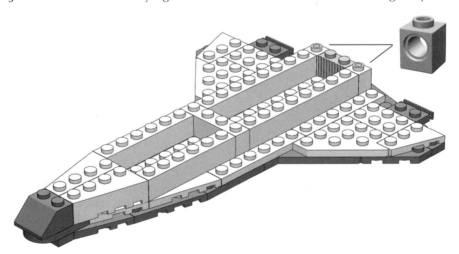

Figure 10-15: The inserted image in the top right corner gives you a building hint, since it's hard to see just what pieces should go at the end of the craft. In this case, it's two 1×1 Technic bricks that go on either side of the 1×2 grille brick.

The 1×4 brick across the middle helps support the plates that you'll add in the next step. You need to make similar decisions about detail when you create your own models. Don't be afraid to design as realistically as possible, but don't overwhelm a small model with more details than it can handle.

Ultimately you need to ask yourself, "Does this model *look* like what I want it to look like?" As long as the answer is yes, then you've got a successful design.

Step 4

Because this model is for display purposes and isn't meant to be functional, creating a hollow cargo bay isn't important to the success of the design. Instead, use 4×N plates (see Figure 10-16) to join the side walls together.

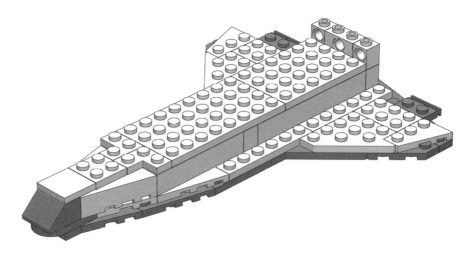

Figure 10-16: More Technic bricks near the back of the body. This time it is obvious which pieces to use, so no insert is necessary.

This gives you a ship that is sturdier and holds up better to being whooshed about the room. A larger-scale model of the shuttle might have included such things as retractable landing gear or movable wing flaps. But it might have been difficult to try to make them work on the small scale you're working with here. You need to decide how many details to include or leave out based on the size of your project.

Step 5

The shuttle model that you're building is really fairly small, so it comes together quite quickly. In Figure 10-17, you can see that, by step 5, you're already adding the 45-degree slopes that form the cargo bay doors.

Although it's hard to distinguish in these black-and-white instructions, the 1×2 plate nearest to the nose of the ship is a transparent element. Remember, the doors aren't functional—they are only for show. But at this scale, such a design decision is acceptable as long as it fits with the look and feel of the rest of the model.

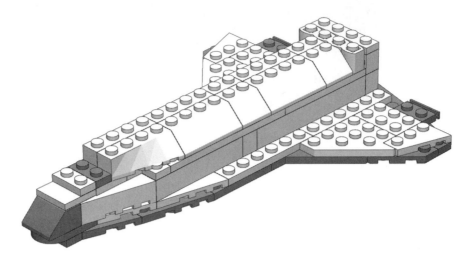

Figure 10-17: The cargo bay doors are already in place.

Step 6

You can sometimes add several unrelated portions of the model all in the same step. Figure 10-18 shows an example of this.

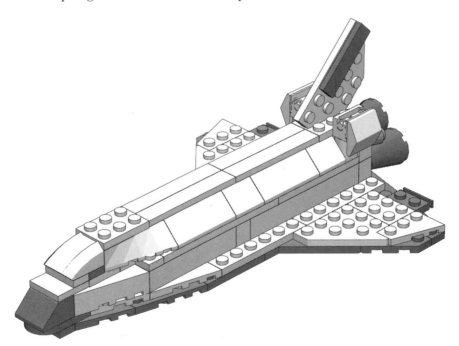

Figure 10-18: As long as nothing is blocked from view by the new elements, you can add any number of pieces in a single step.

In this step, you add the tail (mounted on a 2×3 plate), the cowlings near the engines (the 2×2 33-degree slopes hanging off the 1×2 brick hinges), and also the curved slope that becomes the top of the crew cabin.

Use a black 1×4 tile on the tail to represent some of the protective material that is located there on the real shuttle. Don't worry about re-creating the specific parts of the tail that move (located at the very rear). If you add in too much detail, this may take away from the look of the rest of the model. Remember that you don't want to start adding a greater level of detail in one area if you are keeping other areas sparse.

The tail itself is held in place by the studs on the 2×3 plate below it. The thickness of the plate is nearly identical to the distance between the studs. That's what allows it to be wedged in like that.

Step 7

Sometimes you need to turn the model in one direction or another to more clearly see a building step. Figure 10-19 is an example of this. In this step, turn the ship so that the engines are facing the out. This allows you to see where the 1×1 and 2×2×2 cones that are used to create the engines go.

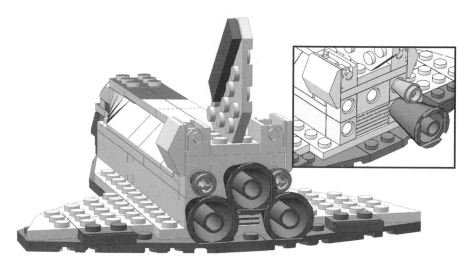

Figure 10-19: You now get to see why I used Technic bricks to build the end of the body. The insert shows the rear of the shuttle without all the cones in place. This should help you understand how I attached these pieces.

Although the engines might not be *exactly* the right size for this scale, they are very close. Additionally, they match the pattern in which the engines are mounted as accurately as possible. That helps better match your micro model with the real thing. Once again, it's about capturing the look, not the minutest detail.

Step 8

Again, in Step 8, reposition the ship as shown in the illustration (Figure 10-20). This time, you're looking at it from underneath so that you can see where to attach the landing gear. In a case like this where you are adding pieces to the underside of another element, you can count the tubes to see where to make the attachment. When you're adding pieces on top of others, you usually use the studs as guides instead.

Figure 10-20: Using only a picture and no words, I can accurately describe where to attach the landing gear on the lower wing.

The two sets of wheels closer to the back are mounted slightly differently than the front landing gear. Each of the rear wheels has a 2×2 cylindrical plate sandwiched between itself and the underside of the shuttle. This causes the nose of the craft to sit slightly lower when you are finished. You can see this effect in Figure 10-21 in step 9. This duplicates the angle at which the real shuttle points when it is taxiing after a landing.

Step 9

Figure 10-21 reveals that step 9 isn't really a step at all; rather, it is an overview of what the completed model should look like.

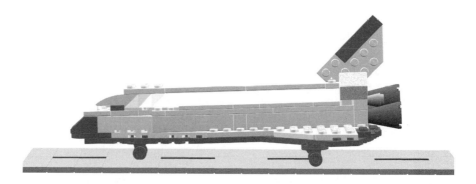

Figure 10-21: The shuttle Triton parked in the classic nose-down position.

You might want to use this last step to determine where to add decals (printed from your computer) or small detail pieces. In this case (Figure 10-21), I just add a runway made of tiles beneath the model to give it a sense of realism.

Something's Wrong: Redesigning Doesn't Mean You've Failed

In the end, don't be concerned if something isn't quite right. This is a model made from LEGO bricks after all. Disassemble the section you feel is lacking and rebuild it using different pieces, different combinations of pieces, or alternate colors. In the case of the shuttle example, I built a prototype for the purpose of documenting it in this book. I rebuilt the nose two or three times before I hit on the combination of plates, tiles, and slopes that I felt best represented the shape I wanted to re-create. Similarly, I adjusted the pattern of plates I used to make the wings several times until I felt they looked right but were also strong enough to support the remainder of the pieces I was going to add on top.

The engines, on the other hand, were the first and only pieces I selected for that portion of the model. They just seemed to work right off the bat. The point is that not every section of a model comes together perfectly on your first attempt. Some turn out exactly as you intend, whereas others require you to change parts or techniques again and again until things begin to look better.

After You're Done

Now you've seen how to design and build an original model from scratch. You've looked at various ways to capture details from real life objects and how to make wise design decisions when translating that object into LEGO pieces. When you're done, you might find yourself asking, "What now?"

The first thing you'll probably want to do is display your model somewhere so that other people can see it. The display might be real, such as in an office cubicle or on a shelf in your LEGO building area. For this, you might want to build something on which to set your model (such as the runway shown in Figure 10-21), or you may want to go even further and build a complete diorama in which to showcase it. Or, perhaps you want to display your model virtually. You can take pictures of it and display them on the Internet for your friends and others to enjoy. The choice is up to you, but chances are that once you've accomplished a successful design, you will want to share it in one way or another.

Review: Taking On the Role of Model Designer

You don't have to be hired by the LEGO company to be a model designer. The moment you decide to build something that's never been built before, you cast yourself into the role of designer. That's really what this book is all about. You will need all of the tools around you—part selection, color choices, scope, and scale—to make good decisions about the models you will design. But working through those decisions adds great dimension to this hobby. Enjoy your new job!

11

BEYOND JUST BRICKS: OTHER THINGS TO DO BESIDES BUILDING

Some hobbies are limited in just how much you can do with them. For instance, if you're a coin collector, you can collect coins, look at them, and not much more. Although there's nothing wrong with this activity, it doesn't offer you many new possibilities if you find yourself getting tired of just looking at your coins. LEGO, on the other hand, allows for activities not always directly related to just building with bricks. This chapter covers three different variations on the LEGO hobby.

Reviews

If you've purchased an official LEGO set, you might want to share your experience building it with other LEGO fans. Writing a good review can be an exercise in both language skills and in learning to evaluate rationally.

Instructions

When you create a model on your own, sometimes you want to share the build information with others so that they can build their own copies. Another way that you can extend the LEGO hobby is to use your computer to create usable instructions for models.

Games

You also have the potential to mix games and LEGO together. You can do this in two ways: either by re-creating some of your favorite existing games or puzzles (checkers, chess, concentration, and so on) or by inventing new games of your own.

"I Give It a Nine Out of Ten": Writing Reviews of LEGO Sets

You've probably discussed a recent movie or a CD with friends. If you really liked the film or the music, you also probably tried to tell your friends why they should take the time to experience it. If this sounds familiar, it's probably not difficult for you to imagine what you'd do if you received a great LEGO set—you'd want to tell other people about it. The easiest way to do this is to write a review of the model that you've bought, built, and enjoyed.

A Simple Review

You may have already seen reviews of LEGO sets posted on the Internet. In some cases, these critiques can be very detailed; they may describe various aspects of the set such as playability, specialty parts, design strengths, etc. However, your review doesn't have to be long and complicated in order to be effective. After all, part of the goal of a review is to express your fondness, or lack of enjoyment, of a particular set.

Your review can take many forms. You may wish to simply write a couple of paragraphs describing what you did and didn't like about the set. If this is the case, your review may end up sounding similar to a movie or book review. You might even decide to give the set a thumbs up or thumbs down as the case may be. On the other hand, you might want to start with something a little more structured, like the simple format described next.

Basic Set Review Form

In this section, you'll find a template you can use to create simple reviews of just about any LEGO set. The bold words indicate the different sections of the form. Keep them as they are. The descriptions that follow each section heading are just ideas of what you might put for your own review.

Set Name/Number

Almost every official LEGO set has a name and product number to identify it.

Number of Pieces

This number is usually printed somewhere on the box. It gives people a sense of how big this particular set is.

Type of Instruction Book

Did the set contain instructions for just one model? Or perhaps it's an "idea" book that just gives you suggestions for things to build.

Price

This is usually given as the before-tax price. Be sure to include the currency to which you are referring.

Set Description

A brief overview of the set. You could include the theme, the overall size, and whether or not it is minifig scale; you could even note things like the type of packaging or where you purchased the set.

Notes

This is the heart of the review. This is your chance to tell everyone what you liked/disliked about the set. Write a few paragraphs as a general commentary about your experience building the model.

Rating

Since it's your review, it's entirely up to you to decide how to rate the set. You can use a scale of 1 to 10 bricks. Or perhaps something like good, better, best. Or you can make it as simple as saying, "I give this set a thumbs up."

Sample Review

This section provides you with a sample review that uses the template that I just described. In this case, I've used the space shuttle model from Chapter 10 as the subject for the review (Figure 11-1).

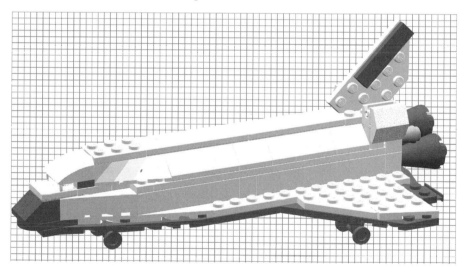

Figure 11-1: The shuttle model we designed and built in Chapter 10 becomes the basis for our sample set review.

You won't normally write reviews about your own sets, but this provides an example with which you're already very familiar.

Set Name/Number

Space Shuttle Triton (Set #0001)

Number of Pieces

99

Type of Instruction Book

Computer generated; 9 steps. Main model only, no alternate models.

Price

N/A

Set Description

The model of the fictional Space Shuttle Triton is much smaller than minifig scale, though not quite microscale. It would make a suitable display model on a shelf or even on top of a computer monitor.

Notes

The model makes good use of wing plates to help create the distinctive shape of the shuttle's wings. The simple color scheme (black and white) of the real vehicle translates well into LEGO bricks. A single bow plate is mounted on an angle to create a realistic-looking tail. I think the landing gear looks a bit too big for this scale, but it does steady the model when it's placed on a table or shelf. Overall, it's a clean, simple model, although it lacks much of the detail that could be captured in a larger scale.

Rating

I'll give this one a thumbs up, ready for launch!

Sharing Your Review

If you're creating your review for your friends, it might be enough to simply send them a copy (perhaps via email) so that they can know your feelings about the set. On the other hand, you may wish to post the review to a LEGO-related website and share it with an even wider audience.

NOTE   *Check out www.apotome.com/links.html for a list of LEGO-related websites where other builders share their reviews, models, and ideas.*

The time and effort you put into providing a fair review of the set will likely help someone else make the decision of whether or not to buy the same thing.

How It's Made: Creating Instructions for Your LEGO Models

In the last chapter, you created a model from scratch. You designed and built a small version of NASA's well-known Space Shuttle. Hopefully, by using some of these techniques you will create your own original models. At some point though, you'll want to take that model apart to re-use the pieces. How will you remember everything you need to re-create the model in the future? It's simple—you just need to document the parts and the steps you used to arrive at your final design.

Many of the LEGO sets you already have probably came with instructions. You might look at them and wonder how you can create such detailed plans for a model. Luckily, there are ways to create these instructions that don't require a degree in fine arts in order to make them useful.

Step-by-Step Pictures

One easy method you can use to create plans for your model is to simply document your building process step by step with a digital camera. The fact that there is no film to develop and print means that you can take as many pictures as you need to fully explain how to obtain the desired results.

First, you can take a picture (or several pictures) of the parts used to build the model, as shown in Figure 11-2.

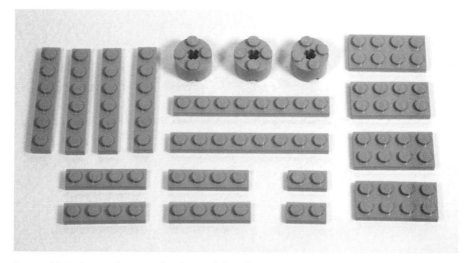

Figure 11-2: Set out the parts for the model and take a picture of them before beginning construction. In this case, I show the pieces needed to build a 4X 1×2 plate.

The elements shown in Figure 11-2 give the builder a clear picture of what parts they'll need to build the model.

Then capture each step, right after you've added the parts for that step to the model. Figures 11-3 and 11-4 show sequential steps for building a 1×2 plate in 4X scale. You saw this same model back in Chapter 5 (Figure 5-19).

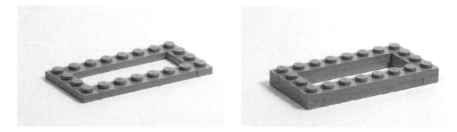

Figure 11-3: Each photograph should show a single step in the construction of the model. Here are steps 1 and 2 of the 1×2 plate in 4X scale.

Figure 11-4: Each subsequent picture should show the model from the same angle but with more parts added. Here you see steps 3 and 4.

You can then import these pictures into a word processor so that you can create instructions for them, all as a single document. Or, alternatively, you can post them to the Internet and let people view them one at a time. Either way, the pictures are an effective way to share your building techniques or even to just remember how to build a favorite model again in a few years.

Computer-Assisted Instructions

Throughout this book, you have seen instructions for a number of different examples. I created most of these images using computer software (LeoCAD) that allows me to build virtual models. Similar to programs that are used to design cars and airplanes, these amazing utilities provide an endless supply of LEGO bricks in every color you need. You can design and build the entire model, as seen in Figure 11-5.

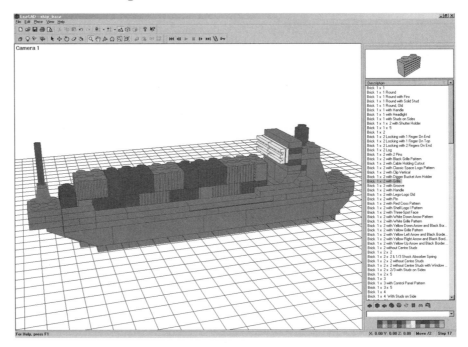

Figure 11-5: LeoCAD is one program available to help you create virtual LEGO models. With this and other programs, you never run out of elements.

NOTE *For a list of software and websites that will help you to create your own computer-generated LEGO models and instructions, please visit www.apotome.com/links.html.*

These programs also enable you to track each step as you go and then use that information to create step-by-step instructions that other builders can follow. Figure 11-6 shows an example of these types of instructions taken from Chapter 5.

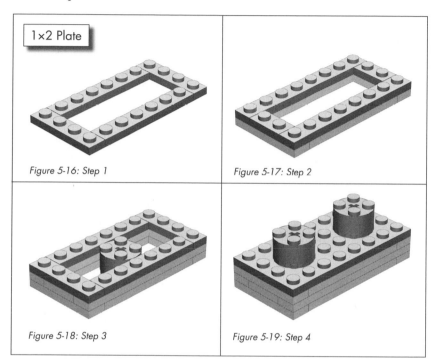

Figure 5-16: Step 1

Figure 5-17: Step 2

Figure 5-18: Step 3

Figure 5-19: Step 4

Figure 11-6: An example of instructions created using computer software. Notice how similar these images appear to Figures 11-3 and 11-4.

Having Fun: Making and Playing Games with LEGO Pieces

The word "fun" is often associated with the LEGO hobby. To take the fun even further, you can combine your LEGO elements with games you already know (by re-creating them in LEGO pieces) or you can create games that are completely original.

Games You Already Know

A number of traditional games are played on a checkerboard-styled playing surface. This board typically has 8 squares along each side, for a total of 64 squares.

Interestingly, the LEGO company makes a waffle-type baseplate that is 32 studs along each side. When you divide 32 by 8, you'll quickly realize that this large LEGO baseplate can be broken up into squares that are four studs long on each side.

As you can see in Figure 11-7, it only takes a few 2×2 tiles to make up each square on the game board.

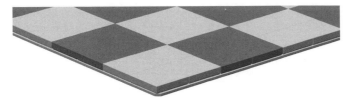

Figure 11-7: Four 2×2 tiles are used to create each different-colored square on the game board.

If you don't have quite as many tiles as you need to completely cover a 32×32 baseplate, you can use two different colors of standard plates. It won't look as smooth, but it should be just as useful for playing games.

Once you've made a board like this, you can use it to play games like checkers or chess. As you can imagine, to play a game of checkers on a LEGO game board, all you really need are simple playing pieces. In fact, they can be as simple as 2×2 bricks in two different colors.

To enjoy a game of chess, however, you might consider creating your own custom set of chessmen. You've probably seen different chess sets, some with traditional style pieces and others that have pieces that reflect a theme of some sort. Using LEGO elements, it's possible to create whatever style chess pieces you prefer. Figure 11-8 shows a simple traditional pawn. It uses mostly common parts, so building eight of them shouldn't tax your collection too much.

And whereas the rook, shown on the right in Figure 11-9, is fairly traditional, it also is a good start to a medieval-themed set of chess pieces. The bishop shown on the left in Figure 11-9 is fairly plain, but it does have the pointed top that is commonly associated with this piece. These are just some examples to get you started. Creating your own themed chess set can be a fun exercise.

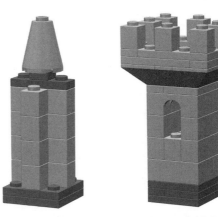

Figure 11-8: A basic chess pawn made from LEGO elements.

Figure 11-9: These two examples are both built on 3×3 bases.

Original Games

In Chapter 10, you tackled the challenge of designing your own LEGO set. For another interesting activity, you might try using LEGO pieces to create your own original game, complete with rules on how to play.

As an example, I'm going to present a game that I originally designed to be played on wooden tiles using glass bead markers. The game is called Connect-Across, and the basic rules follow momentarily. As you'll see, it works just as well when you make it from LEGO pieces.

To get ready to play, you simply need to make 30 tiles or squares similar to those in Figure 11-10.

Figure 11-10: These are two examples of how you can create the tiles. Pick either style or work on one of your own. You'll need 30 identical tiles to play the game.

It's not important which style you use, so long as all the tiles are the same size. Additionally, they don't all need to be the same color; they can be any combination of bricks and/or plates that you have in your collection.

You also need two sets of playing pieces. Each set should consist of 15 identical markers, for a total of 30. You can pick from one of the styles shown in Figure 11-11 or come up with something similar on your own. The only thing to keep in mind is that the two sets of pieces should look different from each other.

Figure 11-11: Several different styles for markers that can be used to play the game.

For example, for the first set, you could use 15 upside-down wheels (with or without the rubber tires) like the one shown on the far left of Figure 11-11. Then, for the second set of pieces, you could make 15 copies of the marker shown on the far right of Figure 11-11.

Once you've built the pieces you need (just described), you're ready to play your first game. Here are the complete instructions to get you started.

An Example of an Original Game: Connect-Across (Basic Rules)

Connect-Across is a game that combines the basic goal of tic-tac-toe with the light strategy involved in checkers. You and your opponent build the board together as the game progresses, while at the same time, you try to get four of your own pieces aligned in a row.

Setting Up

Decide who is going to use which set of markers. You may wish to build one set using light-colored elements and the other using darker elements. Have each player set his or her 15 markers near them on the table.

Set aside four of the square tiles.

Give each player about one-half of the remaining tiles. The tiles are all the same, and it doesn't really matter which ones you get or if you get exactly half of them.

Decide who is going to go first. You can do this with the flip of a coin or by any other means.

The player who is selected to go second actually completes the setup part of the game. They do this by taking the four tiles set aside earlier and arranging them in the center of the table (see Figure 11-12 for an example). These tiles may be set out in any pattern, as long as each tile is touching the side or corner of one of the others. In other words, you can't have any tiles floating free, away from the remainder of the group.

Figure 11-12: Here is only one example of an opening pattern. The tiles can be in any arrangement, as long as they are all touching.

You may wish to use one of the large 48×48 waffled baseplates on which to set your tiles. This keeps them from shifting around too much. However, it's not at all necessary—the game should play just as well on any level surface.

How Is It Played?

It's important to understand that there are really only three basic rules for playing Connect-Across. These rules dictate what you can do any time that it is your turn. During your turn, you can make any *one* of the three following moves:

1. Place one of your markers on any open tile that is already part of the board.

2. Place a new tile on the table, making sure that it touches the side or corner of another tile that is already part of the board.

3. Move one of your markers that is already on the board. This movement can be a single space, to an adjacent and empty tile, or, it can be a capture jump just like in checkers. In this case, your piece leaps from its current position on the board, over an opponent's piece, and lands on an empty square. The piece you jump over is removed from the board and returned to its owner.

And that's it.

Playing the Game

To begin a game, the person who won the coin toss has a choice of either of the first two rules. (There are no markers on the board yet, so rule 3 is unavailable at first.) The first player may either place one of their markers on any one of the four empty squares, or they may instead choose to place a tile on the table, thus increasing the size of the game board. Remember, the tile can be placed anywhere, as long as it touches an existing tile on either an edge or at a corner.

Figure 11-13 shows one example of an opening move. In this case, the player using the light colored markers has placed one of their pieces on the board. They could have chosen to set down another tile instead.

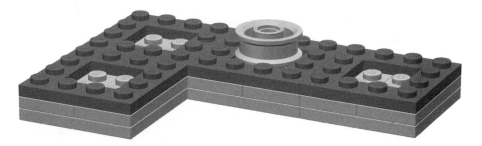

Figure 11-13: The upside-down wheel makes an effective yet simple marker, and it fits perfectly in the center of a tile.

The game then shifts to the other player. Again, they may choose from either rule 1 or rule 2 initially. They can place a marker or place a tile.

Players continue to take turns making moves in a similar fashion. Of course, once either player has placed at least one piece on the board, they may decide to use rule 3 on any of their subsequent turns. Remember that you can pick any of the three moves you want, but you can only make one move during each turn.

What you will notice is that the board soon begins to grow in a rather organic fashion, with rows and columns branching out in many directions. You'll likely find that no two games are ever played on the same shaped board. Figure 11-14 shows a game in progress. You can see that the player using the light-colored markers has a good chance of making four-in-a-row diagonally through the middle.

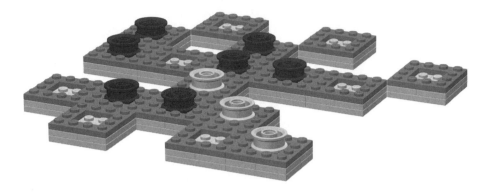

Figure 11-14: Getting four in a row may not be as easy as you think!

Winning the Game

Players continue to add tiles or markers and make single or capture moves until one player is able to get four of their own markers lined up in a row. The row may be vertical, horizontal, or diagonal along four adjacent tiles with touching corners. You can see an example in Figure 11-15. The player using the light-colored markers has created a diagonal row. Follow the wheels from the bottom center of the picture toward the top. The first player to accomplish this wins the game.

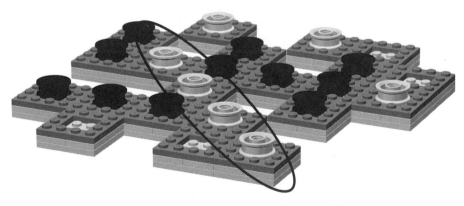

Figure 11-15: The oval highlights the winning move in this particular game.

Designing Your Own Game

Creating your own original game is one part inspiration and 99 parts play testing. A lot of ideas sound good on paper and may even look good if you create the board and playing pieces for them. But many games end up being too complicated, too confusing, or just plain boring. *Play testing* involves actually sitting down with other players and observing your game in action. It helps you find areas that need improvement and allows you to adjust the rules to make the game more fun.

When you're thinking about making your own game, try to think about the following:

- What is the main point of this game?
- How can I use LEGO pieces to help bring this game to life?
- What makes this game different every time it is played?
- Will the game have a theme or will it use abstract pieces like checkers?
- What makes it challenging?
- How can I keep the rules simple but at the same time create interesting twists?

If you can come up with good answers to some of these questions, you are well on your way to designing a fun and exciting game. The next step is too build a prototype of the game. This is essentially a copy of the game you can try out by play testing. Find a friend who enjoys games and get them to walk through the game a few times with you. It won't take long to find the parts that don't work well and to recognize areas that you can tweak to make things more lively. The LEGO system is perfectly suited to building game prototypes; after all, building things is what it does best.

Review: Enjoying Every Aspect of LEGO

How you choose to enjoy LEGO as a hobby is entirely up to you. As you've seen in this chapter, there are ways to add interest to your LEGO elements that don't involve just building models. Just as with the building techniques you've explored in this book, there is no one right or wrong way to enhance your participation in this hobby. That's why writing reviews, playing LEGO-based games, or creating instructions can be just as rewarding as building the models themselves.

12

SORTING, STORAGE, AND SITTING DOWN TO BUILD SOMETHING

When most people think of storing a bunch of LEGO bricks, they think of that plastic tub or maybe that cardboard box a lot of kids have. It's chock-full of assorted parts from a number of different sets and gets dumped on the living room floor when friends or cousins come to visit. It offers ease of use, but it does not really allow any sorting of bricks into meaningful batches.

That box is probably suitable if you have a few thousand LEGO pieces or less. But if you have more than 5,000 or 6,000 elements, you might find that it is getting not only heavy but also crowded. Once you have more than 10,000 bricks, it's time to do some sorting. Figure 12-1 shows that it only takes a few dozen pieces to make a pile that needs sorting.

Figure 12-1: Unruly bricks ready to be sorted

At some point in your building career, you will need to begin the process of sorting your pieces into smaller containers. For some people, this is the least enjoyable part of the LEGO hobby. For others, this process is a pleasant change of pace from building or planning models. No matter what your take on the subject, you must eventually decide how to sort and store your collection.

First let's separate this topic into its three main components:

Sorting bricks
> The system or method by which you separate bricks into piles/ categories.

Storing bricks
> The physical boxes, containers, and drawers that sorted bricks go into.

Setting up a build area
> The type and quantities of bricks you keep readily available and the area you set aside for working in.

Sorting vs. Storing: What's the Difference?

Although sorted bricks are often stored in the manner in which they've been divided up, there is a distinct difference between the system you use to sort and the containers into which you place your sorted pieces. Think of the process of sorting as being similar to that you'd perform on a list of phone numbers and email addresses for your family and friends. You might sort this list alphabetically, by the length of time you've known the person, by where they live, or by group (friends, family, coworkers, and so on). However you approach it, this is your method of *sorting*.

Once it's organized, you might decide to store this information in a small book with lined paper and lettered tabs, you might type it onto one long sheet of paper so you can keep it in your wallet, or you might decide to use some computer software (like an email program) to store it electronically. Whatever you decide on is your system of *storing*.

In the next section, you will focus exclusively on sorting. You can, for the moment, assume that you're just making piles of bricks on the floor or on a table, such as the small piles shown in Figure 12-2.

Figure 12-2: These pieces have been sorted but not yet stored.

You will look at various ways to determine what goes into each pile. Later, I'll talk about what kinds of containers you can use to store these piles.

Sorting Bricks: Divide and Conquer

The most common question asked when people begin to talk about sorting is, "Should I sort by color or by shape?" The answer is not as cut and dry as just choosing one style or the other. The answer depends upon such things as the size of the collection being sorted, the space and containers you have available in which to store your bricks, and even what type of models you're building at any given time.

The first thing to look at is the collection of bricks that you're attempting to sort. Let's sort two imaginary collections, with simplified inventories, to help illustrate the techniques.

Small-Sized Collections

Collection #1 (Table 12-1) presents an interesting challenge. For whatever reason, you have a particular piece that is present in very large numbers; you've got about 500 2×4 red bricks. If you decided to store all the pieces from this collection in a single pile, it might be tricky to find a 1×4 plate when you needed one. However, if you create two piles, one for the 2×4 bricks and one for everything else, it's more likely that you can find a part that isn't a 2×4. When you need a 2×4, of course, you know that they are in their own pile.

Collection #2 (Table 12-1) is a bit different. Here you have a limited supply of red bricks but a slightly larger and more varied list of red plates. If you mix all the bricks and plates together, it might make it harder to find some of the small plates. In this case, your plates are not really dominated by a huge number of any one particular piece. In other words, your collection falls into two camps: bricks and plates. Why not create two piles to represent that fact?

Table 12-1: Inventory for Two Small Collections

Collection #1		Collection #2	
Quantity	**Type of Elements**	**Quantity**	**Type of Elements**
10	1×1 red bricks	10	1×1 red bricks
5	1×4 red bricks	5	1×4 red bricks
500	2×4 red bricks	20	2×4 red bricks
50	2×6 red bricks	25	2×6 red bricks
6	1×4 red plates	50	1×1 red plates
10	1×8 red plates	200	1×2 red plates
20	2×4 red plates	6	1×4 red plates
		10	1×8 red plates
		20	2×4 red plates
		20	2×6 red plates
		10	2×8 red plates
		4	4×4 red plates
		4	4×6 red plates

These examples are a little simple. Let's look at some larger lists of bricks to see others way to sort them.

Medium-Sized Collections

In *Collection #3* (Table 12-2), you have about the same number of red bricks as you had in Collection #2 (Table 12-1) but a few more red plates. In addition, you now have two additional colors to deal with as well; there are both blue and white plates in this collection. The quantity of red plates still dictates that they have their own pile. The bricks, since they are different types of pieces, belong in their own pile as well. This leaves you with just the blue and white plates.

Table 12-2: Inventory for Medium Collection

Collection #3

Quantity	Type of Elements
10	1×1 red bricks
5	1×4 red bricks
75	2×4 red bricks
25	2×6 red bricks
50	1×1 red plates
200	1×2 red plates
6	1×4 red plates
10	1×6 red plates
10	1×8 red plates
20	2×4 red plates
20	2×6 red plates
10	2×8 red plates
4	4×4 red plates
4	3×3 red diamond-cut plates
16	1×4 blue plates
30	2×4 blue plates
25	2×6 blue plates
2	2×8 blue plates
2	4×4 blue plates
20	1×2 white plates
10	2×4 white plates
5	2×6 white plates
6	2×8 white plates
4	4×4 white plates

There really aren't enough of either color to warrant a separate pile just yet. Because the two colors are far apart in tone, you can safely mix them together, confident that such a small pile will be easy enough to search for a piece of either hue.

Let's look at one more example.

Large-Sized Collections

In *Collection #4* (Table 12-3), you'll look at a wider variety of parts and try to see what the best way is to break them down into separate piles.

Table 12-3: Inventory of Larger Collection

Collection #4

Quantity	Type of Elements	Quantity	Type of Elements
100	1×1 red bricks	4	2×8 red plates
5	1×4 red bricks	4	4×4 red plates
175	2×4 red bricks	16	1×4 blue plates
25	2×6 red bricks	30	2×4 blue plates
250	1×1 yellow bricks	25	2×6 blue plates
15	1×4 yellow bricks	2	2×8 blue plates
20	1×6 yellow bricks	2	4×4 blue plates
70	2×4 yellow bricks	20	1×2 white plates
125	1×1 white bricks	10	2×4 white plates
20	1×2 white bricks	5	2×6 white plates
20	1×3 white bricks	6	2×8 white plates
30	1×4 white bricks	4	4×4 white plates
10	1×8 white bricks	5	1×3 33 deg white slopes
80	2×4 white bricks	4	1×2 45 deg white slopes
50	1×1 red plates	10	4×3 33 deg black slopes
20	1×2 red plates	6	2×3 33 deg black slopes
10	1×6 red plates	2	1×4 red arches
2	1×8 red plates	2	1×6 red arches
10	2×4 red plates	4	red bullnose bricks
6	2×6 red plates	6	white headlight bricks

Now this is a more realistic collection. Your own collection will almost certainly have a wide variety of pieces. It will probably include more colors and types of pieces than are showing here, but for this exercise, this pretend collection will suffice.

Start with an easy decision. If you look at the top of the list, it's clear that there are a lot of 1×1 bricks, in three different colors. To make them easy to keep track of, give them their own pile. 1×1's can, in fact, be mixed in with other larger bricks, but when you do this, they have the tendency to filter down to the bottom of the container and, as a result, become more difficult to find.

Next, you have a little more complicated decision to make. Take a look at just the 1×N and 2×N bricks near the top of the list. How you split these up can go a couple of different ways. You can separate all the 2×4 bricks into one pile since, collectively, they contain more pieces than the rest of the bricks put together. Doing so would leave the 1×N bricks (of all three colors) to make a pile of their own. On the other hand, you can sort them exclusively by color. Doing so would give you one pile each of red, yellow, and white bricks. It is likely, that no matter which of these choices you prefer, you'll still want to have your 1×1's set aside so they don't get lost.

A subtle twist on the last separation is to take all of the smallest bricks (the 1×1's and the 1×2's) and set them apart as one pile. Then, no matter whether you go with the 2×4/1×N split or you decide to separate by each of the three colors, you still have your less visible bricks separated from the rest, thus making them easier to find.

Now it's time to sort the plates. This collection has fewer red plates than did the others. As a result, it might be reasonable to make a single pile that gathers all of the plates together. Once again, you are looking at the current quantities you have on hand so that you can decide how best to find a certain piece in a particular color when you are building your next great model later on.

Collection #4 has a few things you didn't see in the other lists. First are the slopes. The black slopes are larger than the white ones, but there is not a significantly larger number of the black ones for them to require a pile of their own. In fact, because the two colors are exact opposites, storing them together is not a problem. A single pile will do for all the slopes.

Finally, look at the very bottom of the list; you'll see some bricks that you have yet to categorize. Based on what you learned in Chapter 1, you know that each of the last four items in this collection are specialized elements. In some ways the specialized elements category is the miscellaneous category for classifying bricks that don't meet other criteria. As the name suggests, almost all of these bricks provide a special function unmatched by typical bricks, plates, or slopes. Based on the small number of specialized elements in this collection, they can simply share one pile.

In a larger actual collection, however, a particular service element may require a pile unto itself. An example might be the offset plates. These relatively common parts are available in a wide variety of colors. Once you have a few dozen or maybe even several hundred, you may want to keep them separate from other pieces. You'll find that this becomes doubly effective when your many offset plates are in 6, 8, or 10 different colors. Keeping them in their own pile allows you to more easily find a handful in just a single color.

The specialized parts in Collection #4 are probably just as noticeable when you keep them together. This remains true until you find that the quantity of one of them has grown to such a level that it requires its own area as well. This process, of redeciding how to sort some elements pops up again and again. Each time you add a large set (or a number of small sets) to your collection or you buy a number of assorted buckets or tubs, or you find yourself buying parts in lots from an online auction or sales site, you may find that you need to extract one or more parts and give them a pile, or piles, of their own.

Storing Bricks

Until now you've focused exclusively on putting your parts into piles based on a number of guidelines. But unless you have unlimited amounts of table space on which to keep your bricks, it's very likely that you'll want to find a better way to store them. *Storing* refers to keeping the bulk of your collection on shelves or in a closet and bringing out only what pieces you need, when you need them. As we discussed earlier in this chapter, the topic of storage is related to, but also separate from, how you sort your bricks. The shelves in Figure 12-3 show how a medium-sized collection might look when stored in a variety of containers.

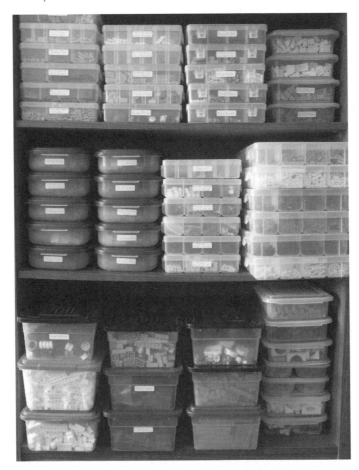

Figure 12-3: Different-sized containers work together to form an effective storage system.

You can see that this collection has been broken down into a number of different-sized containers. Your collection will likely end up stored in a similar manner. But what size boxes should you use? Different pieces have different needs; especially when you take into account how many of each you own. Let's look at several different-sized containers to see how each can be useful.

Start Small, Keep It Simple

One of the smallest boxes that I came across when first storing my collection was an empty videocassette case. No, I don't mean the cardboard sleeve that has the movie's title printed on it; I'm talking about the hard plastic replacement cases that you can often find at stores in packages of 2 or 3 at a time. The best ones I found were translucent white, like the one shown in Figure 12-4. These little boxes are cheap and very handy for those little piles of 20 or 30 pieces—maybe some slopes you have in an uncommon color or perhaps a pile of 1×N's and 1×N plates in some of the new pastel colors. It could be anything, but the point is that there isn't much sense in dedicating huge amounts of space to parts you don't yet have. The videocassette cases are also great for storing tiny things that might get lost at the bottom of a larger, deeper container. These could be things like minifig accessories, small 1×1 plates or tiles, Technic pins and gears, and so on. Additionally, you can store the boxes themselves inside larger LEGO tubs that you may already have. (More about those tubs follows.)

Figure 12-4: Even the smallest container can add a great deal of organization to your collection.

Containers with Compartments

If you are looking for something a little larger than videotape cases, you might want to turn to *leftover containers*. These are plastic containers about the size that you'd find useful for storing leftovers after a big meal, and they are available in your grocery store or discount store. There are brand-name and no-name versions of these, and there is a large range of quality when it comes to how they are manufactured. These containers offer one immediate advantage over almost any of the other types of storage media, however: they are available in a huge number of shapes and sizes.

Some of my favorites in this category are, in fact, not suitable for leftovers at all. They are the right size for a small meal, but they are all a lower quality no-name brand that is not airtight. I wouldn't want to keep last night's lasagna in them, but the lids do stay on. Because LEGO bricks don't need to maintain that just-picked-this-morning freshness, these containers work wonders for storing medium-sized piles.

Some plastic containers, like those in Figure 12-5, have two or more compartments. This allows for some useful storage solutions, such as keeping your standard and inverted slopes separate but also together. This is a case where you can truly merge your sorting and storage techniques in one place. The container maximizes the organization you've been working to achieve. In this example, you can pull a single box out of your main storage area, bring it to your building area, and have at your disposal two or three types of useful, and at the same time related, pieces.

Figure 12-5: No, it's not a TV dinner, but the shape of this container might remind you of food nonetheless.

You may run across all kinds of versions of these containers. Unlike shoebox-sized boxes, leftover containers tend to vary widely in size, shape, number of compartments, depth, and so on. You might want to shop around before buying any of them at all. It's very likely that you can find some of them at dollar stores or other discount retailers for very little money. Or, on the other hand, you may wish to spend a bit more on some brand-name containers so you know that they will, in all likelihood, never wear out. Sometimes you get what you pay for.

In addition, you'll want to have a sense of what sizes and shapes are available in your area and compare that to the piles you have sorted your pieces into. In my case, I have three distinct styles of leftover containers that I use to store my collection. I settled upon each of these because it was useful, inexpensive, and readily available. Your decision on which ones to buy should be based on similar criteria.

Suppose you have a large number of standard blue slopes and inverted blue slopes in your collection. Over time, you've acquired a number of copies of a particular assorted tub of bricks that each contained several pieces of these two elements. During your sorting process, you probably gave these parts their own pile because you had a healthy handful of each. At this point, for storage purposes, you may decide that you want to keep the regular slopes somewhat separate from the inverted ones, while still keeping all of these blue elements together. In a case such as this (similar element with two variations), you could adopt a single container that is or can be divided into two sections. Or, you could use a single container and just divide the slopes and inverted slopes into two different resealable plastic freezer bags before placing them inside.

Shoeboxes: Not Just for Shoes Anymore

In addition to the blue-sloped pieces just discussed, assume that you also have about 50 or 60 red roof bricks (another name for 33-degree slopes) that you won on an eBay auction for a really good price. However, in the rest of your collection, you don't really have many more slopes in any great numbers. Now you've got your blue (regular and inverted, from the last section) and red slopes that you need to keep separate from other elements in your collection. In this case, a small plastic container (one about the size of a shoebox like the one shown in Figure 12-6) might work best; it can hold each of the three distinct elements, each in its own freezer bag. In other words, your red and blue slopes will all share one box, but they'll each be easily accessible since they'll be kept separate by the plastic bags.

The box I'm talking about here can often be one that you find at a nearby dollar store, or perhaps at a home decorating store in the storage aisle. These don't have to cost a lot of money, but they can be enormously effective as storage solutions for a small- to medium-sized LEGO collection. They are available in more expensive brand-name versions, but since you don't require water- or airtight containers, any generic box will probably do just fine.

Figure 12-6: One of the most useful sizes of containers to consider buying

Boxes of this size offer the additional flexibility of being easy to house on shelves, in a closet, or even under a bed if need be. An average sized box of this type can easily hold a couple of hundred 2×4 bricks, several thousand 1×1 bricks, and so on.

These boxes offer other benefits. They are easy to move from a shelf or cupboard to the area where you are going to build. In addition, many of them are translucent, so the contents are not hidden from you. In fact, most of my shoebox-sized bins are not labeled because I can view their contents by looking through their sides. They are also large enough that for many building projects, a single box (of a single color or part type) offers enough pieces that you don't have to go into your deep storage. (More on *deep storage* coming up later in the chapter.)

There is yet another way to make this type of container even more useful. You can store elements that are related in some way, but that you still want to keep separate, together in these containers. You do this by first putting each pile of elements into a zip closure freezer bag and then putting those bags into the shoebox. For example, you may wish to store standard and inverted slopes of the same color in this manner.

Keep in mind that until you've worked with your collection for a while, and have perhaps sorted it once or twice, you may not wish to invest heavily in one specific type of container. For instance, if you're not sure that the shoebox-sized plastic tubs will be big enough, why not use actual shoeboxes for a while? Most households have a handful of such boxes around, and they can be pressed into service to act as test units for your storage needs. You can easily affix a simple piece of paper that lists the contents of the box to the front to help you tell the boxes apart. Although these won't be as uniform or tidy as the plastic boxes, they also won't cost you any money. If, in a few months you find that they are, in fact, useful as a storage medium, you might then want to invest in more permanent versions.

Keeping Track of the Little Pieces: Tackle Boxes to the Rescue

What about all those really small pieces you end up with? They might be 1×1 cylinder plates, or Technic pins, or maybe minifig accessories. They can be difficult to keep track of, even in a very small container. The solution is to use a larger container that is divided into very small compartments. The most common of these are similar to the one shown in Figure 12-7.

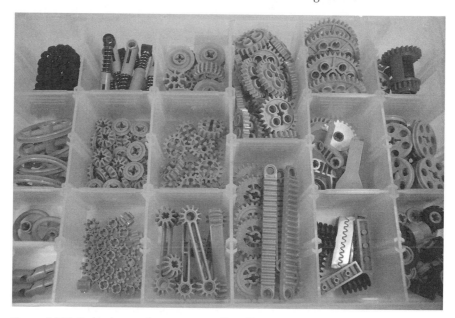

Figure 12-7: Tackle box–style containers offer efficient and organized storage for smaller pieces.

You'll often find these types of boxes in the fishing tackle aisle or sometimes in the craft section of your favorite store. The great thing about them is that they very often have small dividers that allow you to configure the compartments into a variety of sizes and shapes. This enables you to customize the layout of each box to the parts you wish to put in it. This is what makes sure you get the best usage out of each container.

Reuse Containers You May Already Have: Tubs and Buckets

Perhaps you find that you are accumulating large quantities of basic bricks, plates, or slopes and you decide that another size of container is apt to be more useful. Before you go buy any more, remember that you may already have them on hand. If you've bought, or plan to buy, any assorted buckets or tubs from LEGO (they are typically offered in different forms every year or two), then you will have perfect storage containers sitting right in front of you. Figure 12-8 shows the difference between a tub and a bucket.

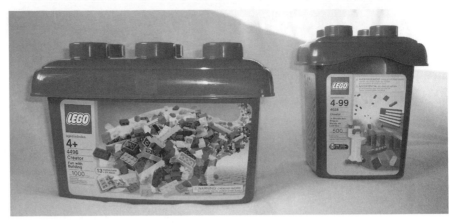

Figure 12-8: The taller square container on the right is a bucket. The wider, but slightly shorter, container on the left is a tub.

A large LEGO tub (shown on the left in Figure 12-8) can hold many times more bricks than it comes with when you buy it. Simply by dumping in loose 2×4 bricks, I have found that a tub can hold 600 to 800 bricks at a minimum.

An average-sized LEGO bucket (shown on the right in Figure 12-8) can hold between 300 and 400 2×4 bricks. However these containers don't always store as nicely as the tubs.

These storage solutions serve an obvious purpose for certain elements that you have, or will eventually acquire, in larger quantities.

Even in the early stages of building your collection, you may want to revisit the examples earlier in this chapter to see how best to fill these handy boxes. For instance, you may have only half a container each of basic 2×N white and black bricks, but you may not have an empty tub for each color. Why not take these two diametrically opposed colors and let them share one tub? Here are some examples of colors that might share a tub well:

Black and white	Red and light gray
Blue and yellow	Dark gray and orange
Green and yellow	Blue and white
Yellow and black	White and red

And so on. Actually, any combination can work so long as you, the builder, can easily tell the difference between them. For instance, putting green and blue in the same tub might, for some, be a bad idea since under less-than-perfect lighting, they might look similar.

By storing two colors in a single tub, you are maximizing the potential storage of that container and, in turn, lessening the amount of space your containers will take up. For some builders, the amount of space in their home that can be devoted to LEGO (both storage and building) may be limited. In that case, there's no sense having a tub capable of holding hundreds of bricks sitting on a shelf only one-sixth full.

Deep Storage: Taking Care of Larger Quantities

For some builders, even large LEGO tubs may not suffice when it comes to the overflow, or bulk brick, side of their collection. There are those who eventually acquire massive quantities of basic bricks. For them, a single color might occupy five, ten, or even more standard LEGO tubs. In these cases, a better solution may be the large, chest-style storage containers—once again available in either brand-name or no-name varieties. As with the leftover-style boxes, the chest-sized versions range in size, thought not as much in shape. They may hold 15, 20, or even 30 gallons worth of bricks. They are effective for *deep storage* of certain elements.

Deep storage is that realm where you keep these large-volume containers filled with bricks that you might only use when you're working on large-scale projects. This might mean that most of the time, these chest-style boxes are in storage somewhere, possibly away from the rest of your collection. They might be in a basement, a cold storage area, or perhaps even at the home of a relative if your own home lacks the room to keep them handy. This contrasts with all of the other containers you've looked at, most of which are generally not that far from where you want to set up to do your building and are, for the most part, easily accessible. It may require a bit of planning to retrieve the contents of deep storage containers so that you can have them on hand at the time they, or rather their contents, are needed.

Setting Up a Building Area

At the end of all this sorting and storing, you still need to conquer the most important task of all: building something. If you're like me, at some point in your life building with LEGO bricks was no more complicated than plopping yourself down on the floor and digging through your boxes of pieces. But now, having reached the stage where you've sorted and more efficiently stored your elements, you may also want to set up an area where you can build models and perhaps even leave bricks out between building sessions. As well, you have probably already realized that keeping most of your pieces in large storage containers, either on a shelf or in a closet somewhere, makes it more difficult to just sit down and create a model. That's the main reason most builders eventually set up a specific area for their LEGO hobby.

A building area does not need to be an entire room; in fact, it doesn't even need to be an entire table! You can make good use out of just about any amount of space that you can set aside for your hobby. Figure 12-9 shows a building table that's not even three feet wide, but it serves the purpose nonetheless.

Figure 12-9: Your LEGO building area doesn't need to be fancy or large. It only needs to be a place where you can work effectively.

First, and most obviously, you need to decide how much space you've got to work with. Maybe you're lucky enough to have a small spare bedroom available, or perhaps a corner of a basement that you can call your own. On the other hand, your LEGO building area might be just an area under a window or along one wall of a spare room. Or, you may have to share a large table with someone else's hobby. No matter what space you find yourself dealing with, the basic ideas behind setting up your workshop are the same.

1. **Decide which LEGO elements are most important to the style of building you do.** Maybe you want lots of gray and brown elements for building castles. Or perhaps you want most of your plates handy because you like to work on sculpture or mosaics. Or perhaps you want several common colors and sizes of basic elements available because you can never decide what you're going to build next.

2. **Decide how much of your work area you want to set aside for keeping the elements from step 1 close at hand.** Remember, it's great to be surrounded by thousands of pieces of LEGO, but if you're only left with one or two square feet of building space, then you're not going to enjoy yourself very much.

3. **Find storage bins or containers that are suitable based on the decisions made in both step 1 and step 2.** These may be small, open-front sorting bins (as in Figure 12-9), or they may storage units that feature lots of small drawers (as in Figure 12-10) in which you can keep your most needed bricks.

Figure 12-10: Sets of small plastic drawers offer great organization solutions that allow you to see your bricks from the front.

To make your building area most effective, you should also give at least some consideration to the following:

Lighting

If at all possible, try to illuminate your building table/area with lights that give off simulated natural daylight. These are a bit more expensive than normal light bulbs, but they offer you a better view of all your colorful LEGO pieces.

Chair

Assuming you are going to sit at your table (and you may not), you will want to get the most suitable seat you can find. This may be a swiveling, office-type chair or nothing more than a simple stool with a backrest. The point is that you are comfortable during your building sessions.

Atmosphere

This can be anything from the overall lighting of the room (sunlight vs. artificial light) to whatever other things you bring into it (for example, is this room strictly for LEGO or does it share space with your other hobbies?). As with the chair, this is all about making yourself comfortable. If you set up a huge LEGO table in the darkest corner of a damp, musty basement, you may not be as inspired as you would be if you picked a smaller space in an upstairs spare bedroom that has a good-sized window.

In addition, think about having the ability to play some music when you build; that can also create an environment that's more suitable for your creative endeavors.

As with the decisions about how to sort and what to use for storage, the decisions about setting up your work area will be a mix of different answers. Not every solution noted here will work for you, but parts of one or more may work very well. Adapt your work area to your style of building, and your collection and you can't go wrong.

Review: Unique Solutions for Every Builder

Early on in this chapter, I brought up the question that many builders ask, "Should I sort by color or by shape?" I think you can see, based on the many different solutions provided throughout the chapter, that the answer is completely dependent on you, your LEGO bricks, and your needs. No one answer is completely correct, and you may need to revisit a solution that works for you now as your collection expands or as your building style changes. Experimenting with and refining how you store and sort your bricks is a great addition to an already fun hobby. Resorting bricks, from time to time, is a good way to remind yourself of what elements you have available. Seeing a particular type or color of piece move from a small box to a larger storage container is a rewarding way of watching your collection grow along with your involvement in LEGO building.

13

MAKING AND USING TOOLS FOR LEGO PROJECTS

For many hobbies, you need some type of tool or combination of tools to work with the basic materials. When you build a car or an airplane from a plastic model kit, you need to use things like glue, paint, and perhaps even a knife to complete the project. To assemble models using the Meccano construction system or similar things out of Erector, you need screwdrivers and wrenches to tighten nuts and bolts.

One thing that has always made LEGO bricks easy to use is the fact that they require no tools to connect pieces together. Does that mean you can't use tools? Not at all. In some cases, you may find it useful to add some small implements to your building environment. One of the very simplest of LEGO tools is little more than a standard brick or plate that can be used to measure other LEGO pieces—most often Technic axles.

As you're building a model from an official LEGO set, you may find an image within the instructions that looks something like Figure 13-1.

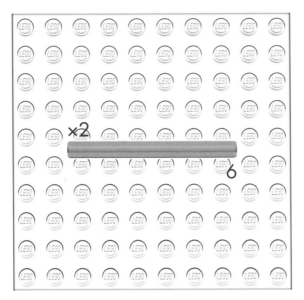

Figure 13-1: This illustration tells you that you need two axles that are six studs long each.

As you can see, there are (usually) two numbers next to the picture of a Technic axle. The number with the letter X in front of it represents how many of that piece you need to use in this step of the instructions. The other number, with no letter next to it, indicates how long the axle should be. The length is measured in studs. Figuring out if you've got the right piece is easy—simply use a LEGO brick as your measuring tool as shown in Figure 13-2.

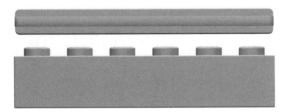

Figure 13-2: It's easy to see that this axle is six studs long.

Using the brick, you can quickly confirm the length of the axle. This allows LEGO to manufacture the axles without worrying about any identifying marks. Although it may not seem very high tech, using a LEGO piece as a measuring device is using a tool nonetheless. This is a simple, yet elegant, solution, and one that has always struck me as another example of making something no more complicated than it needs to be.

There are also tools that can be made from . . . you guessed it, other LEGO pieces!

Presser Tool

One item that always sits on my building table is a presser tool; I find this useful when I'm working with small elements, especially in tight corners. The *presser tool* is handy for those times when you need to push down on a small tile, plate, or maybe a panel in a recessed corner or one that is between other elements where your fingertip just can't reach. This tool is simple to build and is something you may wish to leave together so that it is always available when you need it. The pieces used to create this tool are shown in Figure 13-3.

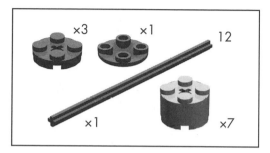

Figure 13-3: Bill of Materials for the presser tool

Actually assembling the tool is quite simple. Figure 13-4 shows how the 2×2 cylinder bricks and plates slide onto the axle. You can use any combination of these elements to create your own customized patterns and color schemes.

Figure 13-4: Assembly instructions for the presser tool

The 2×2 inverted cylinder tile shown on the right side of Figures 13-4 and 13-5 forms the end of the tool giving it a nice, rounded look and feel.

Figure 13-5: Ready to press!

In Figure 13-6, you can see the tool being used to seat a stubborn 1×1 plate. You can loosely align the part in question, and then, using the presser tool, gently apply a downward force that helps set the piece in place.

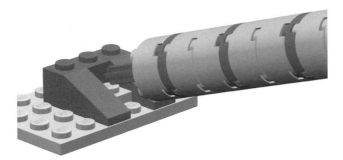

Figure 13-6: The presser tool in action. The 1×1 plate is dropped in and then pressed into its final spot using the tool.

The Ruler

Simplicity, as you've already seen, often provides for the best solutions.

You can use a ruler made of LEGO to measure distances between pieces of large models. For instance, perhaps you're laying down the foundation for a large LEGO house. You can use the ruler to check the distances between the walls. Or, when you're working on a sculpture, you can use it to check proportions of different parts of the model.

In the case of making your own ruler out of LEGO, it couldn't be much simpler. Figure 13-7 shows you the Bill of Materials for this tool.

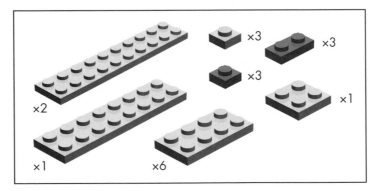

Figure 13-7: Bill of Materials for the ruler

The construction of this little project is almost self-explanatory. Any colors can be used, as long at the 1×1 and 1×2 markers are different than the reset of the elements, as you see in Figure 13-8.

Figure 13-8: The completed ruler

The bottom layer of our LEGO ruler is made up of a 2×8, a couple of 2×10's, and a 2×2. The remainder of the plates go on the top layer to form the patterns shown in Figure 13-8. Measuring is just a matter of looking at the contrasting colored plates. The first dark 1×1 represents 5 studs in length, the first dark 1×2 indicates 10 studs, and so on. The ruler shown here can measure something up to 30 studs long.

Pin Stand Tool

In some of the official LEGO sets you may own, and eventually in some of your own original models, you may find situations where Technic pins, axles, and so on are inserted into various other elements. Sometimes getting these pieces out simply requires using another longer axle to give the piece a bit of a push from one side so that you can then grasp it in your fingers.

For other part combinations, perhaps ones in which you want to apply a bit more force to the stubborn piece, you might want to build yourself something to help. No normal combinations of LEGO elements should ever become fully and permanently stuck, but from time to time, two pieces find a snug fit that can be difficult to undo.

The pin stand tool itself can sit on your building table. You can then push a part down onto it from above. The parts you'll need to build one of these are shown in Figure 13-9.

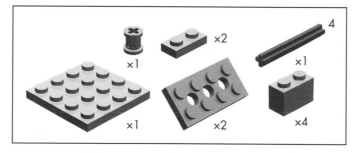

Figure 13-9: Bill of Materials for the pin stand tool

The instructions are easy to follow and the result is a small, but useful, tool that can sit nearby until you need it. To make your own version, simply follow steps 1 through 6 in Figure 13-10.

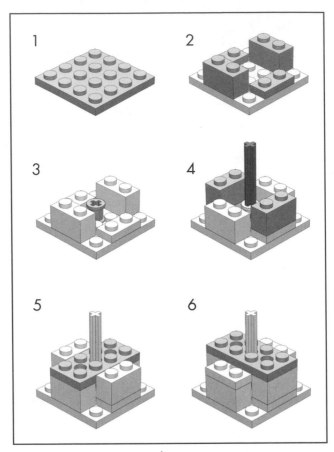

Figure 13-10: Instructions for building your own pin stand tool

With the tool sitting firmly on the table, or even resting on the floor, you can use both hands to center a part over it and push down until the piece is forced out. Figure 13-11 shows how simple it is to use this tool.

Figure 13-11: Pin stand tool in action. Align parts over the axle sticking up from the tool. Push down, and the small axle is pushed out of the Technic brick.

Brick Separator

Sooner or later you're going to want to take one of your LEGO creations apart, whether it's an official set that you built out of the box and put on a shelf for a few months, or a robot that you built last weekend. Eventually you're going to want to reuse the pieces contained in it.

Although there's nothing wrong with displaying your work, there is also a great deal to be gained by taking advantage of one of the other great qualities of the LEGO system—its reusability. Any piece can connect to almost any other piece. Working out all of these arrangements is part of what makes exploring and using the system so satisfying.

Now that you know it's okay to take that model apart, what are you waiting for? Just start by pulling off large sections of bricks, breaking those down into smaller chunks, and finally separating individual bricks from one another. At some point, however, you are very likely to come across two or more pieces that are stuck together so tightly that you can't pry them apart or even get a fingernail between them. Often these will be two small plates that are proving just how well the stud and tube mechanism works. Despite their best efforts to stay together, it is almost certain you'll want to separate them. Let's look at how best to do that.

In some official LEGO sets, and in some assorted tubs of bricks, you'll find a rather odd looking piece of plastic (Figure 13-12). It isn't quite a brick, but it does have some studs on it. It's a *brick separator.*

Figure 13-12: The brick separator—a tool for builders of all skill levels

If you haven't got one of these little tools, you may want to consider buying one. Better yet, you may want to consider buying two since they work well in pairs. If you haven't found one in a LEGO set, you can normally purchase them directly from the LEGO company's Shop at Home service, http://shop.lego.com. Look for item #630.

Brick separators sell for a couple of dollars each. They will save you much more than that in dental fees by helping you separate bricks and plates without resorting to yanking them apart with your teeth.

Take, for example, two 2×2 plates stacked neatly together. They've been part of a model for months, and now they're stuck together and won't budge. Start by taking one of your brick separators in one hand; then place the 2×2 stacked plates studs down on top of it. Then bring the second separator down from above; this creates something that looks like the handles of a pair of pliers (see Figure 13-13). And, like the handles of a pair of pliers, you want to squeeze the two separators together. With very little effort and not much movement, you should find that the two plates begin to disconnect at the edge facing *away* from the brick separator tools. The forces you are applying—along the top surface of the upper plate and along the bottom surface of the lower plate—quickly create a gap at one edge of the two plates that generally allows the two pieces to separate from each other.

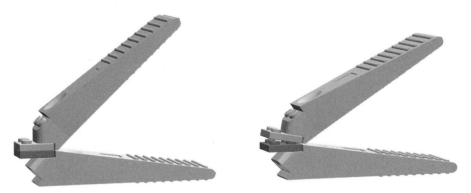

Figure 13-13: Two brick separators working to take apart two 2×2 plates. Gently squeezing the two handles is usually enough to quickly separate even the most stubborn pieces.

Perhaps your problem isn't two small parts stuck together, but rather one small part firmly affixed to a larger one. Take the case of a 1×2 plate stuck in the middle of a 4×6 plate, as shown in Figure 13-14.

Figure 13-14: Sooner or later you'll find yourself faced with the task of trying to remove a 1×2, like the one shown here, from the middle of a much larger piece.

A single brick separator can be of great use here; it can simply apply a bit of leverage so you can free the little piece. In Figure 13-15, I've included a close-up shot that shows the separator working its magic.

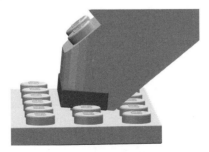

Figure 13-15: The brick separator's unique design allows it to get close to the 1×2 plate and then lever it away from the larger plate beneath it.

Of course, it goes without saying that you can also use these separation techniques when you are constructing a new model for those times you put two pieces together and then quickly change your mind.

Also remember that not having a brick separator doesn't mean stuck pieces have to remain like that forever. Take a look at Figure 13-16 for another example of how to separate such pieces. This time, I'm using two 1×2 plates. Because the plates are so small, it's often hard to use your fingers to separate them. Instead of scratching away with your fingernails at the joint between them, try placing a 1×2 brick on the top and bottom of the plate combination.

Figure 13-16: 1×2 bricks on top and bottom of two 1×2 plates. This easy solution uses pieces you already have.

The bricks now give you enough leverage to cause a small separation between the plates. This is very similar to how the brick separator works; the gap that forms is usually enough to allow you to then separate the plates completely.

You can also use a brick instead of the separator in the other example I noted earlier—the one where you have a small plate stuck in the middle of a larger plate. To make this work, put the brick on top of the 1×2 plate (as demonstrated in Figure 13-17), and gently apply downward pressure as you tilt the brick toward the surface of the larger plate. If you do this without lifting up on the brick, you should find that the 1×2 plate loosens sufficiently from the studs of the 4×6 plate.

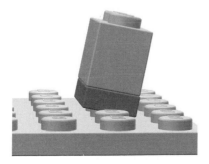

Figure 13-17: Here a standard 1×2 brick is being substituted for a brick separator.

Non-LEGO Tools

I mentioned earlier that *some* of the tools we'd talk about in this chapter are made from LEGO, but that must mean some are not. The ones that are not might be things you already own; you just haven't put them to use in LEGO building yet.

An example is a simple ruler. You may wish to measure part of your model, in real terms, inches or centimeters, especially if you are dealing with building something to a particular scale. We talked about scale at length in Chapter 3, so this next example should be easy to follow.

Suppose you are building a model of your favorite die cast metal car. You've measured the wheels on the real car and they are almost exactly one-half the size of the smallest wheels you have in your LEGO collection. So you can build a LEGO model, using those wheels and based on that car, so it is twice the scale of the die cast car. (You know from further discussion of scale in Chapter 5 that this is a 2:1 scale model.) That means that everything you put on the car (roof, hood, doors, and so on) should also be twice as long and wide as the real thing. By using just an ordinary ruler, you achieve the result you are hoping for. Once again, tools don't have to be complicated to be extremely effective.

A basic protractor (Figure 13-18) may also be handy from time to time, especially when you are trying to replicate things like large, arched structures or the roof of a building. (I talked about creating simulated arches using inverted slopes, near the end of Chapter 3.) If you are able to find a picture of the thing you are building, or if you can take one of your own, you can then use the photo as a reference document. Hold the protractor up to the arch or shape you want to re-create to find out the angle at which it curves or rises. Then, as you build the LEGO version, use the protractor again to see that your angles match those of the building that is the inspiration.

Both the ruler and the protractor aren't really so much tools that you use to build the model as they are devices you use to transfer measurements and ideas from the original source material to your own work.

If you're building a really large model involving a lot of 2×N bricks (perhaps a castle or a tall tower) you may want to think about getting a non-marking rubber mallet. These are available at hardware or home improvement stores and probably have an off-white colored head. That head is important; it's the part you don't want to be leaving marks on your bricks. You will want to stay away from the black rubber mallets for this reason. To use this tool, simply set the bricks down in the way they are to be connected. Give them enough of a downward push with your fingers so that you know that the studs are matched up. Then gently (keyword = *gently*) tap them into place with the mallet. This isn't so much a technique that will improve your building skills as it is one that might save some skin from being worn off your fingertips during long construction sessions.

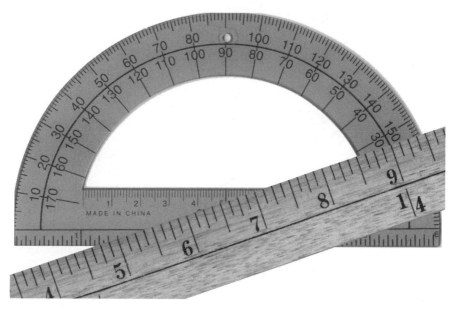

Figure 13-18: A protractor and a ruler—two basic measurement tools that can help you achieve accuracy in almost anything you build

Other Useful Items

Though not specifically used for building models, you may find a couple of other things handy to have on or around your building area. I've listed them below and then included a picture of them in Figure 13-19.

Pencil and paper

Nothing beats good old-fashioned pencil and paper when it comes to sketching out an idea for a model or maybe writing down a list of parts you need to make it. If you're sketching out plans for a model, you might want to use some of the Design Grids discussed in Appendix B of this book, or you may just want to draw freehand on some plain paper.

Calculator

You may find times when your brain just needs some help. This could be when you have to figure out a particular scale (as we discussed in Chapters 3, 4, 5, and 6), or it might just be when you want to make some rough calculations about how many bricks you'll need for a particular project.

Paintbrush

If you're going to use a paintbrush, preferably use one that's never seen paint before. Look for one that is an inch or perhaps an inch and half wide. These are great for dusting models on display or partly built models after they have been sitting on your build table for a few days.

Small zip-closure bags

These are useful for storing small parts either during a build or after you've taken a model apart.

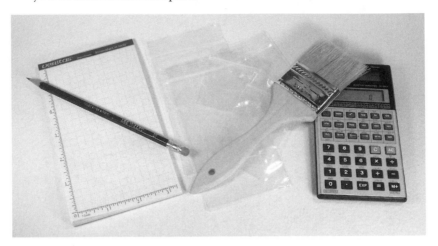

Figure 13-19: Some items you might find useful to have in or around your work area

Review: The Right Tools for the Job

The most important lesson to take from this chapter is to simply surround yourself with the tools, of any description, that help you build as easily as possible. They might include devices made from LEGO that help you build or take apart models more easily, or they might be other tools or objects that help you organize your thoughts and make plans to build models of your own design. Use only the tools you're comfortable with, but use them freely. They will add enjoyment to your building sessions and, in turn, enhance your enjoyment of the hobby itself.

A

BRICKOPEDIA

The LEGO system is made up of thousands of
elements. You've already seen many of them used
and/or described throughout this book. Some are
different sizes of the same type of piece (for example
2×3 and 2×4 are two different sizes of standard bricks),
whereas others are exactly the same size but have different decorations
or patterns printed on them. To catalog every piece in the system would
require an entire book. However, at the same time, it's useful to try to
capture a sense of the various sizes, shapes, and configurations of pieces
that exist. To that end, I have included illustrations of nearly 300 elements
in this Brickopedia. They cover the range from basic bricks, slopes, and
plates, to specialized elements, arches, and even a number of decorative
elements.

I have categorized the Brickopedia from the perspective of building with
LEGO pieces. As a result, I suggest that you do not use the Brickopedia to
plan purchases of LEGO pieces from any type of store either online or at a
real location; its categories and terminology may not match. Also, this
catalog is not suitable as a device with which to record the contents of official

LEGO sets because they may contain specialty parts I have not listed here. In other words, some of the categories and descriptions used here are unique to this text.

Instead, my hope is that this Brickopedia is a tool that you can use (most specifically offline, without the use of a computer) to help categorize, organize, and utilize your most common and most useful elements. As noted, this does not cover the entire spectrum of available LEGO pieces. Rather, it focuses exclusively on standard, common, and highly reusable elements, thus helping you acquire a core knowledge of the LEGO system and its most important aspects.

Brickopedia Breakdown

Each category has a separate entry for each element that contains several pieces of information. The Brickopedia notation system is shown in Figure A-1.

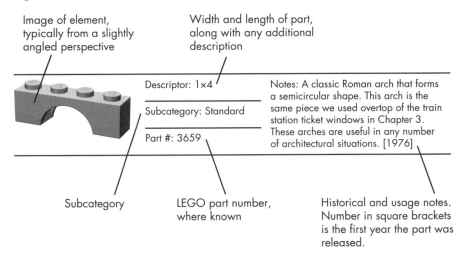

Image of element, typically from a slightly angled perspective

Width and length of part, along with any additional description

Descriptor: 1×4

Subcategory: Standard

Part #: 3659

Notes: A classic Roman arch that forms a semicircular shape. This arch is the same piece we used overtop of the train station ticket windows in Chapter 3. These arches are useful in any number of architectural situations. [1976]

Subcategory

LEGO part number, where known

Historical and usage notes. Number in square brackets is the first year the part was released.

Figure A-1: A sample Brickopedia entry

This information is not intended to value the parts, but only to hint at why you may or may not have certain pieces in your own collection.

I have kept the categories and subcategories lean and have made every attempt to use titles that suggest the nature of the pieces. Where possible, I have cataloged similar parts together to show their relationship. For example, I show standard and inverted slopes of the same size on the same page. This is different than many other categorization systems used for LEGO elements.

The Brickopedia divides LEGO elements into several broad categories; within each of these areas are subcategories that help refine the way pieces are classified (see Table A-1). The following tables (Tables A-2 through A-11) describe the major categories and subcategories. This information may be useful when you are sorting and storing your LEGO pieces and also when you are building with them. It may also give you a better sense of how the whole system works together, one part at a time.

Table A-1: LEGO Elements Categories and Subcategories

Category	Subcategory	Description
Bricks	Standard	Rectangular sides, same height as a 1×1 brick.
	Adapted	Irregular sides/shape or taller than a standard 1×1.
Plates	Standard	Square or rectangular shape, same height as a 1×1 plate.
	Adapted	Irregular sides/shape. "Quarter cut" or "diamond cut" describe pieces that can be put together to form a circle or a diamond shape, respectively.
	Bow	One edge has symmetrical angles cut away whereas the opposite edge is straight or indented in the center.
	Wing	Come in left and right varieties, shaped like airplane wings.
Slopes	Standard	The angled face is generally on the top portion of the element.
	Inverted	The angled face is generally on the underside of the element.
	Peaks	Two or more angled faces meet at the top of the element. When in place, there are no exposed studs.
	Compound	Two or more flat-angled faces.
	Curved	Angled faces have a curve.
Specialized Elements	Junctions	Elements that have studs on their sides or have a portion of themselves that is perpendicular to another part. These pieces allow you to make a bend or a change in shape in a model where they create a junction of two or more pieces.
	Odd Face	Elements that have one or more faces that are irregularly shaped, contoured, or textured.
	Hinges/Turntables	Hinges are bricks or plates that meet at a flexible joint. Turntables allow attached elements to rotate.
	Pin-Enabled	Bricks or plates with a Technic-style pin attached on one or more sides, the top, or the bottom, or elements capable of accepting a pin.
	Wheels/Tires	Pieces that add motion to vehicles.
Technic	Bricks	Pieces similar to standard bricks, but with axle holes running through them.
	Plates	Identical to standard plates except that there are axle holes inserted between the studs.

Table A-1: LEGO Elements Categories and Subcategories (continued)

Category	Subcategory	Description
Technic, continued	Beams	Elements with axle holes running through them but lacking traditional studs.
	Gears	Parts that function exactly as metal gears found in clocks, bicycles, and other real machines.
	Pins/Axles	Thin shafts used to mount gears and wheels onto Technic elements or connect Technic elements to each other.
	Bushings	Elements used to keep axles in place.
	Couplers	Pieces that connect two or more axles, often providing a change of angle between the axles.
Arches	Standard	A single piece that creates a complete arch shape.
	Half Standard	A piece that forms only half of the complete arch shape. Studs are on top as they are with the standard variety.
	Half Inverted	A piece that forms only half of the complete arch shape. Tubes are on the bottom, and no studs are showing. The arch shape is effectively on top of the element.
Tiles and Panels	Tiles	Flat elements that are the same height as a plate but that have no exposed studs.
	Panels	Thin elements that can create a division without occupying the same space as a full-width brick.
Cylinders and Cones	Cylinders	Elements with a cylindrical shape that resembles a coffee can or a drum.
	Cones	Elements shaped like upside-down ice cream cones.
Baseplates	Brickplates	Baseplates that are one full brick in height and have dimensions of 8×16 studs or larger.
	Waffleplates	Any of the thin baseplates with waffled undersides that do not accept studs.
Decorative	Fences, Rails, and Rungs	Latticework or ladder-like elements that can be used as fences, grilles, hand rails, and so on.
	Bars, Clips, and Elements with Handles	Bars are the diameter of a minifig hand and the clips are any bricks or plates capable of holding them in place. Handled elements are those where the bar-sized portion is attached to an otherwise standard piece.
	Foliage	Any element representing or appearing to be flowers, trees, shrubs, or any other greenery.
	Doors/Windows	Self-explanatory.

Table A-2: The Bricks Category

	Descriptor: 1×1	Notes: This part is the basis of the LEGO system as laid out in this book. Measurements and categorization of other parts are based on its 1×1 size. It is also the second most common part in existence. Just don't step on it barefoot in the dark! [1958]
	Subcategory: Standard	
	Part #: 3005	
	Descriptor: 1×2	Notes: The most common part in the entire system, having been used in more than 3,000 different official sets. Mosaics, sculptures, minifig scale buildings, and just about every other thing you build will probably include some of these. [1958]
	Subcategory: Standard	
	Part #: 3004	
	Descriptor: 1×3	Notes: Something of an oddball simply because of its uneven number of studs. However, never overlook three-stud-long parts, simply because not every model or structure is always an even number of studs. [1969]
	Subcategory: Standard	
	Part #: 3622	
	Descriptor: 1×4	Notes: Like its half-size cousin, the 1×2, this part is common and very effective in a variety of situations. On the list of most common parts, this one shows up at number five. You should find lots of these in your collection. [1967]
	Subcategory: Standard	
	Part #: 3010	
	Descriptor: 1×6	Notes: A short stretcher-style brick. Not as common as the 1×4 but not rare either. Extremely useful for creating large sections of walls for minifig-scale dwellings or the walls of macroscale bricks. [1958]
	Subcategory: Standard	
	Part #: 3009	
	Descriptor: 1×8	Notes: A longer stretcher-style brick. Not as common as the 1×4 but not rare either. Like the 1×6, it is very useful for quickly extending walls of minifig buildings. [1958]
	Subcategory: Standard	
	Part #: 3008	

	Descriptor: 1×10	Notes: A fairly new addition to the standard 1×N bricks. Not as common as the 1×8 but not rare either. Longer walls become short work with a long brick like this. [1993]
	Subcategory: Standard	
	Part #: 6111	
	Descriptor: 1×12	Notes: The second longest 1×N brick, because at the time of writing, a 1×14 brick does not exist. Uncommon in smaller sets. It provides a huge overlap for smaller bricks resulting in a stronger model. [1993]
	Subcategory: Standard	
	Part #: 6112	
	Descriptor: 1×16	Notes: Not often found in smaller sets, but if you can get your hands on some, you'll probably find them useful as your own projects grow more complicated. [1988]
	Subcategory: Standard	
	Part #: 2465	
	Descriptor: 2×2	Notes: The "stubby" is another brick that is sometimes overlooked. Several 2×2's can be placed where needed, then tied together with a lesser numbers of larger bricks. It is also the third most common part in the LEGO system. [1958]
	Subcategory: Standard	
	Part #: 3003	
	Descriptor: 2×3	Notes: As is true with the 1×3, this brick is far more functional than you might think. Time and again you'll run across situations requiring pieces of unequal length. Two of them together equal a 2×6—obvious, but easy to forget. [1958]
	Subcategory: Standard	
	Part #: 3002	
	Descriptor: 2×4	Notes: The characteristic 2×4 is often the first brick people think of when discussing LEGO pieces. Introduced with the earliest bricks in 1958, it continues to be a core building element. You can never own too many of these. [1958]
	Subcategory: Standard	
	Part #: 3001	
	Descriptor: 2×6	Notes: A midsized beam that seems to show up in a lot of assorted tubs and buckets. Despite its rather common length, it's interesting to note its late arrival into the system. You might have expected it to be around from the beginning. [1990]
	Subcategory: Standard	
	Part #: 2456	

Descriptor: 2×8	Notes: This beam-like brick has been around since the beginning. It was first seen in the late 1950s when the stud and tube connection mechanism was first patented. [1958]
Subcategory: Standard	
Part #: 3007	
Descriptor: 2×10	Notes: Another one of the original elements that first helped define the modern LEGO system of building. Useful for bracing large models or for finishing a wall above windows or doors. [1958]
Subcategory: Standard	
Part #: 3006	
Descriptor: 4×6	Notes: First seen in the mid-1990s but is more common in some sets released after the year 2000. One of only three standard bricks that are four studs wide. [1995]
Subcategory: Standard	
Part #: 2356	
Descriptor: 4×10	Notes: Introduced the same year as the 4×6 brick. Tends to show up in assorted tubs and buckets. [1995]
Subcategory: Standard	
Part #: 6212	
Descriptor: 4×12	Notes: Seen a few times during the early 1980s but then not again routinely until the mid 1990s. A relatively uncommon brick. [1981]
Subcategory: Standard	
Part #: 4202	
Descriptor: 2×2 elbow	Notes: One of the so-called "elbow" pieces. Handy for shoring up the corner of a wall where columns of stacked pieces come together. Although it's the same pattern as the 4×4 elbow, the smaller version didn't arrive until the late 1980s. [1987]
Subcategory: Adapted	
Part #: 2357	
Descriptor: 4×4 elbow	Notes: This brick is included simply as a comparison to the newer smaller 2×2 elbow. The larger version has not been seen in regular sets for more than 35 years. Sounds like it's about time for it to reappear. What a handy element this would be. [1958]
Subcategory: Adapted	
Part #: 702	

	Descriptor: 3×3 diamond cut Subcategory: Adapted Part #: 30505	Notes: The descriptor lists this piece as being diamond cut because if you arrange four of them with their longest sides together, you get a somewhat diamond-shaped pattern. It's curious that this piece exists but that there isn't a 3×3 standard brick. [2001]
	Descriptor: 3×3 zig zag Subcategory: Adapted Part #: 2462	Notes: Depending on which way this brick faces, it can provide texture because of its indented side. The reverse side gives a realistic bevel to a square corner where two walls meet. [1988]
	Descriptor: 2×3 left beveled Subcategory: Adapted Part #: 6565	Notes: In some cases it's useful to look at two elements as a pair of similar pieces. That is certainly true when you're talking about these two beveled elements. Introduced in the mid-1990s, they can be used on cars, planes, spaceships, and the like to help contour the body providing greater realism than traditional bricks that always meet at 90-degree angles. Also available in the larger sizes 41767 and 41768. [1994]
	Descriptor: 2×3 right beveled Subcategory: Adapted Part #: 6564	
	Descriptor: 2×4 left beveled Subcategory: Adapted Part #: 41768	Notes: Although the 2×3 versions of these pieces were found in sets around 1994, the longer 2×4 versions shown here didn't arrive until 2002. As with virtually all parts of the LEGO system, they remain fully compatible and, in fact, the longer and shorter types work well together to create subtle shapes and angles on your models. [2002]
	Descriptor: 2×4 right beveled Subcategory: Adapted Part #: 41767	

Table A-3: The Plates Category

	Descriptor: 1×1	Notes: At one time LEGO referred to plates as "slim bricks," and you can see why—they are much shorter than regular bricks. Although the 1×1 pictured here looks enormous, it's really not much bigger than the stud on top of it. That makes it one of the smallest elements in the system. [1963]
	Subcategory: Standard	
	Part #: 3024	
	Descriptor: 1×2	Notes: Ranked at number four when talking about the most common parts, this element also ranks highly when you're talking about the most useful parts. Don't let its small size fool you—this part has a tremendous number of possibilities. [1963]
	Subcategory: Standard	
	Part #: 3023	
	Descriptor: 1×3	Notes: As important and useful as the 1×3 standard brick. Pieces with odd numbers of studs are relatively uncommon. For instance, there is no 1×5- or 1×7-sized brick or plate. [1977]
	Subcategory: Standard	
	Part #: 3623	
	Descriptor: 1×4	Notes: Ranks at number nine on the list of most common parts. You can never have enough small-sized bricks or plates. Interestingly, this very common part was not one of the original elements released in 1958. [1975]
	Subcategory: Standard	
	Part #: 3710	
	Descriptor: 1×6	Notes: This piece may have arrived as early as 1969 but was only seen in one set. It came into regular usage around 1977. It's amazing that such a common-sized piece wouldn't have been available right from the start. [1977]
	Subcategory: Standard	
	Part #: 3666	
	Descriptor: 1×8	Notes: Although available sooner than the 1×6, it is still interesting to note that this piece did not come into being until the early 1970s—more than a decade after the launch of the modern system. [1972]
	Subcategory: Standard	
	Part #: 3460	

Table A-3: The Plates Category (continued)

	Descriptor: 1×10	Notes: If it were any longer, a 1×N plate might start to have too much flexibility. Among the standard plates, this piece is one of the less common, though it is by no means rare. [1983]
	Subcategory: Standard	
	Part #: 4477	
	Descriptor: 2×2	Notes: The plate version of the 2×2 stubby brick. This was one of a number of different plates to first appear in the early 1960s. [1963]
	Subcategory: Standard	
	Part #: 3022	
	Descriptor: 2×3	Notes: This one rounds out the list of basic elements with an odd number of studs on one side. Its usefulness will reveal itself as you advance to models that require pieces that aren't always an even number of studs. [1963]
	Subcategory: Standard	
	Part #: 3021	
	Descriptor: 2×4	Notes: The plate version of the venerable 2×4 brick. A piece that has appeared in more than 2,500 different sets over the years. This is another case where it's hard to imagine the system without this piece. [1963]
	Subcategory: Standard	
	Part #: 3020	
	Descriptor: 2×6	Notes: Like its 2×6 brick counterpart, this element is used to bridge the gap between elements four studs and shorter and those that are eight studs or more. It can therefore end up in models of all sizes and shapes. [1969]
	Subcategory: Standard	
	Part #: 3795	
	Descriptor: 2×8	Notes: In the late 1950s and early 1960s, this part, among others, was available as one of the early parts packs. The availability of bulk parts has waxed and waned over the years, but it seems to be on the increase again. [1958]
	Subcategory: Standard	
	Part #: 3034	
	Descriptor: 2×10	Notes: What about making a roof with a gentle slope by staggering a number of plates? You can do that, and when you do, this piece will come in handy for covering lots of real estate all at once. [1977]
	Subcategory: Standard	
	Part #: 3832	

	Descriptor: 2×12	Notes: Like the 3832, this piece helps build plate roofs among other things. And just like the 1×12 standard brick, this piece represents the second longest element in its category. In other words, there is no 2×14 plate. Not sure why, but there isn't. [1987]
	Subcategory: Standard	
	Part #: 2445	
	Descriptor: 2×16	Notes: Sometimes there is a limit to just how long a piece can be. In this case, 2×16 is probably getting close to that limit. Like the 1×10 plate, it's easy to imagine that anything longer than 2×16 might become too prone to bending and breaking. [1984]
	Subcategory: Standard	
	Part #: 4282	
	Descriptor: 4×4	Notes: Although first introduced in 1969, this part was not seen in wide usage until 1973. It then began appearing in more official LEGO sets. [1969]
	Subcategory: Standard	
	Part #: 3031	
	Descriptor: 4×6	Notes: This piece was introduced in 1970 and was featured in a number of sets that first year. [1970]
	Subcategory: Standard	
	Part #: 3032	
	Descriptor: 4×8	Notes: The first year of the modern system featured only two larger plates. The first was this part and the second was the 6×8 plate. [1958]
	Subcategory: Standard	
	Part #: 3035	
	Descriptor: 4×10	Notes: Nice to use when you want to build small minifig vehicles. You can simply attach wheels underneath and then build a passenger cab on top. [1969]
	Subcategory: Standard	
	Part #: 3030	
	Descriptor: 4×12	Notes: Long minifig vehicle or short section of a much larger wing of a much bigger aircraft? You decide. Also handy for filling in sections of floors for buildings. [1967]
	Subcategory: Standard	
	Part #: 3029	
	Descriptor: 6×6	Notes: Square plates start as small as the 1×1. There are, of course, also 2×2 and 4×4 plates. For many years, the 6×6 was the largest of the perfectly square plates. It is now joined by the 8×8 plate. [1978]
	Subcategory: Standard	
	Part #: 3958	

Table A-3: The Plates Category (continued)

	Descriptor: 6×8 Subcategory: Standard Part #: 3036	Notes: The second of the two larger plates featured in sets released during the first full year of the modern system. [1958]
	Descriptor: 6×10 Subcategory: Standard Part #: 3033	Notes: The late 1960s and early 1970s brought us several welcome additions to the 6×N-plate family. The next five parts were all released within 5 years of each other. [1971]
	Descriptor: 6×12 Subcategory: Standard Part #: 3028	Notes: Another of the 6×N plates released between 1967 and 1975. [1967]
	Descriptor: 6×14 Subcategory: Standard Part #: 3456	Notes: How strange that neither a 1×14 brick nor a 2×14 plate exist and yet here is a 6×14 plate. This just goes to show that the LEGO system is organic enough to allow for these little oddities and yet maintain its functional side at the same time. [1972]
	Descriptor: 6×16 Subcategory: Standard Part #: 3027	Notes: This plate is good for making train cars, fire trucks, and maybe even a piece of a roof made from plates attached to hinges. [1967]
	Descriptor: 6×24 Subcategory: Standard Part #: 3026	Notes: Transport trucks, train cars, or even airplane wings all benefit from the availability of such a long, wide plate. [1967]
	Descriptor: 8×8 Subcategory: Standard Part #: 41539	Notes: The largest of the perfectly square plates . . . for now. Is there a 10×10 plate on the horizon? You never know. [2001]
	Descriptor: 2×2 elbow Subcategory: Adapted Part #: 2420	Notes: Can't figure out how to tie together two 1×N walls at a corner? Maybe you've used the stacking technique and now need to hold two sections together. The 2×2 elbow may be just what you need. [1987]

Table A-3: The Plates Category (continued)

	Descriptor: 4×4 elbow	Notes: It's interesting to observe that although the 4×4 elbow is only 2 studs longer on each side than the 2×2, it has nine more studs. This gives it a greater surface area and allows it to hold together larger sections that meet at a vertical seam. [1991]
	Subcategory: Adapted	
	Part #: 2639	
	Descriptor: 2×3 hitch	Notes: Can be built into a trailer hitch or used as a connection for Technic pins. Its curve matches a 2×2 cylindrical brick or plate. [1967]
	Subcategory: Adapted	
	Part #: 3176	
	Descriptor: 3×3 quarter cut	Notes: Useful for rounding corners of wings, fenders, or even walls. [1999]
	Subcategory: Adapted	
	Part #: 30357	
	Descriptor: 4×4 quarter cut	Notes: The only one of the three quarter-cut plates that forms a circle when you place four of them with their flat sides together. [2001]
	Subcategory: Adapted	
	Part #: 30565	
	Descriptor: 6×6 quarter cut	Notes: This larger quarter-cut plate can create shapely balconies for minifig apartments or other structures where a large, rounded corner is an important feature. [1992]
	Subcategory: Adapted	
	Part #: 6003	
	Descriptor: 3×3 diamond cut	Notes: Four of these pieces, placed with their longest sides together, form a multifaceted diamond shape. This is a pattern you might not always use—they are handy in pairs or alone—but it's always good to remember the potential combinations. [1988]
	Subcategory: Adapted	
	Part #: 2450	
	Descriptor: 4×4 diamond cut	Notes: The diamond-cut family grew in 2001 with the addition of the 4×4 version. This piece is handy for helping to define complex shapes of wings on planes and the like. [2001]
	Subcategory: Adapted	
	Part #: 30503	

	Descriptor: 6×6 diamond cut	Notes: Observe the subtle difference between this diamond-cut element and the others in its subcategory. On the 6×6 version, there are two studs at each of the smallest pointed ends, rather than one, like on the other pieces. [1995]
	Subcategory: Adapted	
	Part #: 6106	

	Descriptor: 8×8 diamond cut	Notes: Big pieces can be beautiful too. This monster diamond-cut plate has been seen making up part of the wings of a space shuttle and it can certainly add a similar shape to your models. [2001]
	Subcategory: Adapted	
	Part #: 30504	

	Descriptor: 3×4	Notes: This piece predates the 2×3 wing plates (43722 and 43723), but it forms essentially the same shape as a pair of them put together. The nose portion of airplanes, helicopters, and so on are just a few uses for this little plate. [1985]
	Subcategory: Bow	
	Part #: 4859	

	Descriptor: 4×4	Notes: As with the 4859 above, this piece is roughly the same shape as a pair of similarly sized wing plates. The biggest difference here is the 2×2-cutout section into which you can put a minifig pilot's seat or an internal substructure. [2003]
	Subcategory: Bow	
	Part #: 43719	

	Descriptor: 3×6	Notes: Calling this a bow plate simply describes its shape; it doesn't limit its function. This piece could just as easily be the stern of a small ship or winglets on the sides of a small landing craft launched from a larger spaceship. [1987]
	Subcategory: Bow	
	Part #: 2419	

	Descriptor: 4×6	Notes: Although this is a bow plate by definition, its shape is also suggestive of the stern of a ship or perhaps a small deck area jutting out from the side of such a vessel. [1998]
	Subcategory: Bow	
	Part #: 32059	

	Descriptor: 2×3 left	Notes: In the Brickopedia, I consider wing plates to be any plate elements that individually have the shape of a scalene triangle. In other words, each of their three sides is a different length. Additionally, wing plates must come in pairs that, when arranged with their two shortest sides together, form the shape of a pair of airplane wings. The exact shape may not be perfectly aerodynamic, but as long as they give the sense of wings, they fit into this category. [2002]
	Subcategory: Wing	
	Part #: 43723	
	Descriptor: 2×3 right	
	Subcategory: Wing	
	Part #: 43722	
	Descriptor: 2×4 left	Notes: These two pieces, when used together, cover the same area as the 43719 bow plate. In fact, they cover slightly more, because they don't have the 2×2 area cut out from the inside. The drawback of using them as a substitute is that you need to make sure they are held together tightly by other elements. With the similarly shaped bow plate, the opposite is true—it can be used to hold other elements stable. [2001]
	Subcategory: Wing	
	Part #: 41770	
	Descriptor: 2×4 right	
	Subcategory: Wing	
	Part #: 41769	
	Descriptor: 4×4 left	Notes: I must admit a personal fondness for these stubby little wings. They were part of a model that was released with the classic space sets back in the late 1970s, and it was such a model that holds great memories for me. In that model, two pairs of these pieces were used, with the second piece on each side fitting nicely into the notch that you see in each of the pieces. This creates an unbroken edge that makes for great wing shapes. [1979]
	Subcategory: Wing	
	Part #: 3936	
	Descriptor: 4×4 right	
	Subcategory: Wing	
	Part #: 3935	

Table A-3: The Plates Category (continued)

	Descriptor: 4×8 left	Notes: This pair of wing plates were also seen in some of the early classic space sets. They have the same basic size and shape near the notch, but they then extend out twice as long as the 4×4's shown above. Of course, just because they're called "wing" plates doesn't mean that's the only role they can fill in your models. [1978]
	Subcategory: Wing	
	Part #: 3933	
	Descriptor: 4×8 right	
	Subcategory: Wing	
	Part #: 3934	
	Descriptor: 6×12 left	Notes: Classic space sets gave us two classic shaped wing plates, both of which are shown here. Twenty years later, sets based on a blockbuster movie franchise gave rise to what are sure to become classic plates in their own right. The 6×12's shown here are long enough to be the only piece you need to form the entire wing for many minifig-scale ships. [1999]
	Subcategory: Wing	
	Part #: 30355	
	Descriptor: 6×12 right	
	Subcategory: Wing	
	Part #: 30356	

Table A-4: The Slopes Category

	Descriptor: 4×2 18 degree	Notes: One of the newest elements in the slope family is also one of the lowest. In fact, as of this writing, this is the only size of 18-degree slope currently available. Imagine entire roofs made from this slightly angled slope. [1999]
	Subcategory: Standard	
	Part #: 30363	
	Descriptor: 2×2 33 degree	Notes: The early 1970s ushered in a whole new series of sloped pieces— these were raked at 33 degrees as opposed to the 45-degree ones that preceded them. This particular example is a peak element that typically caps off a sloped roof. [1971]
	Subcategory: Peak	
	Part #: 3300	

	Descriptor: 2×4 33 degree	Notes: The longer of the two 33-degree peaks. Although the 33-degree slopes are available in odd-numbered widths (one and three studs), the peaks come only in even-numbered lengths. [1971]
	Subcategory: Peak	
	Part #: 3299	
	Descriptor: 3×1 33 degree	Notes: It wasn't until the early 1980s that 33-degree roofs with odd lengths became possible. However, it wasn't the 3×1 slope shown here that gave us that opportunity; it was the 3×3 shown further along in the Brickopedia. [1982]
	Subcategory: Standard	
	Part #: 4286	
	Descriptor: 3×1 33 degree	Notes: It was noted in Chapter 1 that many standard slopes have matching inverted varieties. We see one here for the first time. The 3×1 inverted slope is a near mirror image of part 4286. [1982]
	Subcategory: Inverted	
	Part #: 4287	
	Descriptor: 3×2 33 degree	Notes: Among the first of the 33-degree slopes to be released in the early 1970s. Commonly referred to as *roof bricks*, they are certainly used in that context. But as with most elements they are never limited to just one use. [1971]
	Subcategory: Standard	
	Part #: 3298	
	Descriptor: 3×2 33 degree	Notes: The undersides of boats, pontoons, airplanes, and more all benefit from inverted slopes like this. Although the 3×1 slope was released in both standard and inverted styles in the same year, the 3×2 standard had to wait 8 years for its inverted match. [1979]
	Subcategory: Inverted	
	Part #: 3747	

Descriptor: 3×3 33 degree	Notes: Allowed roofs to be made at a 33-degree slant with odd numbers of studs for the first time. [1980]
Subcategory: Standard	
Part #: 4161	

Descriptor: 3×3 33 degree	Notes: Surely one of the more graceful looking slope elements. Low-angle, pagoda-style roofs just wouldn't be complete without this corner piece. [1980]
Subcategory: Outer Corner	
Part #: 3675	

Descriptor: 3×4 33 degree	Notes: As a kid, these were the parts I thought of as roof bricks. I had many of them in classic red. They remain an effective element to this day. [1971]
Subcategory: Standard	
Part #: 3297	

Descriptor: 2×1 45 degree	Notes: This peak can stand alone, capping off fences, castle walls, or even the backs of dinosaurs, or it can become part of the peak of a standard 45-degree roof. [1976]
Subcategory: Peak	
Part #: 3044	

Descriptor: 1×2 45 degree	Notes: A perfect companion for the 2×1 peak shown in the previous entry. This piece can be used to finish off the end of a row of peak elements. [1965]
Subcategory: End Peak	
Part #: 3048	

Descriptor: 1×2 45 degree	Notes: Used for those cases where one peak meets another peak or a portion of sloped roof. The side facing front butts up against a piece like 3043 or against other 45-degree slopes. [1969]
Subcategory: End Peak	
Part #: 3049	

Table A-4: The Slopes Category (continued)

	Descriptor: 2×1 45 degree	Notes: Perhaps the only unusual thing about this element is that it was introduced to the system three years *after* its inverted counterpart. Of course it goes without saying that it's now a common element that helps round out the system. [1979]
	Subcategory: Standard	
	Part #: 3040	
	Descriptor: 2×1 45 degree	Notes: Useful for creating subtle inverted detail under the nose of a small airplane or the hip portion of a miniland figure; this piece can also help shape many small sculptures. [1976]
	Subcategory: Inverted	
	Part #: 3665	
	Descriptor: 2×2 45 degree	Notes: Standard 45-degree peak. It matches and uses the 3048 element to create a contoured roof. [1965]
	Subcategory: Peak	
	Part #: 3043	
	Descriptor: 2×2 45 degree	Notes: One of the earliest slopes to be introduced to the modern system, although it's important to point out that these weren't there from the beginning. Roofs in the late 1950s and early 1960s had to depend primarily on staggered bricks to form their slope. [1965]
	Subcategory: Standard	
	Part #: 3039	
	Descriptor: 2×2 45 degree	Notes: The inverted match to 3039. When you look down at the top of elements like this, you'll notice that part of the top is open and that some of the studs are actually hollow, like tubes sticking out of a small open box. [1975]
	Subcategory: Inverted	
	Part #: 3660	

	Descriptor: 2×2 45 degree	Notes: Another graceful slope element. Though this piece could also be considered a compound slope, it is probably best described as an outer corner because that's the portion of a roof it will most often become. [1965]
	Subcategory: Outer Corner	
	Part #: 3045	
	Descriptor: 2×2 45 degree	Notes: What happens when two sections of roof meet? Simple—you just need to join them together with an inside-corner slope like this. This is a unique piece in many ways because there is currently no similar element in any of the other angles. [1965]
	Subcategory: Inner Corner	
	Part #: 3046	
	Descriptor: 2×2 45 degree	Notes: You can find many uses for this piece, not the least of which is creating a turret effect near the top of a castle tower. [1984]
	Subcategory: Inverted Outer Corner	
	Part #: 3676	
	Descriptor: 2×3 45 degree	Notes: You can never have too many elements with odd numbers of studs. This piece is no exception. [1965]
	Subcategory: Standard	
	Part #: 3038	
	Descriptor: 2×3 45 degree	Notes: A peak element that's three studs long? Not common, but they do exist. [1965]
	Subcategory: Peak	
	Part #: 3042	
	Descriptor: 2×4 45 degree	Notes: If you're building a roof of any significant size, you'll need longer slopes like this one to cover the bulk of the surface. [1965]
	Subcategory: Standard	
	Part #: 3037	

Descriptor: 2×2×2 65 degree	Notes: Though this element was originally released without a center tube inside, a newer version appeared in 2003 that did include this important feature. This is also currently the only piece that is raked at 65 degrees. [1978]	
Subcategory: Standard		
Part #: 3678		

Descriptor: 2×2×2 75 degree	Notes: No, it's not a dunce cap for square-headed people; it's an interesting and very steep peak element. This is useful for everything from castle towers to Santa hats. Although the other 75-degree slopes are three bricks high, this one is only two. [1986]	
Subcategory: Peak		
Part #: 3688		

Descriptor: 2×1×3 75 degree	Notes: Yet another piece commonly found in castle walls, but also the perfect angle for the rear end of a classic style of fire truck. [1984]	
Subcategory: Standard		
Part #: 4460		

Descriptor: 2×1×3 75 degree	Notes: Currently the only 75-degree inverted element. Its interesting feature is that the entire face opposite the sloped side is hollow so that it accepts studs at a 90-degree angle. [1988]	
Subcategory: Inverted		
Part #: 2449		

	Descriptor: 2×2×3 75 degree	Notes: A solid piece in both look and structure. This is perfect for the lower walls of any castle or any other building that requires a sturdy foundation. [1977]
	Subcategory: Standard	
	Part #: 3684	
	Descriptor: 2×2×3 75 degree	Notes: A perfect match for the 3684 and 4460. This one gives you the angles you need to create a corner. You can even use 75-degree slopes to create a very steep roof, perhaps for a ski chalet. [1978]
	Subcategory: Outside Corner	
	Part #: 3685	
	Descriptor: 1×3×2	Notes: A unique new piece that hasn't yet found its way into a large number of sets. Hopefully that will change as the years go by. This element perfectly matches the curve of the 1×3×2 half-arch piece (6005) shown in the arches category. [2003]
	Subcategory: Curved	
	Part #: 33243	
	Descriptor: 3×2 bullnose	Notes: Another element that really has no equal in terms of shape. This element is perfect for giving a more subtle rounded edge to buildings or vehicles. [1995]
	Subcategory: Curved	
	Part #: 6215	

	Descriptor: 2×4 left 45 to 90 degree	Notes: In my mind, these two elements are some of the most interesting to be released in many years. They are unique in that they have the ability to act as intermediaries between standard bricks and 45-degree slopes. That is because one end of each of these left/right elements is a perfect 90 degrees. Then, along its four-stud length, that 90 degrees transforms to 45 degrees, becoming one full stud wider at the base as it does. [2002]
	Subcategory: Curved	
	Part #: 43721	
	Descriptor: 2×4 right 45 to 90 degree	
	Subcategory: Curved	
	Part #: 43720	

	Descriptor: 6×2 left	Notes: Spaceships, airplanes, and other flying machines all became more streamlined with the addition of this pair of pieces to the system. The compound shape—which has a curving slope from tip to studs and a matching curved side—provides a very sleek and realistic shape for traveling machines. [2002]
	Subcategory: Compound	
	Part #: 41748	
	Descriptor: 6×2 right	
	Subcategory: Compound	
	Part #: 41747	

	Descriptor: 6×2 left	Notes: The year 2002 was obviously an important one for new slopes; these two slopes and the four preceding them in this table all made their debut during that year. This pair of elements helps add contours to boats of all sizes, whether as parts of the bow or parts of pontoons to help keep it afloat. They can be used together, side by side, or separated by piece 500 (6×1 curved inverted) to make a wider profile. [2002]
	Subcategory: Compound Inverted	
	Part #: 41765	
	Descriptor: 6×2 right	
	Subcategory: Compound Inverted	
	Part #: 41764	

Table A-4: The Slopes Category (continued)

	Descriptor: 6×1 Subcategory: Curved Part #: 464	Notes: Flat-sided slopes are great, but at times you may want something a little more delicate. These two pieces offer just such a quality. Given their shape, they obviously create a more rounded, and therefore a smoother, angle. [2002]
	Descriptor: 6×1 Subcategory: Curved Inverted Part #: 500	
	Descriptor: 6×2 Subcategory: Curved Part #: 44126	Notes: Matching exactly the slope of part 464, the 6×2 version is also suited for nose cones, wings, and other models that require its gentle arch. [2003]
	Descriptor: 4×4 original style Subcategory: Compound Part #: 4858	Notes: This element is older than the 6069 and is certainly somewhat boxier in the way that its sloped sides meet. [1985]
	Descriptor: 4×4 new style Subcategory: Compound Part #: 6069	Notes: Sometimes new parts come along that make older versions look somewhat dated. Although the 6069 shown here isn't an exact replacement for the 4858, it certainly creates a more sporty projection. [1992]
	Descriptor: 4×4 Subcategory: Compound Inverted Part #: 4855	Notes: Although released at the same time as the 4858 compound slope, this inverted element is a much closer match to the more modern-looking 6069 shown previously. [1985]

Table A-5: The Specialized Elements Category

Image	Details	Notes
	Descriptor: 2×2 macaroni Subcategory: Odd Face Part #: 3063	Notes: Among the most beloved pieces ever produced. Its only real drawback is that it is often difficult or expensive to acquire in large quantities. Maybe someday a bulk pack of these will be available in common colors. [1958]
	Descriptor: 4×4 macaroni Subcategory: Odd Face Part #: 48092	Notes: It's tempting to think that this piece could have been created anytime in the last 40 years, but for whatever reason, it took until 2004 for it to appear. An excellent companion to the original 2×2 macaroni brick. [2004]
	Descriptor: 1×1 with indented stud on one side Subcategory: Junctions Part #: 4070	Notes: The famed headlight brick shown here in two different views—from both the front and the back. Of course front and back are not always important when you're using this piece because it can attach to other elements in a variety of ways. Similarly, it offers various options by which you can attach other pieces to it. The indented stud on the side can become home to transparent 1×1 cylinder plates to create faux headlights. You can use a row of these to attach a 1×N element horizontally and, of course, the opening in the back can accept a single stud of any kind. [1979]
	Descriptor: 1×1 with indented stud on one side Subcategory: Junctions Part #: 4070	
	Descriptor: 1×1 with studs on two sides Subcategory: Junctions Part #: 47905	Notes: This piece was long awaited by many builders. It brings the usefulness of the headlight brick to another level by moving the side stud flush with the face of the brick. Having these studs on only two sides allows this piece to become part of any wall. [2004]

	Descriptor: 1×1 with studs on all sides	Notes: Having been around much longer than the 47905 shown in the previous entry, this element is sometimes called the hydrant brick. Although amazing in its design, it does have a drawback; often the studs you aren't using just get in the way. [1985]
	Subcategory: Junctions	
	Part #: 4733	
	Descriptor: 1×4 with studs on one side	Notes: Although it may not be the most elegant part, this piece just might be one of the most functional. It's small enough to build into almost any structure, yet at the same time, it offers four horizontal studs onto which you can then securely attach other pieces. [2000]
	Subcategory: Junctions	
	Part #: 30414	
	Descriptor: 2×4×2 with studs on three sides	Notes: You might not need one of these pieces every day, but that shouldn't stop you from searching for new uses for such an unusual element. This solid piece can form the core of junction substructures. [1990]
	Subcategory: Junctions	
	Part #: 2434	
	Descriptor: 2×4×2 with tubes on sides	Notes: The creation of the 2×4×2 with studs on all sides (part 2434) left an obvious opening for the opposite part. Thus the 2×4×2 with tubes on two sides was born. Its rather industrial look earns it the nickname "engine block." [1992]
	Subcategory: Junctions	
	Part #: 6061	
	Descriptor: 1×2 single-stud offset plate	Notes: A tiny piece with one lowly stud might not seem that useful, but think again. With this element, you can have parts of a model that are recessed one-half stud in depth offering greater subtlety to the shape and feel of your work. [1977]
	Subcategory: Junctions	
	Part #: 3794	

	Descriptor: 1×1 to 1×1 bracket	Notes: Need to change directions within a very small space? This is your part of choice. The hole on top is exactly one stud in diameter, and the area around it is exactly the height of a stud as well. [2002]
	Subcategory: Junctions	
	Part #: 554	
	Descriptor: 1×2 to 2×2 bracket	Notes: You can easily insert these pieces into a vertical wall leaving the four-studded side exposed and available for attaching other parts. Although it's relatively new, this is likely to become a valuable member of the bender class of parts. [2002]
	Subcategory: Junctions	
	Part #: 44728	
	Descriptor: 2×2 to 2×2 bracket	Notes: This was one of the earliest parts to ever offer studs that were perpendicular to the base of the part. This gem showed up in some of the classic space-themed sets of the late 1970s. [1978]
	Subcategory: Junctions	
	Part #: 3956	
	Descriptor: 1×2 to 1×4 bracket	Notes: Similar in many respects to part 44728. The difference is that the four horizontal studs are now in a single row rather than in two rows of two. Again, this part is useful when you're trying to attach something directly to a vertical wall. [1987]
	Subcategory: Junctions	
	Part #: 2436	
	Descriptor: 1×2 Log	Notes: Odd Face was the name given to this subcategory because the "face" or front surface of these bricks is something other than standard studs or just a smooth wall. The log brick is, of course, useful in brown, but gray versions are interesting too. [1996]
	Subcategory: Odd Face	
	Part #: 30136	

	Descriptor: 1×4 Log Subcategory: Odd Face Part #: 30137	Notes: The longer version of part 30136. What's unfortunate is that as of this writing, there isn't a 1×1 log brick. However, you can sometimes substitute a 1×1 cylinder and get at least some of the effect you're after. [1996]
	Descriptor: 1×2 grille Subcategory: Odd Face Part #: 2877	Notes: A unique piece in that the oddness of its face is different from front to back. Both sides can be described as grille-like. You can use these in groups or rows with similar faces exposed or, alternately, you can mix unlike faces for a great effect. You'll sometimes see these functions as grates on the sides of machinery, roll-up doors on fire engines, or even to replicate corrugated steel panels. [1986]
	Descriptor: 1×2 grille (rear view) Subcategory: Odd Face Part #: 2877	
	Descriptor: 1×2 and 1×2 plate Subcategory: Hinges Part #: 2429/2430	Notes: Although technically two pieces, this pair is almost always seen and used together. [1987/1987]
	Descriptor: 1×2 and 1×2 brick Subcategory: Hinges Part #: 3830/3831	Notes: You can certainly use this pair of parts to create a wall section that swings away from the rest of a building, but you can also used it to create angled sections that don't move. [1977/1977]
	Descriptor: 1×2 brick Subcategory: Hinges Part #: 3937/3938	Notes: You can use this piece to give motion to things like spaceship cockpits or you can angle the studs forward and build the brick into a stationary wall. Once the studs are exposed, you can use them to attach other elements. [1978/1978]

Table A-5: The Specialized Elements Category (continued)

	Descriptor: 2×2 brick	Notes: We saw this pair of elements as part of the alternative section in Chapter 3. In that case, we used the larger top portion to help support the angled alternate roof. [1978/1991]
	Subcategory: Hinges	
	Part #: 3937/6134	
	Descriptor: 2×5 plate	Notes: A classic piece in many respects. This piece is sometimes used to attach things like fire truck ladders, but it is just as capable of being the hinge for wings on a quirky bird. [1967]
	Subcategory: Hinges	
	Part #: 3149	
	Descriptor: 2×2 plate	Notes: A scaled-down version of the larger 4×4 turntable. This is only one plate high and can hide in many inconspicuous areas of a model. [1977]
	Subcategory: Turntables	
	Part #: 3680	
	Descriptor: 4×4 brick	Notes: The part depicted here is actually the "modern" version of a similar element that was first produced back in 1963. Earlier versions did not have the square baseplate seen here; rather, they were cylindrical all the way to the bottom. [1977]
	Subcategory: Turntables	
	Part #: 3403	
	Descriptor: 1×2 channel rail plate	Notes: Momentarily I'll introduce you to the 1×4 channel-face brick. The piece shown here can be used to build a substructure that can then be slid into the 1×4 channel-face element (part 2653) with great precision. Also available in a version that is eight studs long. [1997]
	Subcategory: Odd Face	
	Part #: 32028	
	Descriptor: 1×2 channel face	Notes: This piece is sometimes used as a purely decorative element when put together using the stacking technique. [1981]
	Subcategory: Odd Face	
	Part #: 4216	

Table A-5: The Specialized Elements Category (continued)

	Descriptor: 1×4 channel face	Notes: Although this can certainly be decorative, it can also be quite useful for accepting substructures mounted on the 32028 channel rail plates. [1991]
	Subcategory: Odd Face	
	Part #: 2653	
	Descriptor: 1×2 pin face with one pin	Notes: So you've built a substructure on rail plates and are using the 1×4 channel brick to mount it. Now you need to lock it in place. 1×2 bricks like the one shown here can mate up with 1×2 Technic bricks, which are shown in the Technic category. [1988]
	Subcategory: Pin-Enabled	
	Part #: 2458	
	Descriptor: 1×2 pin face with two pins	Notes: The pin configuration on this piece matches exactly with any two holes on any other Technic brick. Note that its pins are centered under the studs, unlike the 2548 above, whose pin is located between the studs. [2000]
	Subcategory: Pin-Enabled	
	Part #: 30526	
	Descriptor: 2×2 pin face	Notes: When you need a pin to be a secure part of a solid wall, reach for this element. Building it into a 2×N wall gives you a sturdy pin onto which you can attach almost anything. [1985]
	Subcategory: Pin-Enabled	
	Part #: 4730	
	Descriptor: 2×2 pin top	Notes: This is perhaps one of those parts you might not need for the longest time, but when you do, you'll be glad it exists. The same goes for the plate version of this part (2460). [1995]
	Subcategory: Pin-Enabled	
	Part #: 4729	

Descriptor: 2×2 pin top plate	Notes: Sure, this piece can be a place to mount the rotors for a small helicopter, but it can be so much more. Check the description for the pin drop plate in the next entry, then imagine that you've got the bottom of the plates open to build on, rather than the studs. [1988]	
Subcategory: Pin-Enabled		
Part #: 2460		
Descriptor: 2×2 pin drop plate	Notes: Here's what you do: First, build a Technic beam into the side of a model, a beam with three or more holes. Then, join together two or more of the 2476 elements, attach other pieces to them, and finally mount them into the holes of the beam. [1988]	
Subcategory: Pin-Enabled		
Part #: 2476		
Descriptor: Single drop hole plate	Notes: These pieces allow Technic pins or axles to attach below bricks or plates. Those pins or axles could carry gears, wheels, or other Technic bricks with similar holes. The 2444 piece is shown from the side under which is attached its only hole. The 2817 is viewed from the side, showing both holes. [1987/1989]	
Subcategory: Axle Plate		
Part #: 2444		
Descriptor: Double drop hole plate		
Subcategory: Axle Plate		
Part #: 2817		
Descriptor: 2×2 plate with small wheels/tires	Notes: A compact model may still require motion. The wheel/tire set here is mounted on a tiny 2×2 plate that has slender pins sticking out each side. These little wheels may not look like much, but they go around, and that's what counts. [1985/1986/1985]	
Subcategory: Wheels/Tires		
Part #: 4600/4624/3641		
Descriptor: 2×2 wide plate with slick tires	Notes: Are you creating a microsized street machine? Why not include some mean looking slicks? The plate in this figure sets the wheels out wider than the one shown in the previous entry. That gives your street rod a more defined racing look. [1994/1991/1996]	
Subcategory: Wheels/Tires		
Part #: 6157/6014/30028		

Table A-5: The Specialized Elements Category (continued)

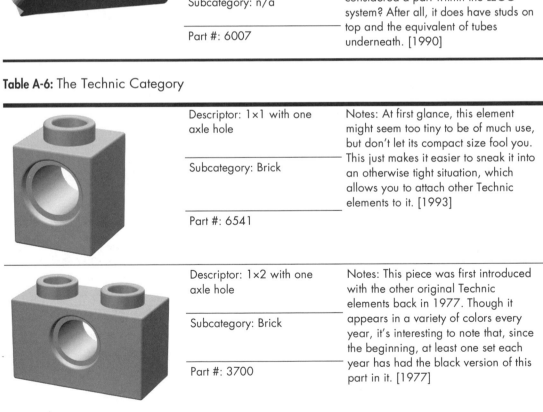

	Descriptor: 2×4 brick with medium wheels/tires	Notes: The wheels you see here (with the four studs showing) are sometimes referred to as Freestyle, named after the series of sets from which they originated. They spin freely on pins jutting out from the sides of the 2×4 brick. [1995/1988/1985]
	Subcategory: Wheels/Tires	
	Part #: 6249/6248/3483	
	Descriptor: Medium wheels with Technic axle holes	Notes: These wheels, with Technic axle holes, can find themselves used in a huge number of ways. Pop some Technic bricks on this axle, and you can mount the wheels on a car. Strip off the tires, and you've got Technic pulleys. [1984/1985]
	Subcategory: Wheels/Tires	
	Part #: 3482/3483	
	Descriptor: Brick separator	Notes: Did you know that the brick separator isn't just a tool, but it's also considered a part within the LEGO system? After all, it does have studs on top and the equivalent of tubes underneath. [1990]
	Subcategory: n/a	
	Part #: 6007	

Table A-6: The Technic Category

	Descriptor: 1×1 with one axle hole	Notes: At first glance, this element might seem too tiny to be of much use, but don't let its compact size fool you. This just makes it easier to sneak it into an otherwise tight situation, which allows you to attach other Technic elements to it. [1993]
	Subcategory: Brick	
	Part #: 6541	
	Descriptor: 1×2 with one axle hole	Notes: This piece was first introduced with the other original Technic elements back in 1977. Though it appears in a variety of colors every year, it's interesting to note that, since the beginning, at least one set each year has had the black version of this part in it. [1977]
	Subcategory: Brick	
	Part #: 3700	

	Descriptor: 1×2 keyhole	Notes: The keyhole brick is unique among the Technic elements, in that it effectively locks an axle in a certain position. You can then use that axle (or axle/pin) to attach wheels, pulleys, or other moving parts. [1998]
	Subcategory: Brick	
	Part #: 32064	
	Descriptor: 1×2 with two axle holes	Notes: Even good ideas can sometimes take a while to see the light of day. Having one axle hole under each stud allows for different connections than those that are possible with other bricks where the holes are centered between the studs. [1996]
	Subcategory: Brick	
	Part #: 32000	
	Descriptor: 1×4	Notes: A common-sized Technic brick that has been incorporated into a wide variety of sets over the years. [1977]
	Subcategory: Brick	
	Part #: 3701	
	Descriptor: 1×6	Notes: Another common element that, like the 1×4 version, has been seen in a large range of sets since first being produced back in the late 1970s. [1978]
	Subcategory: Brick	
	Part #: 3894	
	Descriptor: 1×8	Notes: This is perhaps one of the more commonly available lengths of the standard Technic bricks. It has appeared in nearly 300 different sets over the course of the last quarter century. [1977]
	Subcategory: Brick	
	Part #: 3702	
	Descriptor: 1×10	Notes: Though not introduced in the earliest years of the Technic elements, this was an obvious size to add to the list. [1985]
	Subcategory: Brick	
	Part #: 2730	

Table A-6: The Technic Category (continued)

	Descriptor: 1×12	Notes: Most LEGO builders will tell you that you can never have too many LEGO pieces. And though the medium-length Technic bricks might not feel that different from each other, it's a good bet that you'll want to collect lots of each size if you can. [1978]
	Subcategory: Brick	
	Part #: 3895	
	Descriptor: 1×14	Notes: Although there is no standard 1×14 brick, there is an element of this length in the Technic series of parts. This piece is a relatively new addition to the Technic family. [1997]
	Subcategory: Brick	
	Part #: 32018	
	Descriptor: 1×16	Notes: The granddaddy of the standard Technic beams. These pieces are much sought after by builders of all skill levels, especially those working on things like cranes or bridges. [1977]
	Subcategory: Brick	
	Part #: 3703	
	Descriptor: 2×4	Notes: The invention of the LEGO Technic brick brought about the necessity of inventing a plate to go along with it. The 2×4 version was first introduced in 1977 and since then, there have only ever been three different sizes of this type of part. [1977]
	Subcategory: Plate	
	Part #: 3709B	
	Descriptor: 2×6	Notes: The second in the trio of standard Technic plates. The holes in the plates (centered between the studs) allow for axles to be positioned vertically, though the axles generally spin best when you steady them with a second plate above or below the first. [1996]
	Subcategory: Plate	
	Part #: 32001	
	Descriptor: 2×8	Notes: The longest standard Technic plate yet produced. Note that this version, like the 2×4, was first released in 1977. It's odd that the 2×6 (pictured in the previous entry) would have to wait nearly 20 years to first see the light of day. [1977]
	Subcategory: Plate	
	Part #: 3738	

	Descriptor: 1×3	Notes: An interesting little piece with a single standard axle hole in the center surrounded on either side by plus-sign-shaped holes that are exactly the size of an axle. The middle hole allows pins or axles to spin, whereas the end openings do not. [1995]
	Subcategory: Beam Half-Width	
	Part #: 6632	
	Descriptor: 1×3	Notes: This is the smallest of the full-width pieces. Note that it is the same length as part 6632 but contains only rounded axle holes. Most of the straight full-width beams share this trait. [2000]
	Subcategory: Beam Full-Width	
	Part #: 32523	
	Descriptor: 1×4 liftarm	Notes: This element represents one of the first of the studless liftarm style of pieces to be introduced. In its first year of production, this piece appeared only in a parts pack and not in a set that built any sort of model. [1987]
	Subcategory: Beam Half-Width	
	Part #: 2825	
	Descriptor: 1×5	Notes: The shortest of the half-width elements to feature only smooth axle holes. Contrast this to part 6632, which is shorter but also has holes that lock axles in place. [1997]
	Subcategory: Beam Half-Width	
	Part #: 32017	
	Descriptor: 1×5	Notes: This piece, like the other full-width beams, has only smooth axle holes throughout its length. These allow for pins and axles to rotate freely. For comparison, see part 32348, which also has holes that prevent axles from moving. [2000]
	Subcategory: Beam Full-Width	
	Part #: 32316	
	Descriptor: 1×6	Notes: Like most of the other half-width straight beams, this part consists only of rounded pin/axle holes. [1998]
	Subcategory: Beam Half-Width	
	Part #: 32063	

	Descriptor: 1×7	Notes: The longest of the half-width sized pieces. As seen in Figure 9-6, these slender pieces help introduce rounded and gentler shapes to what might otherwise be boxy Technic models. [1998]
	Subcategory: Beam Half-Width	
	Part #: 32065	
	Descriptor: 1×7 single bend	Notes: Most of the bent beams share the common feature of having fixed-axle holes at each end and open holes in between that allow axles to rotate. [2000]
	Subcategory: Beam Full-Width	
	Part #: 32348	
	Descriptor: 1×9	Notes: Like its longer cousin (the 1×15), this is not a piece that appears in large numbers in single sets. [2001]
	Subcategory: Beam Full-Width	
	Part #: 120	
	Descriptor: 1×9 single bend	Notes: This piece is identical to part 6629, other than the fact that the bend on this piece occurs at the third axle hole. [1999]
	Subcategory: Beam Full-Width	
	Part #: 152	
	Descriptor: 1×9 single bend	Notes: Identical to part 152, other than the fact that the bend on this piece occurs at the fourth axle hole. [1996]
	Subcategory: Beam Full-Width	
	Part #: 6629	
	Descriptor: 1×15	Notes: The longest of the full-width beams currently available. These are not terribly common pieces and rarely show up in large quantities in any one particular set. [2000]
	Subcategory: Beam Full-Width	
	Part #: 32278	

	Descriptor: 1×11.5 double bend	Notes: I've always thought this part had the obvious resemblance to the forks on the front of a forklift vehicle. [1997]
	Subcategory: Beam Full-Width	
	Part #: 32009	
	Descriptor: 2×4 single bend	Notes: Proof that Technic beams come in all manner of variations. Note that this one has a 90-degree bend near one end but that only one of its ends has the X-shaped axle opening. The remaining openings are pin-type holes. [1999]
	Subcategory: Beam Full-Width	
	Part #: 32140	
	Descriptor: 3×3 single bend	Notes: I find this element quite pleasing to the eye. It has a natural symmetry, and the openings (mostly of the locking axle type) give it the look of fancy metal work. Oh, and it's handy for building Technic models too! [1998]
	Subcategory: Beam Half-Width	
	Part #: 32056	
	Descriptor: 3×3 braced	Notes: Elements like this one and part 32250 combine the traditional square geometry of LEGO elements with more natural curved shapes. They are especially useful in small models where you want to achieve complex angles in small spaces. [2000]
	Subcategory: Beam Half-Width	
	Part #: 32249	
	Descriptor: 3×5 single bend	Notes: A simple variation of part 32140. Many of the elements in this category seem to be different combinations of length, hole type, and number of bends along their length. [2000]
	Subcategory: Beam Full-Width	
	Part #: 32526	

	Descriptor: 3×5 braced	Notes: A long, more sloped version of part 32249. This one lends itself well to large-scale automobiles or flying machines. [2000]
	Subcategory: Beam Half-Width	
	Part #: 32250	
	Descriptor: 8 tooth	Notes: Barely bigger than the axles on which it is mounted, this little gear is handy for so many things. It helps create the steering for the model in Figure 9-1 and helps with changing speed and/or power within a gear train when used with larger gears. [1977]
	Subcategory: Gear	
	Part #: 3647	
	Descriptor: 12 tooth bevel	Notes: This is the more modern incarnation of the 12-tooth bevel gear. The earlier version was not as strong and was prone to breakage under stress. [1995]
	Subcategory: Gear	
	Part #: 6589	
	Descriptor: 12 tooth double bevel	Notes: Properly positioned, a double-bevel gear can provide input to two single-bevel gears. [1999]
	Subcategory: Gear	
	Part #: 32270	

	Descriptor: 16 tooth	Notes: Another standard gear from the earliest days of Technic. [1977]
	Subcategory: Gear	
	Part #: 4019	

	Descriptor: 20 tooth bevel	Notes: This gear can be used with an identical piece to change the direction of movement between two axles, or it can be paired up with the double-bevel version to create even more elaborate combinations. [1999]
	Subcategory: Gear	
	Part #: 32198	

	Descriptor: 20 tooth double bevel	Notes: The late 1990s saw an explosion in the number and type of gears available. This is probably due, at least in part, to the 1998 release of the programmable robotic LEGO set known as Mindstorms. [1999]
	Subcategory: Gear	
	Part #: 32269	

	Descriptor: 24 tooth	Notes: This is the original design (released in 1977) of the standard 24-tooth gear. When first produced, it lacked enough support for the openings in the center, and this led to some pieces breaking under heavy loads. In 1995, it was replaced with a stronger version. [1977]
	Subcategory: Gear	
	Part #: 3648	

	Descriptor: 24 tooth clutch	Notes: The dark gray core of this element actually rotates, with some friction, within the center of the gear. This allows the gear to slip a bit under high stress and may keep the axle or other gears from breaking. [1997]
	Subcategory: Gear	
	Part #: 60C01	
	Descriptor: 24 tooth crown	Notes: A crown gear, like beveled gears, can be used to change the direction of motion. A standard gear, or another crown gear, can meet with it at a 90-degree angle. [1977]
	Subcategory: Gear	
	Part #: 3650A	
	Descriptor: 40 tooth	Notes: The granddaddy of all LEGO gears both in terms of size and age. Like most gears, it appears primarily in gray, but recent years have also seen it released in such colors as red, blue, green, and white. [1977]
	Subcategory: Gear	
	Part #: 3649	
	Descriptor: Worm	Notes: Worm gears are most useful when power is important but speed is not. They do well when heavy loads are placed on them but may bind if spun too fast. [1985]
	Subcategory: Gear	
	Part #: 4716	

	Descriptor: 1×4 Rack	Notes: What is a gear rack? In reality it's nothing more than a round gear that has been flattened out so that all of the teeth are lined up next to each other. Useful for creating rack and pinion steering for Technic models. [1977]
	Subcategory: Gear	
	Part #: 3743	
	Descriptor: Classic pin	Notes: Don't confuse the classic light gray pin with a nearly identical part that is typically molded in black. The piece shown here allows other parts to spin freely. The black friction pin is larger by just enough for pieces to hold more tightly. [1977]
	Subcategory: Pin/Axle	
	Part #: 3673	
	Descriptor: Pin/axle	Notes: Need to attach a bushing or keyhole brick to a regular Technic brick? This isn't a problem with this unique piece. The need for such conversions (one type of connector to another) is a common concern when you're working with nonstandard elements. [1978]
	Subcategory: Pin/Axle	
	Part #: 3749	
	Descriptor: Three-stud-long axle with stop	Notes: Sometimes you want to mount gears or bushings on a short axle but ensure that they won't slip off. The stud at the end of this element makes sure other pieces won't fly off at the worst possible moment. [1995]
	Subcategory: Pin/Axle	
	Part #: 6587	
	Descriptor: Three-stud-long pin	Notes: This element often forms critical connections where you need three pieces held together. When inserted in the pinhole of a brick or beam, this piece has a certain amount of friction that makes it less prone to spinning freely. [1993]
	Subcategory: Pin/Axle	
	Part #: 6558	
	Descriptor: Two-stud-long axle	Notes: Believe it or not, the version of this part that was available from 1977 until 1996 didn't have the little notches you see above. The result was that often this small piece got stuck more often than it got loose. Thankfully LEGO corrected this problem. [1997]
	Subcategory: Pin/Axle	
	Part #: 32062	

	Descriptor: Four-stud-long axle	Notes: The standard axle arrived with other Technic parts as part of the original Expert Builder series of sets in 1977. It is available in lengths from as small as 2 studs right up to versions that are 12 studs long! [1977]
	Subcategory: Pin/Axle	
	Part #: 3705	
	Descriptor: Bushing	Notes: Sometimes you'll use this piece to hold axles in place and at other times, you'll use it as a tiny pulley. The center of both the half and full bushings are exactly sized to the standard axle. [1980]
	Subcategory: Half-Width	
	Part #: 4265C	
	Descriptor: Bushing	Notes: The full bushing is just about the height of a 1×1 brick and predates the half-sized one by just a few years. This part offers greater resistance for holding axles and gears in place. [1977]
	Subcategory: Full-Width	
	Part #: 3713	
	Descriptor: Axle joiner	Notes: This piece is used, quite simply, to join two axles together end-to-end. Basically, it allows you to make one longer axle out of two shorter ones. [1993]
	Subcategory: Coupler	
	Part #: 6538	
	Descriptor: Axle joiner	Notes: This piece shares a common trait with the other coupler elements. One hole runs through the piece and allows axles or pins to spin freely. The hole running perpendicular to it is like a bushing and holds axles tight. [1993]
	Subcategory: Coupler	
	Part #: 6536	

	Descriptor: 0 degrees (#1)	Notes: The most basic of the coupler elements. It creates a simple T connection between two axles. An axle placed through the round hole is free to rotate whereas the other X-shaped hole holds an axle locked in one position. [1997]
	Subcategory: Coupler	
	Part #: 32013	
	Descriptor: 180 degrees (#2)	Notes: This piece accepts two axles, one on either end, pointing toward each other, and, as with all the pieces in this group, it has a hole running through the middle that allows a pin or axle to spin if need be. [1997]
	Subcategory: Coupler	
	Part #: 32034	
	Descriptor: 160 degrees (#3)	Notes: If you read the descriptor for each of the pieces in this section, you'll notice a number in degrees. This is the angle of the two axle openings, and it is measured on the side facing up, as pictured here. [1997]
	Subcategory: Coupler	
	Part #: 32016	
	Descriptor: 135 degrees (#4)	Notes: Each descriptor for this group of parts also includes a number, written in brackets. You can also find these numbers printed on the actual elements, which makes it easy to keep them separate. [1999]
	Subcategory: Coupler	
	Part #: 924	
	Descriptor: 110 degrees (#5)	Notes: Different combinations of couplers and axles can become everything from the roll cage for a racecar to the landing gear for a rugged spacecraft. [1997]
	Subcategory: Coupler	
	Part #: 32015	

Table A-6: The Technic Category (continued)

	Descriptor: 90 degrees (#6)	Notes: More interesting geometry notes: The end of each of the couplers in this section is also the exact size and shape so that it fits just perfectly in between four standard studs on a plate or baseplate. [1997]
	Subcategory: Coupler	
	Part #: 32014	

Table A-7: The Arches Category

	Descriptor: 1×3	Notes: Perfectly suited for archer's windows built into thick castle walls. This piece probably represents the smallest possible arch piece that can be both practical and elegant. [1976]
	Subcategory: Standard	
	Part #: 4490	
	Descriptor: 1×4	Notes: A classic Roman arch that forms a semicircular shape. This arch is the same piece we used overtop of the train station ticket windows in Chapter 3. These arches are useful in any number of architectural situations. [1976]
	Subcategory: Standard	
	Part #: 3659	
	Descriptor: 1×6	Notes: The radius on this arch is much greater than that of the 1×6×2 shown in the next entry. In other words, if you kept following the arch shape, the imaginary circle under the brick would be much larger on this piece. [1972]
	Subcategory: Standard	
	Part #: 3455	
	Descriptor: 1×6×2	Notes: Like the 1×4 arch the 1×6×2 arch represents a classic Roman shape that is extremely pleasing to the eye. A series of these can create a pleasing arcade for any building. [1971]
	Subcategory: Standard	
	Part #: 3307	

Table A-7: The Arches Category (continued)

	Descriptor: 1×8×2	Notes: Like the 1×6 arch, this piece uses a slightly larger radius to form the arch shape. Therefore the arch appears to be still spreading outward as it reaches the edge of the span. [1971]
	Subcategory: Standard	
	Part #: 3308	
	Descriptor: 1×12×3	Notes: Now that's an arch! Impressive in its very size, this piece adds a grand opening to train tunnels, fire stations, or other buildings requiring this type of architectural detail. [1993]
	Subcategory: Standard	
	Part #: 6108	
	Descriptor: 1×2	Notes: Tuck this compact piece under part 6005 shown next, and you can create interesting shapes, either in matching or complementary colors. [1992]
	Subcategory: Half	
	Part #: 6091	
	Descriptor: 1×3×2	Notes: A natural partner to the 6091 element shown previously. In fact, 6091 fits nicely under the arch of the 6005. By itself, this 1×3×2 piece can also be considered a flying-buttress type of arch. [1995]
	Subcategory: Half	
	Part #: 6005	
	Descriptor: 1×5×4	Notes: Used alone, this is another flying-buttress arch due to the fact that it starts at a point away from a wall or structure and then meets up with it at the top of its half arch. Used in pairs, these pieces become essentially a 1×10×4 arch. [1986]
	Subcategory: Half	
	Part #: 2339	

Table A-7: The Arches Category (continued)

	Descriptor: 1×5×4	Notes: Another case where nearly a decade separates the release of a standard part (such as the 2339 shown previously) and its inverted counterpart—the half arch shown here. [1997]
	Subcategory: Half Inverted	
	Part #: 30099	

	Descriptor: 1×6×2	Notes: No, it's not the handle from a LEGO lunchbox . . . though it could be. Instead, it's an arch with gently curved corners that can be used as a wonderful decorative piece. [1994]
	Subcategory: Standard	
	Part #: 6183	

	Descriptor: 1×6×3	Notes: Another and perhaps the most suited piece capable of being a flying buttress. This one really extends outward from the top until it reaches the bottom of the half arch. This is yet another piece that is simply elegant to look at. [1992]
	Subcategory: Half	
	Part #: 6060	

Table A-8: The Tiles and Panels Category

	Descriptor: 1×1 tile	Notes: Although a similar part was actually released in 1971, this is the modern version that includes the tiny groove around the base, which makes it easier to remove. [1978]
	Subcategory: Standard	
	Part #: 3070B	

	Descriptor: 1×2 tile	Notes: Similar to the 1×1, this is the second-generation version of this part. The first, without the groove around the bottom, was first seen in 1968. [1977]
	Subcategory: Standard	
	Part #: 3069A	

	Descriptor: 1×4 tile	Notes: Run some of these in a series down the middle of a few rows of black tiles, and you've got yourself the lines of a divided road. [1987]
	Subcategory: Standard	
	Part #: 2431	
	Descriptor: 1×6 tile	Notes: This is a surprisingly new piece, given the desirability of tiles as part of the LEGO system. [1995]
	Subcategory: Standard	
	Part #: 6636	
	Descriptor: 1×8 tile	Notes: Want your small helicopters to look more real? Why not equip them with these pieces as rotors rather than similar lengths of 1×N plates? [1980]
	Subcategory: Standard	
	Part #: 4162	
	Descriptor: 2×2 tile	Notes: Sidewalks are just the start of the many uses for standard 2×2 tiles. Mix them with 1×N tiles of different colors and you can create the lines you need to represent streets or parking lots. [1976]
	Subcategory: Standard	
	Part #: 3068B	
	Descriptor: 2×2 cylindrical	Notes: It's a manhole cover and more! Like many other tiles, this one also has a small groove around its bottom edge making it easier to remove from a model once you're done with it. [1983]
	Subcategory: Standard	
	Part #: 4150	
	Descriptor: 2×2 cylindrical	Notes: This piece isn't exactly a true inverted plate. As you can see in the illustration, it has a curved underside. Sometimes called a boat plate, it can be affixed under various craft to allow them to skim over carpet or other surfaces. [1991]
	Subcategory: Inverted	
	Part #: 2654	
	Descriptor: 1×1×1 panel	Notes: This piece sort of looks like someone let the air out of a 1×1 brick. But it's ultimately a very useful piece for creating hollowed-out areas along the face of an otherwise solid wall. This piece works well with part 4865 shown next. [1995]
	Subcategory: Standard	
	Part #: 6231	

Table A-8: The Tiles and Panels Category (continued)

	Descriptor: 1×2×1 panel	Notes: What may look like a tiny little couch is actually a very handy piece for creating steps on the sides of vehicles, or tiny accents on large open spaces. [1985]
	Subcategory: Standard	
	Part #: 4865	

	Descriptor: 1×4×1 panel	Notes: A longer couch? No, just a longer version of the 4865 piece. [2000]
	Subcategory: Standard	
	Part #: 30413	

	Descriptor: 1×2×2 panel	Notes: Panels like this really shine when they are used to represent part of an outside wall while leaving more room inside of a model for moving parts or other substructures. [1997]
	Subcategory: Standard	
	Part #: 4864	

	Descriptor: 1×2×3 panel	Notes: Panels are quite useful no matter which direction they're facing. Turned like the 2362 piece shown here, they look solid, but when turned 180 degrees, they can add an indent to an otherwise dull wall. [1998]
	Subcategory: Standard	
	Part #: 2362	

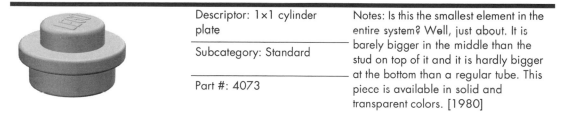	Descriptor: 3×2×6 panel Subcategory: Standard Part #: 2466	Notes: Not all panels are flat. Some, like the 2466 element shown here, are made up of several thin flat sides meeting at interesting angles. [1988]
	Descriptor: 1×4×3 panel Subcategory: Standard Part #: 4215A	Notes: Many parts are available in transparent colors, but some are perhaps more worth mentioning than others. The 4215A panel shown here is available in a number of opaque colors but most notably in a clear version (same part number) like the second illustration. This allows you to use it as a window for a large office building or another minifig structure where you need to let a lot of light shine in. [1994]
	Descriptor: 1×4×3 panel Subcategory: Standard Part #: 4215A	

Table A-9: The Cones and Cylinders Category

	Descriptor: 1×1 cylinder plate Subcategory: Standard Part #: 4073	Notes: Is this the smallest element in the entire system? Well, just about. It is barely bigger in the middle than the stud on top of it and it is hardly bigger at the bottom than a regular tube. This piece is available in solid and transparent colors. [1980]

	Descriptor: 2×2 cylinder plate	Notes: Observe the keyhole-shaped opening in this piece. It matches perfectly with a similar feature found on 2×2 cylinders. I used that opening to help create the presser tool in Chapter 13. [1980]
	Subcategory: Standard	
	Part #: 4032	
	Descriptor: 1×1 cone	Notes: You may use this piece as the nose cone of a very small rocket, but even if you don't, it's a handy shape nonetheless. It's worth pointing out that the tip is just the right size to fit into the bottom of an identical piece or the underside of nearly any regular brick or plate. [1985]
	Subcategory: Standard	
	Part #: 4589	
	Descriptor: 1×1 cylinder	Notes: Shown here is the updated version of a part that was originally released with the earliest parts in 1958. The difference here is that the stud is hollow, whereas the original was solid. [1977]
	Subcategory: Standard	
	Part #: 3062B	
	Descriptor: 2×2×2 cone	Notes: Another part that underwent a face-lift after its original release. In this case, as with the 1×1 cylinder, the newer version has a hollow stud. [1984]
	Subcategory: Standard	
	Part #: 3942	

Table A-9: The Cones and Cylinders Category (continued)

	Descriptor: 2×2 cylinder	Notes: Sort of like a tiny coffee can, only with studs on top. This piece, like some of the other cylinders and cones, has a hole running vertically through it that matches exactly to the size of standard Technic axle. [1978]
	Subcategory: Standard	
	Part #: 3941	
	Descriptor: 3×3×3 cone	Notes: These pieces are sometimes used as the engines on a rocket or space shuttle. [1995]
	Subcategory: Standard	
	Part #: 6233	
	Descriptor: 4×4×2 cone	Notes: This lampshade-like piece can be used as the engine of a spaceship or it can also be a transitional piece that joins 4×4 cylinder pieces to 2×2 cylinder pieces. [1982]
	Subcategory: Standard	
	Part #: 3943	
	Descriptor: 4×4 cylinder	Notes: The holes on the sides of this piece easily accept a Technic pin or axle or even the studs from any standard piece. The only real problem is that when you stack a bunch of these, they tend to look like a column of Swiss cheese. [1995]
	Subcategory: Standard	
	Part #: 6222	
	Descriptor: 4×4 quarter-cut cylinder	Notes: Another case where the existence of one part highlights the absence of a similar part. There is, for example, no 3×3 quarter-cut cylinder, nor is there a 2×2 for that matter. Maybe someday? [1990]
	Subcategory: Adapted	
	Part #: 2577	

Table A-10: The Baseplates Category

	Descriptor: 8×16 brick plate Subcategory: Standard Part #: 4204	Notes: A newer version of a similar element (700). The updated brick plate illustrated here features extra bracing beneath it. This bracing, along with the normal studs, helps make this part very rigid and strong. [1985]
	Descriptor: 8×16 waffle plate Subcategory: Standard Part #: 3865	Notes: This baseplate is perfect for smaller buildings like gas stations or bus stops to help complete your minifig town. [1971]
	Descriptor: 10×20 brick plate Subcategory: Standard Part #: 700	Notes: As a kid I nearly wore out my green 10×20 brick plates. They were the base for countless houses, factories, and shops that all eventually met with some disaster that inevitably resulted in my LEGO fire apparatus coming to the rescue. [1965]
	Descriptor: 16×16 waffle plate Subcategory: Standard Part #: 3867	Notes: Large baseplates like this are also found in sizes such as 32×32 and 48×48. The latter is perhaps one of the largest LEGO elements ever produced. These form the base, literally, for all manner of buildings and scenes. [1978]

Table A-11: The Decorative Category

	Descriptor: 1×4 lattice Subcategory: Fences, Rails and Rungs Part #: 3633	Notes: This one could become a small garden fence or the decorative guardrail on a microscale ship. [1976]
	Descriptor: 1×4×2 lattice Subcategory: Fences, Rails and Rungs Part #: 3185	Notes: Another pretty element. This one looks great when built into a wall, quickly becoming the grate over an air conditioning system or perhaps just a vent of some kind. Being useful doesn't mean you have to be unsightly. [1967]

Descriptor: 1×2 ladder plate		Notes: A tiny ladder-like piece that is easy to incorporate into most models since you really only need to find room for the 1×2 plate. The rungs of the element can then rest against the side or end of the model to form a ladder or grille of some kind. [1980]
Subcategory: Fences, Rails and Rungs		
Part #: 4175		

Descriptor: 1×2 grille plate		Notes: This piece was rereleased in the mid-1990s with a tiny groove around the bottom edge. This groove is handy since this little grille-like piece ends up getting used on many surfaces. Want to make it more interesting? Mount it on another piece that is a contrasting color. [1987/95]
Subcategory: Fences, Rails and Rungs		
Part #: 2412B		

Descriptor: 1×6 hand rail		Notes: A handsome element that is often used on train models but can just as easily be the handrail on the sides of a small bridge or perhaps a guard-rail on a ship. [1996]
Subcategory: Fences, Rails and Rungs		
Part #: 6583		

Descriptor: 1×8×2		Notes: Sort of like the type of fencing you might find in parking lots or maybe the railings you'd find along the upper decks of a fancy passenger liner. Of course, it could just be a plain old bicycle rack for a minifig park. [1988]
Subcategory: Fences, Rails and Rungs		
Part #: 2486		

Descriptor: 4 brick high basic bar		Notes: Light saber? Baseball bat? Hand rail? Yup, it's all that and more. The diameter of this bar is exactly the size of a minifig hand and is also the right size for any of the following clip elements. [1999]
Subcategory: Bars		
Part #: 30374		

	Descriptor: 4 brick high basic antenna	Notes: How about a self-attaching bar? The round-tipped antenna has a sort of socket at the end that attaches easily to any studded element. It's also the same width (along the main section) as the basic bar shown in the previous entry. [1977]
	Subcategory: Bars	
	Part #: 3957	
	Descriptor: 1×1 clip plate horizontal	Notes: Then there are parts that just keep evolving. The 1×1 clip plate is on its third incarnation in the 25-plus years since it was introduced. This piece is often used to hold handled parts and bars onto models. [1979/1987/ 1993]
	Subcategory: Clips	
	Part #: 4085C	
	Descriptor: 1×1 clip plate vertical	Notes: It's worth noting that clip plates don't necessarily just have to clip to ordinary bars such as part 30374. They can also be attached to handled parts such as part 2540 or 30236. [1990]
	Subcategory: Clips	
	Part #: 6019	
	Descriptor: 1×1 with studs	Notes: This is the modern version of an earlier part. The rounded part that is attached to the side has two stud-sized areas that allow any number of other elements to connect. In addition, the hole through those studs is exactly bar size. [1980/1988]
	Subcategory: Clips	
	Part #: 4081B	
	Descriptor: 1×1 with clip top	Notes: This piece highlights the main difference between the Brickopedia and other classification systems. This piece is typically called a "1×1 tile with clip," but that label then causes it to be in a category that doesn't include its clipped cousins shown here. [1989]
	Subcategory: Clips	
	Part #: 2555	

	Descriptor: 1×1 brick	Notes: Some pieces in this category have clips whereas others, like this one, have the bar attached instead. [1992]
	Subcategory: Handles	
	Part #: 2921	
	Descriptor: 1×2 plate	Notes: This piece can be decorative or functional depending on what you attach to the handle. Of course, it takes up very little space (only that of a 1×2 plate) and therefore may sometimes be more useful than the brick version (part 30236). [1989]
	Subcategory: Handles	
	Part #: 2540	
	Descriptor: 1×2 brick	Notes: What's good for the plate is usually good for the brick too. This piece has the same sized handle as the 2540 plate. Rows of this brick make great decoration on the tops of buildings or even some vehicles. [1999]
	Subcategory: Handles	
	Part #: 30236	
	Descriptor: 1×2 plate with braced handle	Notes: Another case where parts are sometimes separated, despite having similar features or functions. The 2432 is often called the "1×2 tile with handle." Of course that means it's not often seen in the company of the other handles elements. [1987]
	Subcategory: Handles	
	Part #: 2432	
	Descriptor: Bush	Notes: Decorative gardens, rustic western settings, or mountainous train layouts all benefit from this little scrub brush element. [1992]
	Subcategory: Foliage	
	Part #: 6064	

Table A-11: The Decorative Category (continued)

	Descriptor: Fruit tree	Notes: Need an apple orchard? How about some well-groomed bushes for the sides of a posh minifig mansion? The fruit tree element comes to your aid with style. [1977]
	Subcategory: Foliage	
	Part #: 3470	

	Descriptor: Pine tree (small)	Notes: Some parts are only ever produced in a single color. This little pine tree is one of those elements and has only been seen in standard green since its introduction more than a quarter century ago. [1976]
	Subcategory: Foliage	
	Part #: 2435	

	Descriptor: Pine tree (large)	Notes: Like the small version, the large pine tree has only ever been manufactured in green during the last 30 years. Mixing large and small versions together in a scene will add realism and interest. [1973]
	Subcategory: Foliage	
	Part #: 3471	

Table A-11: The Decorative Category (continued)

Descriptor: 3×5 stem	Notes: Using several of these pieces together can help give you the look of an ivy-covered wall when you're building a library or perhaps an old home where nature has begun to reclaim part of her territory. [1987]
Subcategory: Foliage	
Part #: 2423	

Descriptor: Sea grass	Notes: True, it can be used as sea grass, if you're building a sea. But why not also think of it as a cactus, or maybe a yet-to-be-discovered creepy-munga bush on a planet first explored by a minifig ship of your own design? [1997]
Subcategory: Foliage	
Part #: 30093	

Descriptor: Basic flag	Notes: Castles, carnival rides, and parade floats alike all need colorful flags that look like they're blowing in the wind. This simple but effective ornamental element is most often placed atop part 3957, the four-brick-high antenna. [1984]
Subcategory: Ornamental	
Part #: 4495	

Descriptor: Lion head carving	Notes: Decorative pieces reached a new level of sophistication and elegance in 2000 with the introduction of this lion head ornamental piece. Perfect for classy downtown buildings where minifigs gather to do business. [2000]
Subcategory: Ornamental	
Part #: 30274	

Table A-11: The Decorative Category (continued)

	Descriptor: 1×2×2 window	Notes: A staple of the LEGO system from the beginning. You can use them in groups so that they look like large office windows, or you can use them alone to add character to even the smallest minifig dwelling. [1958]
	Subcategory: Windows	
	Part #: 7026	
	Descriptor: 1×4×3 train window	Notes: This is the newer version of the train window shown with the original version of the glass insert (the insert arriving 13 years prior to the new window). This part combo also works well as windows for buses or even spaceships. [1993/1980]
	Subcategory: Windows	
	Part #: 6556/4034	
	Descriptor: 1×2×2	Notes: These pieces are often called plane windows, but they can just as easily be used in models of trains, fire trucks, ships, helicopters, and so on. These are useful with or without available glass inserts. [1987]
	Subcategory: Windows	
	Part #: 2377	
	Descriptor: 1×4×2	Notes: What's better than one plane window? How about two joined together? As with 2377, this element can find its way into a variety of vehicles. It's best if you think of it as a panel with cutouts. It allows great function in very little space. [1985]
	Subcategory: Windows	
	Part #: 4863	

Table A-11: The Decorative Category (continued)

	Descriptor: 1×2×2 2/3 window	Notes: Do the occupants of your castle need to let some light in? This beautiful pair of elements will certainly help with that. Don't forget you'll want to use a 1×4 standard arch over top of this window to make it look like part of the wall. [1996]
	Subcategory: Windows	
	Part #: 30044/30046	
	Descriptor: 1×4×3	Notes: The old reliable 1×4×3 basic window is shown with inserts that look like panes of glass. You can also replace those with ones that are latticed, or even turn the part around. You can then add shutters to give them a homier look. [1977]
	Subcategory: Windows	
	Part #: 3853	
	Descriptor: 1×4×5 four pane door	Notes: Minifig-scale buildings aren't much good if your characters can't get in and out of them. This often-used part is strangely only available in the version shown above that opens from the left. [1977]
	Subcategory: Doors	
	Part #: 3861	

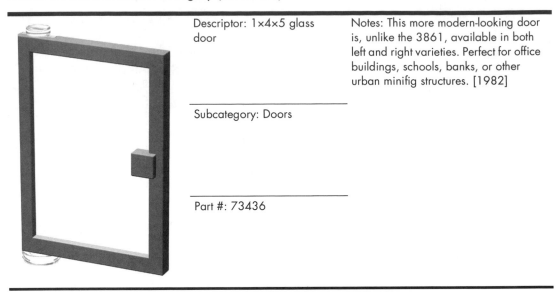

Descriptor: 1×4×5 glass door

Notes: This more modern-looking door is, unlike the 3861, available in both left and right varieties. Perfect for office buildings, schools, banks, or other urban minifig structures. [1982]

Subcategory: Doors

Part #: 73436

Review: Bricks, Plates, and So Much More

Although it contains more than 250 different LEGO elements, it's worth repeating that the Brickopedia does not include an entry for every piece ever made. My intention when creating it wasn't to make it a reference guide for the entire LEGO system, but rather to give you a *sense* of the core pieces that provide the best opportunities for builders of all skill levels. I hope that as you browsed through it you saw pieces you recognize, ones you wish you had, and ones you forgot about but you're now going to dig out of the bottom of one of your buckets of LEGO bricks.

B

DESIGN GRIDS: BUILDING BETTER BY PLANNING AHEAD

Sometimes just a little bit of planning can save a lot of headaches. The Design Grids discussed here are intended to save you some of the frustration that comes from not mapping out the direction you want your work to take. The grids are made of special graph paper created with dimensions that match those of LEGO elements. You may find them useful when you are experimenting with different part combinations in advance of actually getting your bricks out onto the table. This planning might be for a small part of a large model or it may be for the layout of an entire mosaic image. How you use these grids is up to you. What follows are some suggestions on how to use them effectively.

Downloading the Grids

Because the individual squares on each grid are exactly the same size as real LEGO elements, it is not practical to reprint them in this book. By downloading and printing out your own copies, you will ensure that the grids are sized correctly. In the following pages, you'll see why that is so important. You can download the Design Grids (as Adobe Acrobat files) from www.apotome.com/grids.html.

About the Grids

Each of the four Design Grids has been engineered to serve a different purpose. Grids #1 and #2 are most useful when you are sketching out mosaic images or planning a model that will be viewed from the top looking down. Grids #3 and #4 take a different approach and allow you to imagine a LEGO model as seen from the side.

Design Grid #1

Grid #1 allows you to look down on a model from above, straight down on the studs. As you can see by the sample shown in Figure B-1, each square is exactly the size of a real 1×1 brick.

Design Grid #1 – 1:1 Scale
[Studs Up/Top Down Orientation]

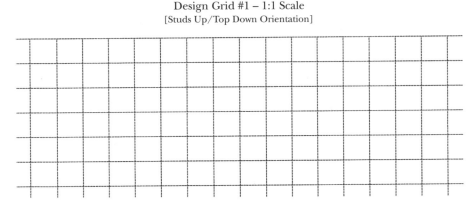

Figure B-1: The squares on Grid #1 are all the same size as the top surface of a 1×1 brick.

Design Grid #2

Grid #2 is unique among the Design Grids in that it is the only one of the four that does not have lines drawn to exactly the size of real LEGO elements. Instead, it is made up of a 32×32 field of squares that are sized to fit on a single page. You can use it to help you plan a mosaic that fits onto LEGO's common 32×32 waffle baseplate. As you can see in Figure B-2 the grid also has another special feature.

The added feature of this grid is that it makes it easy for you to give any location on the baseplate a name by which you can reference it. You can use the letters (along the left side) and numbers (along the top) next to the grid to pinpoint a particular location within the design. For example, in Figure B-3, you can see that I have marked an X in some of the squares on the grid.

I can identify these locations by the letter/number combination. In other words, you simply find the row and column that meet at the square you want to think about and you see which letter and number match that square.

	1	2	3	4	5	6	7	8	9	10	11	12	13	14	15	16	
a																	
b																	
c																	
d																	
e																	
f																	

Figure B-2: Just like the reference markers found on a real map, the numbers and letters help you determine where bricks need to go.

You may also find these identifiers useful when transferring your mosaic design from paper to actual elements. You can count out the numbers and letters on your actual baseplate and use them to distinguish where you should place certain bricks or plates. In Figure B-3, you can see elements indicated on the Design Grid at locations A1, B2, and C3. On the right, you see the actual LEGO pieces in exactly the same locations on the baseplate.

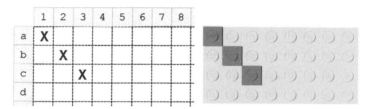

Figure B-3: This side-by-side comparison shows how marks made on the Design Grid translate into the position of real pieces on the actual baseplate.

You may not always need to reference pieces by their exact location, but at other times, you may find this letter and number system very useful.

Design Grid #3

Grid #3 allows you to plan a model as though you are looking at it from the side. A portion of the grid is shown in Figure B-4. You can see that the boxes (also known as cells) on this grid are much shorter. In fact, each box is the height and width of a standard 1×1 plate as seen from the side. This configuration is referred to as *plate view*.

Three of these boxes, just as with the real plates, equal one standard 1×1 brick in height. The page itself is set up just the way you would read a normal book, with the short sides of the page at the top and bottom.

Design Grid #3 – 1:1 Scale
[Plate View – Portrait Orientation]

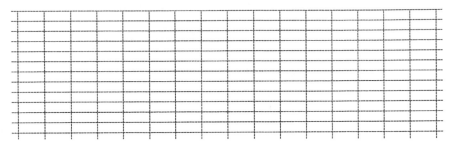

Figure B-4: A portion of Grid #3 shows the layout of the cells.

This is known as *portrait perspective* (see Figure B-5).

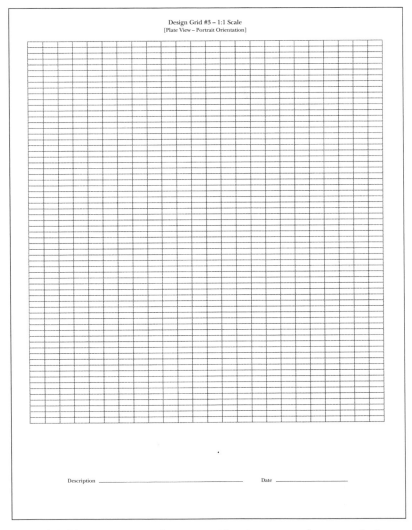

Figure B-5: Here you can see the entire grid as it appears when you print it out on a page.

Design Grid #4

Grid #4 consists of the same sized squares as Grid #3, but the entire page is oriented with the long sides of the page at the top and bottom. This is known as *landscape perspective*. The image of the grid (shown in Figure B-6) has been reduced in size so that you can see the orientation of the squares as they appear on a full page.

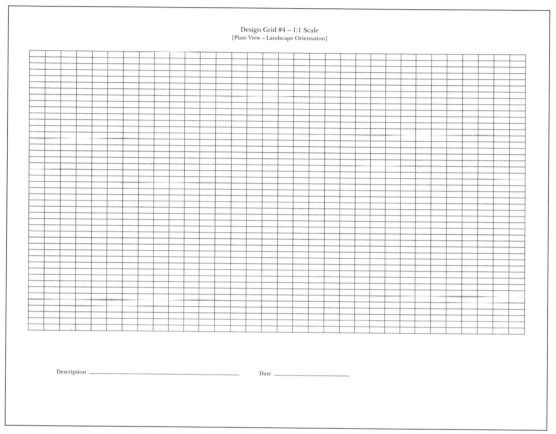

Figure B-6: This grid is useful for planning models that are wider than they are tall.

Using the Grids Effectively

As noted earlier, the grids included with this book fall into two different categories. Grid #1 is useful for creating things like the floor plan for an office building, the shape of an airplane's wings, or the layout of walls surrounding a castle. Grid #2 is most effective for planning small, studs-out mosaics. The last two allow you to plan the height of a model and include the side view of such things as slopes and plates. You can also use them to plan mosaics or help you design custom-sized arches that you make from inverted slopes. Which grid you use depends on what part of the model you are trying to design. A large model may, in fact, not even fit on a single grid. In that case, you can either use the grid to work out only a portion of the model, or you can simply tape several sheets together until you have enough room to complete your design.

Same Model, Different Views

You can and should use two, three, or all four of the different grids when designing a model. For example, if you are sitting down to design the train station model from Chapter 3, you might use Grid #1 to plan the layout of the walls, including the ticket counter and the front door. Grid #2 is, of course, most useful for planning mosaics (see more about mosaics in Chapter 8). Grid #3 is handy for just about any model or even just experimenting with combinations of parts. You might then use Grid #4 to sketch the front of the train station indicating where you plan to put the windows and the bench. Like any tool, the Design Grids are intended to make your life easier, so use them as much or as little as you need.

Sketching or Planning

Because the grids are sized to the exact dimensions of LEGO elements, you can use them effectively in two ways. The first method is to simply sketch out your model on the grid, not worrying about which pieces go where. Then, when you have the basic model drawn out, you can find pieces in your collection that match the shape you've created on the grid.

The second way is to draw specific pieces onto the cells in order to see how they look. You might do this if you don't happen to have a specific piece but are planning on buying some. Or, you might use this method to simply try out some different part combinations without having to get out several of your storage boxes.

Colorize Your Ideas

The grids aren't just effective for planning the *positions* of pieces. You can also use them to test what certain color combinations might look like. To do this, draw the outlines of the pieces with which you want to experiment. Then color them in using colored pencils, crayons, or fine markers. You can even test the look of color combinations for parts you may not yet own. It's an easy and inexpensive way to figure out what parts you may need for future projects.

Description and Date for Future Reference

There are also spaces provided at the bottom of each grid to fill in the description of the model and the date the design sketch was made. Figure B-7 shows an example of the kind of note you can make for yourself using this part of each grid.

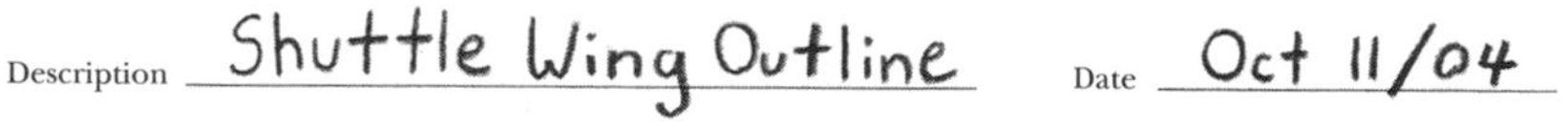

Figure B-7: Descriptions don't have to be fancy. Jot down just enough information to remind yourself of the purpose of this particular design.

You may want to keep some of your designs in safe place. That way, as you design future projects, you can look back to see your past efforts—what did and did not work.

Drawing on Grid #1

Remember, Grid #1 presents a view just like you'd see if you were looking down on the map of a town. You see things as though you are floating high above in a hot air balloon. You can't see the sides of any object from this view, only the tops. For example, if you were to draw the Empire State Building micro model (from Chapter 6) onto a copy of Design Grid #1, you would end up with something like the drawing shown in Figure B-8.

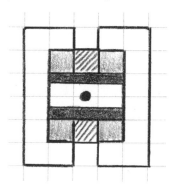

Figure B-8: A microsized Empire State Building as seen from above.

You can use this particular grid in several ways. First, you can use it to determine the various heights of layers within the same model. As you can see in Figure B-8, I've used various shading techniques to represent different levels of the building. Areas are shaded light and dark gray, other parts are indicated by diagonal lines, and still other portions have been left blank. Each of these different patterns or shades indicates that the height of the model is different than it is in a differently colored/shaded area. This treatment reminds me to pay attention to the changing geometry as I construct the building, and it is also a way that I can represent three dimensions on a two-dimensional diagram.

You can also use Design Grid #1 to plan the outline of something, like we did with the shuttle wings in Chapter 10, or to see the distances between walls within a building, as with the train station example from Chapter 3, or even the distance between two small buildings.

If you're going to use it for outlining, then it's really only necessary to draw a line around the outside of the shape and then use the grid to fill in the needed bricks. Figure B-9 shows part of the shuttle wing that we designed back in Chapter 10.

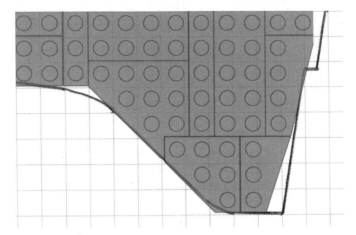

Figure B-9: Using the Design Grids, you can literally piece together a model design by placing real elements on top of your paper sketch.

In the case of buildings, you can use the grids to plan where the walls will be and also how features such as doors and windows will fit in. Figure B-10 shows what a portion of the train station walls from Chapter 3 might look like.

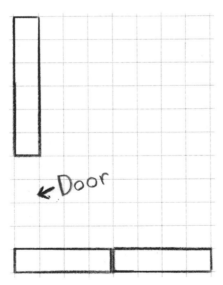

Figure B-10: Make notes to remind yourself of different features or substructures.

Of course another good use for Design Grid #1 is to help plan studs-out mosaics. As I noted in Chapter 8, the studs-out style isn't as subtle as the studs-up variety, but such mosaics can still be fun to plan and build. See Figure B-11 for a simple example.

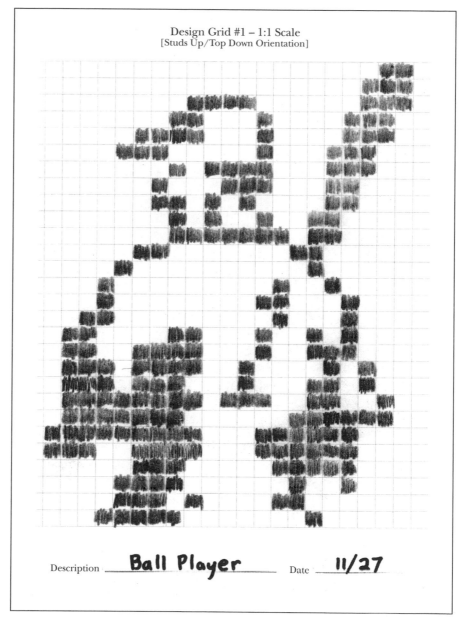

Design Grid #1 – 1:1 Scale
[Studs Up/Top Down Orientation]

Description **Ball Player** Date **11/27**

Figure B-11: Simple characters and themes are good subjects for studs-out mosaics.

Drawing on Grid #2

One way of using Grid #2 effectively is to find an image you want to turn into a mosaic. Print out a copy of the grid and a copy of the image on a separate piece of paper. If possible, resize the image to approximately 6 1/2 inches square and center it in the middle of the page. Then, when you set the grid sheet on top of the printout of the image, the two sheets will be aligned. This will, more or less, cause the image to fall within the length and width of the grid itself. To plan your mosaic, simply trace whatever parts of the image you want to reproduce in bricks. In Figure B-12, you can see that I'm beginning to sketch out a simple example.

Figure B-12: If possible, try to use lightweight paper when printing out Grid #2. This will allow your image to show through from below.

NOTE   *Refer to Chapter 8 for even more information on using Grid #2.*

Drawing on Grid #3

Design Grid #3 represents an entirely different view than you saw on Grids #1 and #2. In this case, you perform the model planning as though you are looking at the bricks and plates from the side. If you were to simply draw a single 1×1 plate, it would look like Figure B-13.

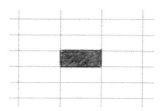

Figure B-13: As simple as it gets. This illustration
shows you what a 1×1 plate should look like.

A standard 1×1 brick would then look like Figure B-14.

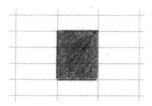

Figure B-14: Three 1×1 plates stacked together
always equal the height of a standard 1×1 brick.

As you can see, each time you want to draw the equivalent of a full-height
1×1 brick, you simply draw a line around three of the cells. You draw longer
bricks, such as a 1×N bricks, by extending the top and bottom lines until you
have captured the length you need. Figure B-15 shows what a 1×4 arch brick
would look like when drawn on this grid. You don't need to limit yourself to
just standard bricks and plates; you can draw other pieces just as easily.

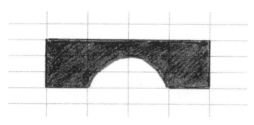

Figure B-15: Parts with complex shapes, such as the arch
shown here, can also be easily drawn on the Design Grids.

You can also indicate slopes on this grid by drawing diagonal lines along
with lines for the bottom and side of the element (see Figure B-16).

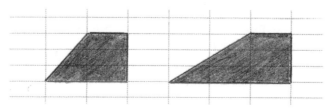

Figure B-16: Follow the geometry of a real element, and your drawings
will always be accurate.

For example, in Figure B-16 you can see a 2×1 45-degree slope and a 3×4 33-degree slope. Notice that the diagonal lines cut across the lines of the grid itself, but that's to be expected. If you are ever confused about which lines to connect to make the sloped side of the piece, just grab an actual slope from your collection and study where the slanted edge meets the rest of the brick. Don't forget to leave a flat line at the top to represent where the stud is located.

Drawing on Grid #4

Once you understand how to use Grid #3, you know how to use Grid #4. The only real difference between the two grids is the way the pages are oriented. As noted earlier, Grid #3 is used in portrait perspective, whereas Grid #4 is in the landscape perspective. You'll find Grid #3 useful when your model is taller than it is wide. Obviously the opposite is true for Grid #4.

Figure B-17 shows an example of testing a particular combination of parts—to view their final shape—without ever taking a piece out of storage. As you can see, the drawing isn't perfect, but it can help you make some key construction decisions.

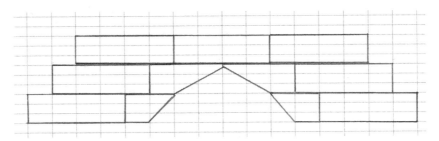

Figure B-17: Inverted slopes are just as easy to draw as their standard counterparts. Here I've sketched out a substitute arch, not unlike the example you saw back in Chapter 3 (Figure 3-25).

Review: From Grids to Bricks

You will always need to tweak your model as you translate it from a sketch into real bricks, but by doing so, you should end up with a stronger design. The drawings you create on the grids should only provide you with a guide; you don't have to follow them brick for brick. The best thing to do is to create your design sketch and then simply start building the real thing. As you work, you can step back, examine the actual assembly, and see which bricks or plates you want to change. The result, whether a small group of pieces or a complete mosaic portrait, will be a work of art that you can call your own.

LIST OF KEY FIGURES

Pieces, Models, and Techniques	Figures	Pages
1×1 standard brick	Figure 1-1	2
1×1 jumbo brick model, complete instructions	Figures 5-3 to 5-5	83
1×2 jumbo plate model		
complete instructions	Figures 5-16 to 5-19	90–91
completed model	Figure 5-15	89
2×2 45-degree jumbo slope model		
complete instructions	Figures 5-20 to 5-24	91–92
completed model	Figure 5-15	89
2×4 standard brick, shown from all sides	Figure 1-3	3
2×4 jumbo brick model, complete instructions	Figures 5-6 to 5-12	84–87
bond patterns for bricks		
stacked	Figure 2-2	20
overlapped	Figure 2-3	20
staggered	Figure 2-4	20
column patterns		
chimney	Figure 2-26	33
compound post	Figure 2-25	33
hybrid	Figures 2-28 and 2-29	34
keyhole	Figure 2-27	33
simple post	Figure 2-24	33
microscale house model		
Bill of Materials	Figure 6-10	110
complete instructions	Figures 6-11 to 6-16	111–112
completed model	Figure 6-9	110

(continued)

Pieces, Models, and Techniques	Figures	Pages
miniland figure model		
complete instructions	Figures 4-4 and 4-5	68–69
completed model	Figure 4-3	65
suggested parts to use	Tables 4-1 to 4-3	66–67
space shuttle model		
Bill of Materials	Figure 10-12	186
complete instructions	Figures 10-13 to 10-21	187–193
completed model	Figure 10-2	176
sphere model		
Bill of Materials	Figure 7-3	117
complete instructions	Figures 7-4 to 7-17	118–125
completed model	Figure 7-2	117
train station model		
Bill of Materials	Figure 3-5	42
complete instructions (main model)	Figures 3-6 to 3-17	43–50
complete instructions (roof submodel)	Figures 3-18 to 3-23	51–54
completed model	Figure 3-4	41
walls, building basic	Figures 2-12 to 2-15	26–27

INDEX

Numbers

1×1 brick, as standard for
       measurement, 2
1×2 plate model (jumbo version),
       90–91
1×N, 3
2×2 45-degree slope model (jumbo
       version), 91–92
2×4 brick model (jumbo version),
       84–87
4X scale, 83–84, 93
5:6 ratio, 13–14
10X scale, 82, 89

A

alternate solutions. *See* substitution
angelfish, mosaic design, 140–43
approximation
    described, 96
    examples of usage, 97–98, 102
arch
    alternate for train station, 56
    elements, 282–84
    parts of, 55
    substitutes, 55
axle (Technic)
    described, 158
    determining length, 228
    elements, 279–80

B

bars, 291–92
baseplate
    described, 12

elements, 242, 290
selecting size for mosaics, 135–36
beam
    composite type, 31
    correct assembly, 32
    defined, 30
    examples of usage, 30, 35, 80
    incorrect assembly, 31
    simple type, 30
    Technic (studless), 157, 273–76
bevel gears, 168–70, 276, 277
Bill of Materials
    defined, 41
    for microscale house model, 110
    for pin stand tool, 231
    for presser tool, 229
    for ruler, 230
    for space shuttle model, 186
    for sphere model, 117
    for train station model, 42
BOM. *See* Bill of Materials
bond patterns, 35. *See also*
       overlapping, stacking,
       staggering
bracing
    defined, 29
    demonstrated, 30, 79–80
brick, 2, 5–6
    as measurement device, 228
    elements, 243–46
    Technic, 156, 270–72
brick hinge
    elements, 266–67
    example of usage, 59–60
brick separator
    described, 233
    element, 270

brick separator, *continued*
    examples of usage, 234
    how to obtain, 233
    using bricks instead of, 235
Brickopedia
    arches listing, 282–84
    baseplates listing, 290
    bricks listing, 243–46
    categories and subcategories, 241–42
    cones and cylinder listing, 287–89
    decorative elements listing, 290–98
    described, 239–40
    plates listing, 247–54
    sample entry, 240
    slopes listing, 254–62
    specialized elements listing, 263–70
    Technic listing, 270–82
    tiles and panels listing, 284–87
brickplate. *See* baseplate
bucket container, 221–22
build area, setup, 223–26
building principles, 35, 175
bushings (Technic)
    described, 159
    elements, 280

C

calculator, 237
candy cane model, 100
cargo ship model, 17
character. *See* miniland figure model
chess pieces, creating from elements, 202
chimney pattern, 33
clips, 292
colonnade
    defined, 45
    used to build train station, 47
colors
    available, 15–16
    choosing appropriate, 181
    combining in storage container, 222

examples of usage, 16–17, 104, 127, 175, 181
    for space shuttle model, 183–84
    in design, 182
    obtaining more, 16–17
    sorting by, 211–16
    substituting, 16, 47, 49–50, 53
    with macro-sized elements, 84
column
    defined, 32
    examples of usage, 29–30, 42, 43, 79–80
    tying to a wall, 80
    types, 32–35
combinations, of 2×4 bricks, 19–20
composite beam, 31
compound post, 33
computer software
    filter to create mosaic blueprint, 144
    for model design, 200
    using to create building instructions, 200–1
cone
    described, 11
    elements, 287–89
Connect-Across game
    creating pieces for, 203
    rules, 204–6
containers, for storage, 216–22
coupler (Technic)
    described, 159–60
    elements, 280–82
curved wall, 27–29
cylinder
    described, 11
    elements, 287–89
cylinder plates, described, 11–12

D

decorative elements
    described, 12
    elements, 290–98
deep storage, 223
design elements, 182–85
Design Grids
    downloading, 299–300

how to use, 303–10
labeled columns and rows for
      mosaic planning, 301
legend, 142
landscape perspective, 303
plate view, 147, 301–2
portrait perspective, 302
purposes, 300–3
top down, 300
using to approximate features,
      96–97, 102–5
using to design models, 177–78,
      180–81
using to plan a mosaic, 136, 137,
      140–43
designer, role of
in creating original models,
      173–74
picking subject matter, 113, 126,
      175
designing. *See also* design elements;
      Design Grids; designer,
      role of
choosing color combinations,
      181–82
finding distinctive features, 107,
      176, 179
LEGO models, 35, 94, 173
original games, 203–7
picking a scale, 181
where to begin, 175
dimensions of elements, 2–3
diorama, defined, 75
doors, 297–98
driven/driver gear, 160–1, 162
Duplo elements, 39

E

element
classifying types, 5–12
defined, 1
understanding sizes of, 2–3
Empire State Building model
designing, 102–4
determining scale of, 108
turning design into model, 105–6
Expert Builder series, 153

F

facade, 75–76
factor, scale, 82, 87, 88, 108
foliage, 293–95
four times scale, 83–84, 93

G

games
Connect-Across, 203–6
creating board for, 201–2
creating pieces for, 202
designing original, 203, 207
gear (Technic)
described, 158
elements, 276–79
gear ratios, 162–64
gear train
described, 160–61
importance of alignment, 162
geometry
5:6 ratio, 13–14
relation of plates to bricks, 14–15
relation of tubes to studs, 14
Great Sphinx of Giza, 126. *See also*
      Sphinx model

H

handles, 293
helicopter model (Technic), 168–71
hinge. *See* brick hinge
house model, microscale, 110–12
hybrid column, 34–35

I

idler gear. *See* gear train
instructions, creating for models,
      199–201
inverted slope, 8

J

joiner, 280
jumbo bricks
1×2 plate model, 90–91

jumbo bricks, *continued*
    2×2 45-degree slope model,
        91–92
    2×4 brick model, 84–87
    building with, 92–94
    comparison of scales, 94–95
    creating studs for, 96–98
    creating walls for, 87–88
    described, 81
    four times scale, 83–84, 93
    other parts, 89
    picking a scale, 95–96
    ten times scale, 82, 89
jumper plate, 8
junction elements, 241, 263–65

K

keyhole pattern, 34

L

ladder plate, 291
landscape perspective, 303
lattice, 290
layer, of elements, 26–27
leftover container, for storage,
    218–19
legend, creating, 142
LEGO company, 64
LEGOLAND, 64
liftarm (Technic), 273
lighthouse model, 17

M

macroscale, defined, 82. *See also*
    jumbo bricks
mallet, 236
manufacturing, precision of, 13
microscale
    1x1 standard, 101
    calculating scale, 101, 102, 107–8
    defined, 99–100
    Empire State Building model,
        102–7
    house model, 110–12
    selecting arbitrary scale, 107–8
    suggested subject matter, 113

technique, 102, 107
    wheels, 109
    windows, 109–10
microscale house model, 110–12
Mindstorms series, 154–55
minifig, basic version, 37
minifig scale
    calculating scale, 38–39
    techniques, 61
    train station model, 40–60
    variations, 38
Miniland, 63–64
miniland figure model
    arms and accessories, 72–73
    basic version, 65–66
    compared to minifig, 65
    creating appearance of motion,
        73–75
    heads and hats, 69–70
    instructions, 68–69
    legs, 72
    most useful pieces, 66–68
    shirts and skirts, 71–72
miniland scale, 64
models, instructions for
    1×2 plate (jumbo version), 90–91
    2×2 45-degree slope (jumbo
        version), 91–92
    2×4 brick (jumbo version), 84–87
    microscale house, 111–12
    miniland figure, 68–69
    space shuttle, 187–93
    sphere, 118–25
    train station, 43–54
modified plate, 8
mosaics
    creating blueprint with computer
        software, 144
    creating letters, 148
    creating patterns with Design
        Grids, 137
    determining size, 135
    geometric patterns, 138–39
    incorporating into a model,
        149–50
    photo, 140
    plates versus bricks, 137–38
    print and trace (design
        technique), 140–43

quartering the image, 145
required elements, 135–36
rotating 90 degrees, 149
studs-out, 133–34, 136–46
studs-up, 134, 146–50
types of, 133–34
uses, 135
using baseplates, 135–36
viewing while building, 143
mosaic filter, 144

N

N, to represent element length, 3
non-LEGO tools
calculator, 237
mallet, 236
paintbrush, 237
pencil and paper, 237
protractor, 236
ruler, 236
zip-closure bags, 238

O

odd-face element, 241, 263, 265–66,
267–68
offset plate, 8, 264
original games, designing, 203, 207.
See also Connect-Across
game
overlapping
described, 22–24
importance when building walls,
25–27
with bricks, 32, 43, 47, 57, 85
with plates, 31, 52, 59, 179
with slopes, 49, 53

P

paintbrush, 237
panel
described, 10
elements, 284–87
patterns, geometric, 138–39
pencil and paper, 237
photo mosaics, 140
photos, use when designing, 131, 177

pin (Technic), 158
pin stand tool, 231–32
pin-enabled elements, 165–67, 241,
268–69
plate
cylinder, 11–12
defined, 6
elements, 247–54
offset, 8
relationship to brick height,
14–15
Technic, 272
uses, 6–7
plate view, 147, 301–2
portrait perspective, 302
precision of manufacturing, 13
presser tool, 229–30
print and trace, 140–43
proportion, 184

Q

quoin, 78

R

redesigning, 193
repeating patterns, 138–39
repetition, 78, 185
reviewing LEGO models, 196–98
rise, arch, 55
roof
alternate for train station model,
57–59
hinged brick technique, 234
roof bricks, 48. *See also* slope
rotation step, 122
round wall, 27–29
ruler
as a non-LEGO tool, 236
made from elements, 230–31

S

scale. *See also* jumbo bricks,
microscale
calculating, 38–39, 64, 108
comparison of various, 100
deciding which to use, 107–8, 181

scale, *continued*
    defined, 38
    demonstrated, 83
    factor, 82, 87, 88, 108
    knowing which is being used, 107
    minifig, 38–39
    miniland, 64
    value, 39, 64
scaling up, 84–89
scope, 174–75
sculpture. *See also* Sphinx model
    choosing a subject, 126
    described, 115–16
    sphere model, 118–25
separator. *See* brick separator
setup, for build area, 223–26
shape, 182–83
shoebox container, 219–21
shuttle. *See* space shuttle model
simple beam, 30
simple post, 32
slope
    defined, 7
    elements, 254–262
    inverted, 8
soffit, arch, 55
software. *See* computer software
sorting. *See also* storing
    by color versus by shape, 211
    by size, 212–13
    large collection, 214–16
    medium collection, 212–13
    small collection, 212
    versus storing, 210–11
space shuttle model
    Bill of Materials, 186
    designing, 176–85
    instructions 187–93,
    naming and numbering, 176
    reasons for picking as subject,
        175
span, arch, 55
specialized elements
    defined, 8
    elements, 263–70
sphere model
    Bill of Materials, 117
    building half at a time, 118

comparing top to sides, 125–26
    instructions, 118–25
Sphinx model
    building foundation, 131
    capturing look and feel, 127
    ears, 129
    head, 128
    headdress, 130–31
    nose, 129
    paws, 129–30
    reasons for picking as subject,
        126–27
    re-creating angles, 127
stacking
    described, 21
    examples of usage, 32, 42, 43, 46,
        109
    problem with, 21, 23
staggering
    described, 24–25
    examples of usage, 24–25,
        118–119, 187
station. *See* train station model
storing. *See also* sorting
    bucket container, 221–22
    deep storage, 223
    different colors together, 222
    leftover container, 218–19
    shoebox container, 219–21
    tackle box container, 221
    tub container, 221–22
    videocassette case container, 217
stretcher brick, 47
structure failure, 31
stud
    defined, 3–4
    position on top of elements,
        86–87
    representing in jumbo models,
        84, 87, 91, 96–98
studless beams (Technic), 157,
        273–76
studless building, technique, 157
studs-out mosaic
    described, 133–34
    designing, 136–46
studs-up mosaic
    described, 134
    designing, 146–50

submodel
    defined, 50–51
    train station roof built as, 51–54
substitution, 61
    defined, 54
    examples of, 41, 54–60
substructure, defined, 30
symbols, legend, 142
system, defined, 1

T

tackle box container, 221
taking apart elements. *See* brick
    separator
Technic
    combining with pin-enabled
      elements, 166–67
    compatibility with standard
      system elements, 154
    defined, 155
    elements, 270–82
    helicopter model, 168–71
    history, 153–54
    Mindstorms series, 154–55
    obtaining elements, 155
    overview of elements, 155–60
    vertical building technique,
      164–65
Technical Sets, 153
ten times scale, 82, 89
test build, 88–89
tile
    described, 10
    elements, 284–87
tires, 269–70
tools, made from LEGO elements
    pin stand, 231–32
    presser, 229–30
    ruler, 230–31
top down Design Grid, 300
train station model
    Bill of Materials, 42
    instructions, 43–50
    other uses for, 40
    roof submodel, 51–54
    substitute arches, 55–56
    substitute roofs, 57–60
    substitute windows, 56

Triton. *See* space shuttle model
tub container, 221–22
tube, defined, 4–5
turntables, 267

V

vertical building technique, Technic,
    164–65
videocassette case container, 217
vignette, defined, 75

W

waffleplate. *See* baseplate
walls
    creating, 22–24, 25–27
    curved, 27–29
    overlap technique, 22–24, 27
    substitutions, 41, 55
wheels
    elements, 269–70
    microscale, 109
windows
    alternate for train station model,
      56
    elements, 296–97
    microscale, 109–10

Z

zip-closure bags, 220, 238

THE LEGO® TECHNIC IDEA BOOKS

Simple Machines | Wheeled Wonders | Fantastic Contraptions

by YOSHIHITO ISOGAWA

The LEGO Technic Idea Books offer hundreds of working examples of simple yet fascinating Technic models that you can build based on their pictures alone. Colors distinguish each part, showing you how the models are assembled. Each photo illustrates a different principle, concept, or mechanism that will inspire your own original creations. The Technic models in *Simple Machines* demonstrate basic configurations of gears, shafts, pulleys, turntables, connectors, and the like, while the models in *Wheeled Wonders* spin or move things, drag race, haul heavy gear, bump off walls, wind up and go, and much more. *Fantastic Contraptions* includes working catapults, crawling spiders, and bipedal walkers, as well as gadgets powered by fans, propellers, springs, magnets, and vibration. These visual guides are the brainchild of master builder Yoshihito Isogawa of Tokyo, Japan.

OCTOBER 2010, 168 PP., 144 PP., AND 176 PP., *full color*, $19.95 EACH
ISBNS 978-1-59327-277-7, 978-1-59327-278-4, 978-1-59327-279-1

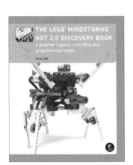

THE LEGO® MINDSTORMS® NXT 2.0 DISCOVERY BOOK

A Beginner's Guide to Building and Programming Robots

by LAURENS VALK

The crystal-clear instructions in *The LEGO MINDSTORMS NXT 2.0 Discovery Book* show you how to harness the capabilities of the NXT 2.0 set to build and program your own robots. Author and robotics instructor Laurens Valk walks you through the set, showing you how to use its various pieces and how to use the NXT software to program robots. Interactive tutorials make it easy for you to reach an advanced level of programming as you learn to build robots that move, monitor sensors, and use advanced programming techniques like data wires and variables. You'll build eight increasingly sophisticated robots like the Strider (a six-legged walking creature), the CCC (a climbing vehicle), and the Hybrid Brick Sorter (a robot that sorts by color and size). Numerous building and programming challenges throughout encourage you to think creatively and to apply what you've learned as you develop the skills essential to creating your own robots.

MAY 2010, 320 PP., $29.95
ISBN 978-1-59327-211-1

THE UNOFFICIAL LEGO® MINDSTORMS® NXT 2.0 INVENTOR'S GUIDE

by DAVID J. PERDUE *with* LAURENS VALK

The Unofficial LEGO MINDSTORMS NXT 2.0 Inventor's Guide helps you to harness the capabilities of the NXT 2.0 set and effectively plan, build, and program your own exciting NXT robots. After examining the pieces in the NXT 2.0 set and the roles they play in construction, you'll learn practical building techniques, like how to build sturdy structures and work with gears. Next, discover how to program with the latest version of the official NXT-G programming language, and how to troubleshoot if something doesn't work right the first time. Finally, follow step-by-step instructions for building, programming, and testing six all-new robots, including Sentry-Bot, a robot guard that shoots balls at intruders; the Jeep, a four-wheeled steering vehicle that avoids obstacles and follows lines; and the Lizard, a large walking robot with a swinging tail that uses the color sensor to detect different colored balls and respond. Each robot can be built using just one NXT 2.0 set, so there's no hunting for obscure parts.

DECEMBER 2010, 336 PP., $29.95
ISBN 978-1-59327-215-9

FORBIDDEN LEGO®
Build the Models Your Parents Warned You Against!

by ULRIK PILEGAARD *and* MIKE DOOLEY

Written by a former master LEGO designer and a former LEGO project manager, this full-color book showcases projects that break the LEGO Group's rules for building with LEGO bricks—rules against building projects that fire projectiles, require cutting or gluing bricks, or use nonstandard parts. Many of these are backroom projects that LEGO's master designers build under the LEGO radar, just to have fun. Learn how to build a catapult that shoots M&Ms, a gun that fires LEGO beams, a continuous-fire ping-pong ball launcher, and more! Tips and tricks will give you ideas for inventing your own creative model designs.

AUGUST 2007, 192 PP., *full color*, $24.95
ISBN 978-1-59327-137-4

PHONE:
800.420.7240 OR
415.863.9900
MONDAY THROUGH FRIDAY,
9 A.M. TO 5 P.M. (PST)

EMAIL:
SALES@NOSTARCH.COM

WEB:
HTTP://WWW.NOSTARCH.COM/

FOR MORE INFORMATION, PLEASE VISIT WWW.APOTOME.COM

To support *The Unofficial LEGO Builder's Guide* I've set up a website at www.apotome.com. There you will find additional information and instructions about the subjects covered in the book. Though the contents are not essential, you may find that things like the Design Grids or the complete instructions for the microscale cargo ship (Chapter 6) will add to your enjoyment of the book.

Throughout *The Unofficial LEGO Builder's Guide* you may have noticed web links included in some of the Notes. Although they appear in many places, there are, in fact, only three unique links:

http://www.apotome.com/grids.html

This is the page you will want to visit when reading any of the sections that refer to the Design Grids. On this page you will find Adobe PDF files that you can download for free. You can then print out as many copies of the Design Grids as needed to help you when creating your own original models or just following along with the examples in the book.

http://www.apotome.com/instructions.html

In some cases *The Unofficial LEGO Builder's Guide* includes an image of a model but not the instructions. Where possible, instructions were included in the published text, but some were left out for editorial reasons. You can visit this page to find complete instructions for some these models (where noted in the book).

http://www.apotome.com/links.html

A large number of the illustrations included in the book were generated using computer software. A complete list of those tools and links to other LEGO building software can be found on this page. Rather than list each of those links here, I will post them on the website where they can be kept up-to-date.

Please feel free to email me at ULBG@apotome.com with any questions you may have about the website or any of the information found in the book itself. I also look forward to hearing from you with comments about your experience reading *The Unofficial LEGO Builder's Guide.* Or, send me an email telling me about your LEGO creations that use techniques found in the book.

COLOPHON

The Unofficial LEGO Builder's Guide was laid out in Adobe FrameMaker. The font families used are New Baskerville for body text, Futura for headings and tables, and Dogma for titles.

Images of LEGO pieces and the instructions for LEGO models included in this book were produced using the following software and methods:

Models were planned and assembled and instruction steps were documented using LeoCAD v0.73.2 as an editor. From LeoCAD these files were exported to the standard LDraw .dat format. The .dat files were then imported into LPub v2.2.0.0. LPub in turn sent each of these files to L3P v1.3 for packaging into .pov files ready for rendering. Where possible the LGEO POV-Ray Library of parts was used to generate higher quality images.

LPub was then used to launch one of two versions of POV-Ray in order to create the ray-traced images. MegaPOV v1.0 was used to generate the step-by-step instruction images for most of the models featured in the book. POV-Ray v3.5 was used to generate the more photo-realistic images of parts such as are featured in the Brickopedia and for many of the other construction examples throughout the book. Regardless of type, all figures were rendered at 2304×1728 pixels.

Raw rendered images (most of which were 11 megabytes in size or larger) were then resized and cropped as needed using Paint Shop Pro version 4.

The book was printed and bound at Malloy Incorporated in Ann Arbor, Michigan. The paper is Glatfelter Spring Forge 60# Smooth Eggshell, which is certified by the Sustainable Forestry Initiative (SFI). The book uses a RepKover binding, which allows it to lay flat when open.

UPDATES

Visit **http://www.nostarch.com/legobuilder.htm** for updates, errata, and other information.